In the Words of the Offender

Peter Tadman

Detselig Enterprises Ltd.

Calgary, Alberta, Canada

In the Words of the Offender

© 1997 Peter Tadman

Canadian Cataloguing in Publication Data

Tadman, Peter, 1944-
    In the words of the offender

ISBN 1-55059-146-0

    1. Prisoners—Canada—Interviews. 2. Life imprisonment —
Canada.   I. Title.
    HV9308.T32 1997   365'.4'0922   C97-910024-0

Detselig Enterprises Ltd.
210-1220 Kensington Rd. N.W.
Calgary, Alberta T2N 3P5

Detselig Enterprises Ltd. appreciates the financial support for our
1997 publishing program, provided by Canadian Heritage and the
Alberta Foundation for the Arts, a beneficiary of the Lottery Fund of
the Government of Alberta

Printed in Canada

ISBN 1-55059-146-0

SAN 115-0324

Cover design by Dean Macdonald.

To young offenders everywhere.
May you learn quickly that crime does not pay.

Acknowledgments

"Everybody has trouble understanding. I have trouble understanding; my parents too. My one aunt and uncle come up and see me and they have trouble understanding. But does that mean that you bail out right away? Maybe go and try and understand it yourself. Go ask. Nobody came and asked me anything."

– Hugh Peters, Saskatchewan Penitentiary

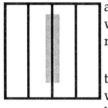 am glad I asked and thankful to all of the offenders who were willing to share their stories for the public record.

I believe Rodney Munro, serving a 60-year sentence, best summed up the feelings of his counterparts when he said: "If just my saying something will help keep one kid out of jail, I think it's worth it. This is not the place to be."

All of the offenders signed waivers allowing me to record their answers to my questions and obtain their criminal records. I felt it was necessary in order to ensure accuracy and consistency with what they had to say.

During the early stages of my writing, Christina Allison (not her real name) provided initial editing advice and suggested *In the Words of the Offender* would be a better title than *Sons Gone Wrong*, which I had carried with me for several years. I thank her and Jan Desnoyers, who spent countless hours transcribing the audio tapes of my first series of inmate interviews.

Robert Grimmelt chose to relay his story in longhand and then explain anything that needed clarification.

I thank my nephew, Jeff Jodoin, for always being available with his computer expertise. Without him – typewriters were my life – I would probably still be bogged down, still composing, trying not to be too many months beyond deadline.

You just don't walk past tight security into a Canadian penitentiary and seek approval, ask if you can start talking with the prisoners, telling everybody you're a nice person and all you want them to do is spend several hours with you, open up their hearts, souls and minds to a stranger. It just doesn't work that way, particularly when prisons aren't exactly known as places where love and trust abounds. It takes a great deal of support, not only at the outset, but throughout the entire process, which in this case spanned more than three years.

Many, including a very supportive, unwavering family, assisted. They are:

- From the Correctional Service of Canada (CSC): Rick Dyhm, warden Jack Linklater, warden Jim O'Sullivan (who has since retired), Al Tessier, John Vandoremalen, Judy Waters and Carole Binette – all of whom made all the difference in the world. Chuck Andrews, Bill Ballantyne, Rob Garrison, Murray Gilmor, Helen Herbert, Dolores Hoff, Rose Kubin, Sheila McBride, Agnes Roy, Chuck Stephenson and Jean Westmacott also helped along the way, as did innumerable CSC staff who put up with my apparently never-ending visits to their prisons during the night, weekends and holidays. I want to specifically thank all of the correctional officers who obligingly unlocked doors, gates, more doors and more gates to let me gain access to the country's most feared men. Equally important, I thank them for going through the same routine to let me out after each of my interview sessions. There are a lot of wonderful moments in the universe, all kinds of great feelings in life. I want to tell you that being allowed to walk away free from prison is among them.
- From the Canadian Centre for Justice Statistics: Shelley Crego.
- From Alberta Justice Corporate Support Services: Dr. Randy Petruk, Rita Lauterbach and Steven Sinclair. Also providing invaluable data were reference centre librarian Eunice Cutting and library technician Mary Leung.
- From the Alberta Legislature Library: all of its forever-aiding staff.
- From the trenches of Canadian Press (CP) and Broadcast News (BN): Bob Colling, who generously agreed to proofread "one more story" in the seeming millions he handled before retiring from a long, distinguished career.
- And finally, from Detselig Enterprises Ltd.: editor Linda Berry, publisher Ted Giles and marketing manager Barry Rust, who deserve much credit for their faith and effort *In the Words of the Offender*.

– Peter Tadman

Contents

Foreword

"Society doesn't know what goes on in these places. They've never lived in here, they don't know, they can't say they know. Society can't say they know how it feels to fly like a bird. They can't say that because they never were a bird so they don't know how it's like to fly. And they don't know what it's like in here."

— Mika Piilila, Edmonton Max

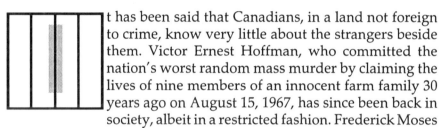t has been said that Canadians, in a land not foreign to crime, know very little about the strangers beside them. Victor Ernest Hoffman, who committed the nation's worst random mass murder by claiming the lives of nine members of an innocent farm family 30 years ago on August 15, 1967, has since been back in society, albeit in a restricted fashion. Frederick Moses McCallum, charged with the axe slaying of seven people on January 30, 1969, was also given freedom with no public announcement.

In truth, little is known about our neighbors, even less about the more than 14 000 adult male convicts who populate the country's federal penitentiaries. Rising prison populations and overcrowded institutions are universal problems. During the past decade, for the most part since 1990-91, the Correctional Service of Canada (CSC) has seen a 27 percent increase in the numbers of prisoners it must house. The rise in prison population in 1995-96, according to a March, 1997, Statistics Canada report, was less than one percent over the previous year. Who are these men, sometimes boys? Where do they come from? What have they done? When and why did these sons go wrong?

Equally important, recognizing that the majority of convicts will ultimately be released back onto the streets from captivity, what do they learn while surviving in their vicious world, locked behind unyielding steel gates for years at a stretch? And should they have the good fortune to make it out alive, to once again taste freedom, which many won't, what can Canadians expect?

Based on more than a million words from unrestricted interviews behind high, impenetrable walls, *In the Words of the Offender* is a unique, long overdue addition to the limited amount most people

Kingston Penitentiary (KP) – "A penitentiary . . . should be a place to lead a man to repent of his sins and amend his life," stated a report to the House of Assembly in 1831. Four years later, Canada's first prison, the largest and most expensive building in the country, opened in the village of Portsmouth on the scenic shore of Lake Ontario. On June 1, 1835, its first six inmates were admitted beyond the grey stone walls. The inmate population in the nation's 42 federal institutions for men reached a high of 13 948 in 1994-95.

know when it comes to crime and those who commit it. News accounts, sensational as a matter of course, are heard and read of the law being broken, someone being arrested, and subsequently being locked away. Curiously, more often than not, that marks the end of it. Nothing more, nothing less. "Of all the public institutions, none is such a closed book to the people at large as the penitentiary," said the Ottawa Citizen almost 80 years ago. The newspaper, which noted that interest in offenders ended once they were sentenced to prison, proclaimed: "That is where interest should begin . . ."

·Young offenders, many destined for solitary life behind bars, have become the bane of Canadians. There has been an outpouring of concern and rage from coast to coast. Study after study has been conducted to find out why Canada's youth have gone wrong and what can be done to stop the seemingly limitless violence. Reporters have continually attempted to interview incarcerated young offenders, but to no avail. According to the law, the protection of privacy, imposing a veil of secrecy, takes precedence. The stories you will read, the result of extraordinary prison access, shatter that barrier in an unprecedented manner.

The following true life accounts of 14 randomly selected federal prisoners, delving into their formative childhood years, is a chance to find out what makes imprisoned men tick. And when you consider the history of some of these offenders – trouble and hopelessness from the playpen to the Big Pen – you will wonder, among other things: How is it humanly possible that so many lives are tragically wasted so soon after they begin?

In the Words of the Offender is a rare opportunity to discover more about humanity, a subject in grave question when left solely to psychiatrists, psychologists and criminologists.

Over and above that, these stories should prove beyond a reasonable shadow of a doubt – considering the diverse backgrounds and mindsets of those who broke the law, and the law won – there but for the grace of God, go I.

—Peter Tadman

*The degree of civilization in a society can be judged by
entering its prisons.*

Fyodor Dostoyevsky (1821-1881)

The Victims

Randy Lafond

"You can get out and more or less everything for you is freedom. But the victims are still suffering. Some have died, some have lived, some are crippled, some will never be the same . . . we're suffering for a little time for what we did to them. That's about all I got."

anadian taxpayers shelled out over $949 million for the operating expenses of federal corrections – which included parole supervision of 8493 offenders on any given day – in 1995-96. The total amounted to $36 million more than during the previous year. The annual cost to keep an offender in a federal penitentiary, someone sentenced to a term of two years or more, was $46 250.

Beyond the federal system, $970 million was spent provincially to incarcerate about 20 000 inmates and supervise 100 800 offenders within the community. Twenty-seven percent of those in provincial custody were awaiting the outcome of charges against them, 73 percent were serving jail terms that averaged 31 days.

The nation's steel and concrete fortresses, where the median time in custody is 46 months, are designed, in part, to get offenders to realize the law of the jungle will not be tolerated; society, as we know it, commands order, demands respect.

On a warm May evening, Randy Lafond, 6'0", 220 pounds, had agreed to meet me deep within the bowels of his dreaded maximum security existence, for the purpose of telling his story, how he had come to know violence so well, why he had savagely beaten other humans, including two victims who barely cheated death.

While waiting by Control 2, having passed through six electronically monitored gateways to get there, inmates flocked in from the yard. It was time for visits, a handful of them were being delayed, cruelly unnecessarily they reckoned. They were trapped behind an immovable metal barrier, angrily milling about, unable to get loose to see their guests. Suddenly, the heavy, barred obstacle lumbered open. Two names were barked out. They could proceed. The others could not, were forced to wait, and began cursing the correctional officers. One of them screamed, "The worst f——in' excuses used by you guys are: 'I work for the government, I don't know, I don't make the rules.'" Instantly, a guard fired back: "The worst f——in' excuses you guys use is, 'I don't give a shit.'" Back and forth it went. Then, three of the remaining four highly agitated convicts were allowed to pass through for their shortened visiting privileges. They had lost sacred time, minutes that were precious. Their cohort, now alone, more sullen than ever, was refused entry. It seemed his expected visitor had not shown up. He told Control 2 that he was going back to the gym, then hurled a few more insults: "Do you want to frisk me? Do you want to feel my balls for the 100th time, you sick bastard?" The correctional officer had heard it all before. He simply ordered the prisoner, much subdued now that his companions were not within earshot: "Go to the gym!" And he did, silently, without further protest.

Randy Lafond, who along with regularly rotating guards and fellow inmates spends 24 hours a day in this type of ongoing, volatile atmosphere, eventually arrived. He had been out in the yard playing baseball on a beautiful, sunny night. We postponed our meeting to the following week, a non-baseball time. When I arrived, Randy was busy in the prison kitchen, then he had a shower. It was beginning to look as though he had changed his mind, decided not to share his story. Finally, an hour late for our rescheduled interview, this 24-year-old, who had come to know prison life so well at such a young age, sat down, and for the first time, willingly reviewed his troubled life for public consumption.

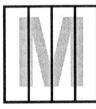y life is on hold. I more or less never had the chance to do the things I wanted to do. Everybody's ideal life would be grow up, get a job, get a house, marry someone, have kids, things like that. I never had that. I never thought of that. I just thought of having girlfriends, getting a place, didn't care how I paid for it. I wanted things quick, and that's the way I went about it.

I was born in Saskatoon, raised there for four or five years, then moved to Edmonton where I spent some time with my uncles and my aunties. Eventually I moved back to Saskatoon. We moved to PA (Prince Albert), usually travelled quite a bit, back and forth.

We had a big family. I had two brothers and three sisters. My cousins were like brothers and sisters. We all hung together, we all stuck together, we were a tight family, all of us.

Saskatoon was the place where my family had always been. They were born there, they were raised there. Our reserve, that's Muskeg, was 40 miles out of town. I lived some time there, back and forth on the reserve, my grandma and my uncles.

There's a lot of difference on a reserve, because of the fact there was not many cops around, there's really no law. There was nothing to be broken out as a law, everybody shares, everybody gives, everybody gives and takes. Everybody helps each other out when they need help.

Randy Lafond – "When I was young, I was doing good. I had no complaints from my family. My relatives encouraged me until about Grade 5. I started slipping from there. There was alcohol involved with my family at that time. I started realizing it. I took advantage of it."

I liked going to school, playing sports and games. It's mostly what I liked, just going to school and waiting until school was over and hang around with my friends.

When I was young, I was doing good. I had no complaints from my family. My relatives encouraged me until about Grade 5. I started slipping from there.

There was alcohol involved with my family at that time. I started realizing it. I took advantage of it.

I had a lot more responsibilities when my mom was drinking, or somebody else was drinking in the family. I more or less had to take control. Watch, make sure something doesn't burn, make sure something doesn't get broken. I more or less had to grow up and watch the young ones: they don't get hurt; they don't fight too much; things like that. I was the oldest out of everybody, out of all my cousins and everything, so I had to watch everybody, while everybody else drank.

I never met my father until I was 18 years old. I guess he was around when I was about two or three years old and then he left. So I'd never known my father. When I was small, when we were moving around, I got letters from him and never knew how he looked or anything, just by pictures and people telling me who he was, that I had a strong resemblance to him.

About age 12, that's the first time I entered a correctional centre. At that time my family was not drinking heavily, they'd drink maybe once a month, whenever they felt they needed a time out. One weekend, my uncle and uncle-in-law come in from Alberta, and they got into a fight in my house. Not a serious fight. My mom kicked everybody out, and I liked my uncle a lot. I didn't want to see him walking in the winter alone, and I knew Saskatoon, he didn't. So I went with him, walking to my uncle's place, his brother's house. He spotted a car running, so we got in and drove. Got in a high-speed chase. Ran into a telephone pole at 120 miles an hour. From there it was all downhill, more or less.

I was knocked out, my uncle brought me back. He just shook me, brought me back into reality. I was taken to the police station handcuffed. I was actually 11 years old, day before my birthday. I didn't go to the hospital. They thought I was just a little somebody, in for big trouble. They told me they was taking me to Kilburn Hall.

When I first got there, I was put in a cell that was maybe, six by eight feet. Just a single cot with a steel frame for a bed. Next day I went to court. I don't really remember much about courts, just remember spending a lot of time at Kilburn Hall.

I was in there for three years. I was with a lot of friends I met in there, couple family members; my cousins I ran in to there. It's closed custody, and you finally get upstairs and get a lot more freedom, you get to move around a lot, go outside and everything. I took advantage of that by talking with friends, saying let's take a walk. So I ended up taking a walk a few times. There was really no fences, there was nothing.

At that time I didn't want to see any of my family, because I was going through a stage where I wanted to be my own boss. I wanted adults to have nothing to do with me. I just wanted to be by myself.

A social worker come and talked to me and asked me, if there was a group home in Regina, if I could go, would I go there? I agreed to it, and he said, "We'll take you there for a year and if that goes good we'll bring you back and you'll just go home." I said all right. I went to Regina, to a group home.

We got to go camping, things like that. Kept me occupied, kept me busy, and it was things I liked. After a year there, they asked me if I wanted to sign for two more years. They had me into hockey, soccer, every sport I could get into that I liked, and so I agreed to stay.

But I ran into my bad parts there, where I took off a couple times, because I didn't like the way things ran. I didn't get my own way sometimes, and I would take off and turn myself back in. In the summer of '86, my time to go, I paid my respects to everybody, left, went back to Saskatoon.

I went back to my mom, and everything was good. I had a new sister. She was about five or six months old. I loved playing with her, having a good time with her; taking her out to the park, things like that. That went on for the summer, and then finally came time for school and I thought I didn't have to go. I wanted to go out, have fun, party with the friends and the family. But my mom stated that I had to go to school, so I went. I was getting back into it and everything, then by about November, December, I got kicked out for fighting, went home, and my mom didn't know. We were muscling people in the school. Didn't really care what we did to people, because we weren't respected in that school. There was racism everywhere. People try to hide it, but you know it's there. All these people got everything, they got first in line, their names were known and respected. That's the way in our eyes they were. So we changed things in our eyes. And this guy went right to the principal and told him what was going on, so the principal come and called me and my friend up to the office and told us we were suspended.

There's racism in every institution, there's racism on the street, there's racism in the classroom, there's racism everywhere. We probably go about it different ways though. Some people will not tell you, some people will talk behind your back, and I myself was put in group homes with different races, put in there with Chinese, blacks, Italians, whites. I was put in there with everyone, and got to respect them and they respected me. So, I felt that, as I grew older, I respected people but I didn't base it on somebody else's race.

My mom wasn't home one day when they came and arrested me and told me I was charged with assault causing bodily harm. From there, I went straight to the correctional centre because I was 16. I went to court the next day and they sentenced me to a year probation, so I was walking the street again.

I was charged with attempted B&E, breaching probation and mischief. I got six months closed custody and three months open custody and was sent to Kilburn Hall again. I stayed for three months, and then me and five other guys escaped.

There was the fences, 12 to 16 feet high with double mesh, an extra six feet from the top going down, and there's fences going outwards from the wall, every door is electric.

They take two guys out with you when you walk the yard, and two guards against 13 guys is pretty hard to control, we thought at that time. The guards weren't touched. They sit in a smoking area in the middle of this field, where the guys play football. The guards usually stay on this little walkway, we went out, started playing football, and some inmates came walking by to go to the other yard, a big area divided into two. They were going by, the guards turned, looked at them, and that's when we sprang to the wall. We climbed, and went over.

You couldn't walk down the street without having your head down, wearing a cap pulled over your face so you could walk around. If you had long hair, you had to put it in a ponytail, it was like that, you have to change everything. I was free for approximately two weeks, arrested in a stolen car with five of my friends, not the same ones I escaped with, and brought back.

I got charged with escape and obstruction, which is not telling on the guy. I got more time. This carried on for three years: escaping; coming back; escaping; coming back. It was to the point where they were shipping me to a different institution and hoping I'd leave from that one, then they'd take me to another institution. I went to three institutions: Kilburn Hall, North Battleford Youth Centre and the Paul Dojack Youth Centre in Regina.

I was just finishing off 46 months, for all the times I picked up charges as a young offender. At the youth centre, they had levels. You do good you get a higher level, you get more freedom. I was on the highest level for the longest time. I could walk around the track whenever I wanted, take out guys to walk around, help people when they needed it. I was more or less seeing myself in a different way when I was on a higher level, helping people.

They asked me if I wanted to go to open custody. It was a farm. We'd feed cows, horses, pigs, sheep, ducks. On the fifth day, I didn't like the way things were running, the inmates taking advantage of everybody. The kids in there were getting on my case: "If you don't do this, I'm going to tell on you." In my eyes, I didn't see that as right, because these kids are going to end up being in the correctional centre one day and they're going to get themselves hurt for being a rat.

I told myself I'm out of here, conned them into letting me go swimming, they let met go, and I walked away. I stayed out for three and a half weeks. I was 18 at that time, and they said to me when I was arrested, that I'm going to the correctional centre. No young offender centres wanted me anymore.

I walked into the adult correctional serving 22 months. I got hit 10 months, I had a year left to do of young offender. Wasn't scared. But when I walked in there, I was told by the guards that I'm young, and that adult offenders don't like young offenders. Apparently a couple years earlier, young offenders escaped, screwed it up for all the inmates.

I was always talked down to. They asked me if I had any friends or family to take care of me. I had to hold on. I said: "I've got family in here, but I got nobody to take care of me." I walked out into population, and run into three family members. By the time they got out, I had been talking with people, getting to know people, and people got to know me.

When I went into the correctional centre, I weighed 145 pounds. I got out at about 198 pounds. I was doing 315 pounds, bench pressing. I was curling about 150 pounds. I was leg pressing about 300, 400 pounds. In five months I was doing all that weight.

I was there for 14 months, and they offered me a release program. I got out onto the street and felt a lot better from when I was young, because I had to hide all the time. I was always worried about who I was running into, if somebody's going to put it on me, rat on me, and what kind of name I had to make for myself. My family had a name, people were scared of them. I changed that around where I'm my own boss. I didn't need no one to be scared of me because I had family. Either they were scared of me because of me, or not scared of me at all. And the reason that I say scared of me is, because if they did something to hurt my family, if they did something like that, I would not do nothing before, whereas this time I would go up to that person and find out what happened. Usually, the guy would throw a punch at me, kick at me, the fight was on. Two or three fights a week, and usually they would end up in both of us standing up, walking away, where there are no knives, no bats, nothing ever used in my fights, because at that time I didn't need a bat or anything, a weapon, to hurt anybody. If I couldn't do it myself, then I didn't feel it was right to do it with anything else.

A few weeks after I got out, I was sitting at home with my girlfriend. Her brother came up to the house and said he just got a gun pulled on him, a shotgun. Some deal went down that he got burned on. At that time I didn't know him too well. He was laughing, he liked lying, liked causing trouble for other people. I was partying with his brother, as well as my girlfriend, so we had to go out to this place. I picked up a stick, he picked up an aluminum bar, and we walked into this house, saying to ourselves, "We're going to get shot." We had two guys behind us. If we're going to get shot, make sure they get us to the hospital in time. We were drunk, so we were thinking that we were going to live from those shotgun blasts. We walked into the house, and lucky enough, these guys were down in the basement, so we called them up. They came walking up the stairs and we hit them over the head, started giving it to them.

One guy ended up with 98 stitches on top of his head, his nose broken, jaw broken. He was messed up pretty bad. The other guy got 87 stitched in line, top of his head, and same thing with him, blood coming out everywhere. Two other people got away, because we didn't know how many were in the house. All we knew was there was these two. When we first heard we were going there, we heard there was eight or nine people there. When we got there, we looked around, there was nobody there, then all of a sudden these two winners. We asked them what happened after we gave it to them.

We took the guns, left the place, got arrested an hour later, guns and everything. Spent a month in remand, went to court, got the charge thrown out, and were back on the street again.

Apparently the charges were dropped because the guys wrote statements saying they wanted nothing done about it. They feared for their lives, and when it came to trial they didn't show up.

I wasn't really working, I was always partying. I was with a girlfriend and liked to party quite a bit. I'd smoke drugs and things like that. Things changed. My head was getting sore. I was getting dizzy and things just weren't going my way. She liked to party, I couldn't put up with this, so we broke up. We ended up getting back together, and I told her at that time, if I go with her, the drinking's got to stop, the dope's got to stop, because I don't like it. I liked booze but never actually liked dope. I didn't like the feeling and also I've been told I've got a heart murmur, and I've been told I had a concussion when I was young, so my body wouldn't really put up with it.

I was partying in a bar. My brother-in-law just finished losing his wife and his daughter in a fire, so I wanted to take him out, let him relax a little bit. We were in the washroom, and some guy come up to him and started making fun of him, and saying: "You're the cause, loser, losing your wife. You started the fire. You killed your wife and your kid." My brother-in-law slapped him, and I jumped in front, grabbed this guy, hit him once, and really, that's all I remember. The guy went down on the ground and we got grabbed by the bouncers and were taken out.

We got charged about two hours later with aggravated assault, heard that some guy's in the hospital with a broken ankle, broken ribs, screwed up face and everything. Went to remand and I was on remand for five months. I got released on bail and started hanging around friends again, trying to work, because I knew I was going back to jail for this charge, because I did hit the guy, and I thought that's what it was. When we went to trial, I saw what happened to the guy, and I couldn't believe it, because I know myself, I didn't do that. Apparently my friend who was with us was the one that did it, but I couldn't say nothing, because it was a brother system, nobody says nothing about nobody. So, he got away and I got two years for that charge because I was picked up on the street for fighting another guy.

I got out of jail at 198, 200 pounds. Three months later I was at 168 pounds. I lost all my weight. I was running around, not eating properly. I was at a party with my girlfriend, a new one, and some guy. I invited this guy to the party and apparently he had a problem with putting some bros in the joint. Ratted on some bros in jail. I just caught the tail end of it, but he was saying to me that he thought I was trying to screw around with him. He was trying to take me out, saying: "I can take you, I can drop you."

I said: "Well let's check it out." We walked outside and my friend started to fight first.

I grabbed the guy and just stood my ground and said: "Listen! The fight's right here." I hit him once, the guy went down. The guy was 225, 230 pounds and I couldn't believe that. I was surprised because the guy went down in one shot and I was 168 pounds. So, I took advantage of that, started beating him.

When I got arrested, I asked the reason why I was getting charged with attempted murder. I said, "It was just a street fight." They stated to me that there was some words of, "wanting to kill him, should have killed him," that's the words I was saying there. I don't remember much of that night.

He was in a coma for three and a half weeks. He had an IQ of a three-year-old. His vision was no longer stable. He couldn't see three feet in front of him without squinting really hard. He had three or four headaches a day. He didn't know how to dress himself, didn't know where he was going when he left the house. When he talked on the phone, he didn't know what he was talking about. That's all the stuff I heard.

When I went to the preliminary hearing, my brother-in-law's girlfriend, three volunteers, and two cops testified against me, and him. I stayed in remand for a while. I was making some calls into the city on remand, trying to find out what's happening with this guy. When it came to trial, they showed up and I copped down to assault causing bodily harm, reduced from attempted murder. I received three years concurrent to the two years I was serving for aggravated assault.

I was taken to Prince Albert Penitentiary. I heard stories, so many stories about the Pen. They say there was people getting killed left and right, you got to watch who you look at, and don't gun people off, don't get mouthy. I was too old to let people do things that shouldn't be done, so I walked in there. I knew I had family in there, and right away I was told, "You have no family in jail. All you have is brothers." So I walked into jail and expected to be on my own, and right away I had some friends in there, and things were all right for a while. Played sports, working out. I spent eight months in there, and they brought a guy in, somebody you don't get along with, incompatible. They moved him on my range, four cells away from me. I went to dinner. I walked by those cells and I looked at him, he gave me a smirk so I walked back to his cell. I asked him: "What the hell are you doing here?"

He said, "F—- you!" The fight was on.

The guy lost two or three teeth, loosened some other teeth. He had a slight concussion, was put in the hospital, and I was charged with assault. I stayed in segregation. You're locked up 23 and a half hours a day. They let you out in the morning for a shower, every second day. You have exercise every day for approximately half an hour and at that time you can take a shower after you come in from your exercise, or when the guards feel it's right that you have a shower. You're mostly locked up. They have you double bunked.

I received three months for assault, and was told that Sask Pen did not want me anymore. They raised my level to maximum security. Then they moved me here to Edmonton Max.

My girlfriend couldn't deal with me being in jail. I lost my family, a lot of friends, people I care about.

What keeps me going is thinking that you're going to get out one day. There's going to be a day when you get out. I know I'm serving time for the crimes I did, but yet I don't want to keep my mind in jail. I keep it other places, like writing my poems, writing letters to family members, friends on the street, seeing how they're doing, seeing what they're doing out there that keeps them busy. I like to hear good things out there, and they write me back, not saying that they miss me, because I don't really like hearing that kind of stuff. I know they miss me, but all I like to hear is that they're having a good time, they're having kids, they're taking care of each other.

If I get paroled, the first thing I'm going to do is just take a long walk, look at the sky, look all around me, without looking at a fence, without looking to see where a guard is, or someone watching you. Just knowing you can walk and keep on walking. Just enjoy it.

My plan would be to leave Alberta, try and start over. Get onto the street and change, because I myself am not thinking about drinking, thinking about drugs, thinking about crime, thinking about people who have done me wrong, because I don't believe in that. I just want to get out of here and try to start a new life, start a family, and one day not far down the line, move back to my reserve.

I know I won't change everything, but I know I can change the way I think and the way I do things. I can't change what already happened, the people who've been hurt. You can get out and more or less everything for you is freedom. But the victims are still suffering. Some have died, some have lived, some are crippled, some will never be the same. The victims out there are always going to suffer, whereas us, we're suffering for a little time for what we did to them. That's about all I got.

I Think I Killed My Wife

Rob Grimmelt

*"I found her and stabbed her again – one last time. It was in the neck.
I do not know why."*

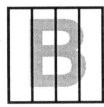 orn August 13, 1958, Robert Romel Grimmelt, a meek, nervous fellow, is one of more than 14 000 men who inhabit the cells of Canada's federal prisons. His crime: killing his wife, who stumbled, screaming, into a neighbor's apartment after being stabbed repeatedly. A scant few minutes earlier, the troubled couple met in their nearby suite to discuss their pending divorce. Court was told that Deborah, as her punctured body lay bleeding from massive wounds, was grabbed by the hair and had her throat slashed. His sentence: life 12, which means he will serve at least a dozen years before he is eligible to apply for parole. If it is granted, a decision that will rest with the National Parole Board, the prisoner, quiet and unassuming, will be subjected to conditions of release for the rest of his natural born days.

His story soon follows. Before that, however, for the record, there are two matters of significance. First, it has been said with accuracy, "the greatest danger to life and limb is when a wife leaves her husband." Second, also true, Rob Grimmelt was put on a waiting list when he sought counselling less than two weeks before his night of rage.

rowing up as a child was a wonderful life in a small mining town, Snow Lake, Manitoba. It was a beautiful little community that was peaceful and the nicest place to live. You may not have heard of Snow Lake, but it's roughly 500 miles north of Winnipeg and when I lived there, the population was about 1500. Since then some of the mines (zinc, copper, ore) have closed and a lot of people have gone.

My dad, a heavy drinker but a good man, was a miner, while my mom, who never really drank, stayed at home with the kids who included me, an older and a younger brother, and my little sister. I had a very happy childhood, with many family activities such as camping, fishing, hunting, playing hockey, swimming and snowmobiling.

In my early teens, I began to drink. When I was 14, I started on marijuana. Until then my grades had been good and I was quite a popular kid in school.

By the time I was 15, my mom left my dad and was soon involved with other men. I still haven't been able to forgive her for that. Maybe I could have, but her marrying a new man resulted in her wanting very little to do with us kids. I sensed great rejection from that. My mother to this day says that she loves me but will not come for an overnight prison visit. She is also "ashamed" of what I've become.

Going back to the divorce, I took off from home, not knowing who to choose to live with, ending up on the streets of Calgary, Edmonton and Winnipeg. I was still 15 years old.

I worked in a car wash for a while, picked bottles and panhandled for money.

By 17, I had learned to steal food from convenience stores when I was hungry. I also began to sell drugs.

I eventually got into a carpenter's helper position in Regina and settled down with a girl, Andrea, who gave birth to Little Robbie who was named after me. He died six months later of Sudden Infant Death Syndrome. It was a terrible loss, so sudden. It was devastating. We loved that little baby a lot. We were really attached to him.

By that time, I had worked for three different framing companies – being ripped off three different times. The one company still owes me $1100.

So I went back to selling drugs, mainly marijuana and hash. I sold for several years, enjoying a lot of good times and money, but that all resulted in approximately five drug charges. I never did any jail time. It was only fines.

By 1983, when I was 25, I attended Henwood, an alcohol and drug rehabilitation facility in Edmonton, to get help for my alcohol problem. Bradley was born in December '83 and I was again trying to straighten my life out. His mother Kathy, who I met a couple of years earlier, would not stop using cocaine or messing around with other men. Our relationship ended by the autumn of 1985.

Back into the booze and broke, I attempted robbery December 14, at a Mac's convenience store, in order to get some money to buy Brad a birthday present. I was arrested on the scene and spent the next six months in the Fort Saskatchewan Correctional Centre just outside of Edmonton. I also got 18 months probation.

As far as the holdup, it was pathetic. I was very drunk and pretended to have a weapon. I didn't have anything, even though I motioned inside my jacket. It was so bad I didn't even get out of the store before the police arrived. They originally charged me with

Rob Grimmelt –
"My mother to this day says that she loves me but will not come for an overnight prison visit. She is also 'ashamed' of what I've become."

robbery with violence, but the only violence was when the shop-keeper and cop beat me up. They finally charged me with attempted robbery. I guess they don't have a charge for being stupid.

After I served my time, I tried again, very seriously, to straighten my life out. I joined a local church and received help to get a car, a good job and a place to live. I also immediately took custody of Brad, raising him as I worked. We attended church regularly. We spent all our time together; going to parks, the playground at the giant West Edmonton Mall, and the kinds of places a father takes a son. I had Brad in daycare in preparation for kindergarten. Kathy was pretty well out of the picture, although she would take our son on weekends.

In January '89, I met Deborah. She was a godsend. She was beautiful, vibrant, witty, intelligent and we both fell in love very fast. She even had a daughter, four-year-old Dezarae. I met Deborah at the daycare and we used to say the children brought us together.

In the spring, about two months after we met, we got married and were an instant family. You could say, we got married in a fever.

I can't say enough about Deborah, the girl I married, the girl whose life I stole. She was a kind, beautiful young woman, full of life. She was very quick to admit her faults and to make up for them. She loved her daughter, grandmother, mother, father and brothers very much. She was very forgiving. She was also very quick to help somebody in need and very generous. She was a very beautiful woman in all respects. Deborah was very vibrant and intelligent. One day a man in the downtown area had a mild heart attack and she was the only one who helped revive him and waited until the ambulance came. She was full of integrity and was very strong-minded. I believe that the main reason she left me for another man was only through the strong influence and persuasion of a careless party girl, who she took a strong liking to. Otherwise she loved her family, she loved me and the kids very much.

It started six weeks after we were married. For no apparent reason, Deborah went back to an old boyfriend who was not the father of Dezarae. I was left with Brad, all the bills and no money in the bank. Deborah had taken it all.

Then everything started going bad. A friend, someone I considered a buddy, babysat and ended up beating my son. He had given him a harsh spanking that left Brad with severe bruising. I went to his house; he would not come out. Next, the welfare system decided they were taking me to court to pay alimony to Kathy for the son who I was raising. Then, as if I needed any more trouble, Deborah's boyfriend began threatening me over the phone, her lawyer was trying to sue me for mental cruelty, and I lost my job. Actually, I quit on the advice of my boss. There had been a lot of disruptions, I was turning into a nervous wreck and my boss thought I should take a break. I had worked for the paint store for two and a half years and was in line for a management position. I took Brad and left town for Vancouver.

Within a couple of months, Deborah had contacted me and wanted to reconcile. I agreed and we were soon a happy family again back in Edmonton.

I loved her dearly and she me, and she said she was truly sorry for what she'd done to me.

But she was also a very high-strung girl with a bad temper. Many times I had to restrain her from punching or hitting me. She would get so upset over the littlest things. And for a time, I went back to drinking and soon became a disgusting drunk – once being arrested for impaired driving – and a short separation happened again.

We were soon back together as a happy family. The kids loved each other as we did them, and Deborah, when she was happy, would treat me like a king. And for the last few months that we were together we were very much in love, and I in turn treated her like gold. I had never hit her and when she hit me, I would only try to restrain her. Even her family knew I treated her very well.

Up until about a month before she left me in November '90, I was beginning to sense that something was terribly wrong, and was receding into a depression.

I came home from work November 15, to find what appeared to be a break and entry into our small one-bedroom apartment in north Edmonton. Deborah had moved out, taking most of everything. I was stunned. I felt horrible. Sick in fact. The rejection was devastating. Totally out of the blue.

After questioning my neighbors and friends, I learned she had told them that I was "abusing" her and that's why she left. It was a lie and hurt me very bad.

Several days later, me and my son ran into her with her boyfriend. They got on the same bus as us and didn't see us. We watched them snuggling and kissing for what seemed like many blocks. I felt sick to my stomach. I thought of going after him, but I had my boy with me and with Brad there I didn't want to cause a scene. Afterwards, I finally confronted her best friend who told me that the affair had been going on for a couple of months.

I was in shock and despair. I had to make new daycare arrangements and change my work schedule.

I decided then to divorce her. But I still loved her and was very shook up about everything. I went to my doctor for medication. I asked him for help to get me through this until the divorce was over.

Exactly one week before that terrible night – January 11, 1991 – I fell off the wagon. I had not had a drink for eight months. In my drunken haze, I phoned Deb's grandma looking for her, as I wanted her to come home. I drank until I passed out and much to my surprise, Deborah appeared in the morning! She stayed for three or four days and I thought we were getting back together again. But she left again on the Wednesday with mutual plans to proceed with the divorce action on Friday the 11th.

I finished off the rest of my whole prescription that night and went to work in the morning. Thursday night I went to have the prescription refilled. It was called Lectopam, similar to Valium as I understand it.

Somewhere between Thursday night and approximately half an hour before Deborah arrived Friday evening, I took that whole bottle (30 pills). I remember swallowing the last seven or eight pills once I knew she was coming, thinking the divorce would be over that night and I could get on with my life. I had plans for me and Brad to move to the Okanagan that spring.

I was very confused, diagnosed later to be in a drug-induced state. I never drank any alcohol. I guess I was starting to black out even before she arrived – not even seeing the man (Kathy's boyfriend) who came over to pick Brad up. He later testified that it was like I was in a trance, looking right through him. He told the court that he was worried about me. The quality of my mind was a big question at my trial. Dr. Louis Pagliaro said I was in a state of automatism,* a robotic mode. In simple terms, the body moves but the mind isn't in control.

---

*This was neither the first time nor the last time that the robot defence of being in a dissociative state – insane or non-insane automatism – entered the annals of the justice system. In a highly publicized 1996 trial, it was used by wealthy Calgary resident Dorothy Day Joudrie, 61, who shot her estranged husband six times with a gun. As upon the floor he did lie, she asked him how long he'd take to die. Miraculously, he lived. Mrs. Joudrie was found not criminally responsible on account of a mental disorder, sent to a psychiatric hospital and released five months later under strict conditions concerning reporting, travel and alcohol counselling.

Apparently, I went to the store and bought a grape Crush for Deb. That was her favorite.

I remember when she arrived by cab, because I paid for it, but for some reason she was shouting at me.

In court, the witnesses said that Deb was there for about 20 minutes. I thought she was there about two or three.

All I remember was her shrieking voice calling me a loser and whatever else. I remember pacing, trying to get away from the noise. All I can say is that I stabbed her twice, then attempted to call 911 when I realized what I'd done.

One doctor later diagnosed me as being hysterical. I remember I could hardly breathe. I remember saying the address and something about stabbing my wife.

The rest of the conversation still has not come back to my memory except the part where I was telling the operator I wanted to phone my dad. They never did let me call him.

I don't remember a lot of what was said on the 911 line. Most of it is a blank even though my defence lawyer got a copy of the tape. It is very upsetting to listen to.

TRANSCRIPT, 911 CALL:

911 Operator – 911 Emergency.

RG –Yeah, we have an emergency. I might have killed my wife. Yeah, this is number eight . . .

911– OK. Just stay on the line. I'm going to connect you with an ambulance. OK?

RG – 'K.

911 – Stay on the line for a minute.

Ambulance Operator - Ambulance.

RG – Number eight, one thirty-six twenty, a hundred and nineteen street.

Ambulance – OK. What's the problem sir?

RG – I think I killed my wife.

Ambulance – OK.

RG – 'K.

Ambulance – Just a sec'. Don't hang up. Don't hang up on me.

RG – There's a guy comin' and he's gonna get it too.

Ambulance – OK.

RG – Just send an ambulance quick, OK?

Ambulance – OK. Now just stay on the line with me.

RG – What?

Ambulance – Stay on the line.

RG – Yeah.

Ambulance – OK. How old is your wife?

RG – Twenty-four.

Ambulance – OK. How do you mean you think you killed her? What happened?

RG – I stabbed her.

Ambulance – Stabbed her.

RG – Yeah.

Ambulance – OK. Just calm down now, we've got a unit on the way.

RG – OK.

Ambulance – Just stay on the . . .

RG – Hold on!

Ambulance – Stay on the line with me.

RG – Stay away Huey – stay away! I'm on the . . . I phoned the police. Stay away. [pause] Just hold on yourself.[pause]

Ambulance – OK. Is your wife alert or is your wife talking to you sir? Hello? Hello? [pause] Hello?

RG – [pause] Hello.

Ambulance – Yes, hi. Is your wife breathing, talking to you?

RG – I don't know.

Ambulance – You don't know. Is she breathing at all?

RG – She's at the neighbor's place.

Ambulance – She's at the neighbor's place.

RG – Yeah.

Ambulance – OK. And that's, where is the neighbor's place? [pause] Hello?

RG – We're gonna need the police, we're gonna hafta know if she's gonna live or what. OK?

Ambulance – OK. Just hang on, we've got the police coming too.

RG – 'K.

Ambulance – OK. Where did you stab her? [pause] Hello? [pause] Hello?

RG – Yeah.

Ambulance – OK. Where, where is she injured?

RG – In the neck, in the body. You guys come and see, OK?

Ambulance – OK, we're on our way.

RG – OK.

Ambulance – Don't hang up on me now!

RG – I'll talk to you when you get here.

Ambulance – OK. Well I won't be there, another crew will be there.

RG – OK.

Ambulance – OK. She's stabbed in the neck and the body?

RG – OK.

Ambulance – OK. How much bleeding, is she bleeding right now?

RG – Yeah. I don't know. I'm goin' to find out.

Ambulance – OK. I'll wait here, you come back and tell me.

RG – 'K. [lengthy pause]

Ambulance – Hello? [pause] Sir, are you there? [lengthy pause] Hello, are you there sir? [pause] Hello? Hello?

RG – Yes.

Ambulance – Yes, are you there?

RG – Yeah.

Ambulance – OK. What's the condition of your wife now?

RG – She's dead.

Ambulance – She's dead?

RG - As far as I know. Phone this number 455-8884.

Ambulance – OK. Is she...where is she at? Is she at apartment number one?

RG – Yeah.

Ambulance – OK. Are you going to stay on the phone with me?

RG – No. I can't.

Ambulance – Yes, you can.

RG – I have to phone my dad.

Ambulance – No. You have to stay on the phone with me sir. OK? How do you know, why do you think she's dead?

RG – [burps] Looks pretty dead to me.

Ambulance - She looks pretty dead to you.

RG – [burps] OK.

Ambulance – Were you fighting? What was the problem there?

RG – We're trying to get a divorce.

Ambulance – Trying to get a divorce. You had an argument is that correct?

RG – Very bad argument.

Ambulance – Very bad argument.

RG – Yeah.

Ambulance – And you stabbed her.

RG – Huh?

Ambulance – And you said you stabbed her.

RG – Yeah. She grabbed a knife.

Ambulance – She grabbed a knife.

RG – I grabbed it back.

Ambulance – OK.

RG – And I retaliated and I went crazy.

Ambulance – Was there anybody else around?

RG – No.

Ambulance – No. Just the two of you?

RG – Yeah.

Ambulance – What's your name sir?

RG – Robert Grimmelt.

Ambulance – Robert Grimmelt.

RG – Yeah.

Ambulance – OK Robert, OK. We've got an ambulance on the way.

RG – 'K.

Ambulance – It'll be there shortly.

RG – OK.

Ambulance – How old . . .

RG – I want to phone my dad.

Ambulance – No. You stay on the line with me sir. How old are you?

RG – Thirty-two.

Ambulance – You're 32 years old.

RG – Yeah.

Ambulance – How old is your wife?

RG – Let me phone my dad, please.

Ambulance – No, no. I've got to keep you on the phone.

RG – Why?

Ambulance – We gotta . . . we gotta talk to you. We gotta keep you talking here.

RG – Why?

Ambulance – Well, I wanna . . . I wanna . . . we need some more information
from you here.
RG – Well, I'm not talking to you.
Ambulance – You're not talking to me. [line goes dead] Sir?

While I was on the phone, I'm not sure exactly when as much of what happened is still a blur, Deborah – with her stomach and neck bleeding – ran to the neighbor's. I think that I hallucinated seeing Huey come to the door and I grabbed another knife. I remember being very afraid.

As I later got a copy of the 911 call, I have been able to figure out that at that point the 911 operator and I agreed for me to go and see how she was. I found her and stabbed her again – one last time. It was in the neck. I do not know why. I have been trying for over three years to figure that out and can only guess about it. To this day I love Deb dearly and miss her more than ever. I do know that in the midst of the 911 call, I swallowed about 170 codeine type aspirins. I also know and thank God for the fact that I was not angry when I did it. It was not out of malice or envy, revenge or anything like that. I take full responsibility for what I've done. I think about her constantly and still love her very much. I should never have killed her. If only I could have stopped myself.

I will say that I was very traumatized by the destruction of my little family and believe I was mentally unstable in the weeks leading up to her death. However, I do not wish to try to excuse myself for what happened, and whatever state of mind I was in, *I* was ultimately responsible for what I did. I should never have killed her, I never ever thought I would kill anyone. There was so much to it, yet it was so fast and unreal. But the bottom line is that Deborah lost her life and I must pay for that. If the death penalty was optional, I'd take it.

I am continually punished for what I did – the loss of my life out there with my son – but I accept that.

It's been more than three years since Deborah died and I've been behind bars ever since. I've served about a quarter of my sentence which means at least nine more years before I would be considered for full parole. It's possible I could get day parole and go to a halfway house before then, but that's unlikely until I've served at least a total of 10 or 11 years.

About 16 hours a day is spent locked in my cell. It has a single cot, sink and toilet. I thank God for the compassion of the Canadian government, allowing us to buy a TV and radio to have in here. In my confined space, I have some pictures of family and friends that I've put up on the walls. I also have a picture of Deborah in my photo album.

I spend a lot of time writing letters, mostly to my dad and mom. My older brother has disowned me, I never hear from my younger brother, and my sister, well, she was supporting me to some degree but that stopped. After she read a news story, she said she was ashamed of me and cancelled a lot of visits. My dad still visits me even though it is difficult, as he lives in British Columbia.

I pray, read my Bible a great deal, go to chapel and do workouts in my cell. We don't have any equipment there. It's pushups and that type of exercise.

It isn't easy believing in God in prison. You get a lot of flak. There haven't been any serious threats, but there's always the danger of a punch to the head. There are taunts. It's seen by some as a weakness, a goody-goody type of thing.

Basically, if you go to prison – at least a maximum security one – you'll spend the few hours out of your cell working at jobs such as cleaning or duties in the kitchen. There is a small payment, about a dollar an hour. I work in the kitchen. As far as the remaining three hours, there is some free time, although as you can appreciate it is not exactly free, to visit, if there are visitors, go to chapel, the gymnasium and that sort of thing. It's back to our cells at 9 p.m. and the process repeats itself for as many years as you are held behind bars. It's like living in hell in here.

The days are full of drudgery, apprehension and fear. One never knows what's going to happen in a day. Tension is very high and we have very few ways to vent our frustrations. Most people who get stabbed in here get stabbed in the back. That's just the way it is. I've been lucky. I've only been in one fight. I had been in prison for about a year and some guy was bullying me. I threw the first punch, he tumbled down the stairs and that was it. He turned out to be a skinhound, a sex-offender. I then had to go to kangaroo court, that's what we call the prison justice system, and was fined $25. As far as personal safety in here, there is a constant threat of getting beaten or stabbed. It's hard to get away from it. You try to resolve any differences as peacefully as you can, pretty well on your own. If there is a fight, no one interferes until the guards come.

I suffer from anxiety and depression. My nerves are shot and I get many headaches. I am very lonely. Some people are gay, but I'm not. I've never been approached in a serious way. There's a lot of joking about it. You know it happens, but you don't actually see it, at least I haven't.

Because I'm not gay, I never get touched in a compassionate way. I long to have a massage or someone to rub my neck when I have a headache. I pace the floor of my cell several hours a day. I have started to rub my own feet and rock myself on my bed. Sometimes, I talk or sing to myself.

Lately, my mind wanders away so easily. It's very hard to concentrate on any one thing for any length of time. I am always worried about things. The food is terrible and mealtimes are always quite stressful. Many of the prisoners get mad about the food.

Many times I feel like I complain too much. Do I have a reason? I don't know. A lot of prisoners are actually very understanding people. They've been there. But most of them all have big problems of their own, so I really can't talk to them too much.

The medical staff here is a mockery. They've refused to treat me for my nervous anxiety condition. Instead they provide Tylenol 2s to treat one of the symptoms and anti-depressants that seem to foul up my stomach. I think I have permanent damage, plus my mind is very forgetful.

I go through very serious bouts of wanting to end it all. I thought about it for about two hours one night, but kept telling myself not to hurt my dad or Bradley. Or Jerry and Leah or Rick and Bev. They're two Christian couples who I know from the street. They're middle-aged, responsible citizens and are very supportive, bringing Brad to visit me about once a month.

As far as ending it all, I've got the means to do it and know it would be fast. I'm almost at the point where I think the Lord would forgive me because I just can't carry the load any more. I really hope you understand, my God. Unless something happens, I can see it's only a matter of time. I've been fighting it off for three years now. Last fall I told my psychologist about it, but then had to quickly restate that I wasn't serious about it, because he told me their solution is to put you in the hole for a while until it "passes." What a joke!

As I conclude my story, it's yet another day. I've seen the prison psychiatrist and I'm feeling a little better. For how long, I don't know.

What I do know is I would like to state just a few more things and then leave you with a poem I wrote.

My son Brad will be 19 when, and if, I get out. I will have missed 12 years of his life, his whole growing up pretty well, except when he was little. His natural mother, Kathy, is raising him.

I take full responsibility for what I did, but now that it's over and the smoke has cleared I can see a connection with rejection. I felt terribly rejected when my mom left my dad. I felt I had lost my mom. Maybe it was that fear of rejection when it was clear Deborah was leaving. There's quite a bit of similarity.

I pray for Deborah and her family; especially Dezarae, all the time. I can't imagine what I've done to those wonderful people.

I feel strongly that I should make some reference to God. It is important for me to state that all my hope lies in the compassion and forgiveness of Jesus Christ (Ps. 32:5; Prov. 28:13). Psalm #116 says so much for me. But best of all, I know that He has Deborah now in peace, and I will see her again (First Thes. 4: 13, 14).

POEM

I live these days in sorrow and want
Forever realizing the pain I've caused
Not just for them but for myself
Relentless grief for the son I've lost

Continually confined to hope and want
To cry and miss and wish for not
She was so dear, so full of life
She's with you now, my darling wife

Maybe, somehow, it's fitting gain
To make me breathe the heavy rain
And remind me of forever more
The family she loved, oh help them Lord.

I search my soul for a place to hide
Oh God, I wish it was me that died.

I Didn't Even Think About It

John Mackenzie

"I pulled the trigger, he went back against the wall, put his arms to his chest, looked up and said 'You bastard' – and died."

t happened February 26, 1982, at Newcastle, New Brunswick. John Norman MacKenzie, 22 at the time, wielding a sawed-off shotgun, a long way from his British Columbia birthplace, blew away another human being. It was during a futile attempt to rob the victim. A few days later, underneath a sleeping bag, on top of a sawed-off loaded shotgun stolen from Saskatchewan, a peaceful arrest was made in the attic of a garage.

Before this, John MacKenzie had worked in a stereo shop, had spent four years in the military reserve specializing in weapons and explosives, and had been admitted to university. At the time of the killing, he was on the loose from a Calgary jail. His record consisted of convictions for theft, mischief, joy riding, dangerous driving, break & enter, possession of a prohibited weapon and possession of stolen property. Additionally, there were more than 20 outstanding warrants for alleged crimes in British Columbia, Alberta and Ontario, ranging from hit & run to armed robbery to prison escape.

Throughout the Newcastle murder case, the youthful, self-proclaimed career criminal, who has since admitted committing dozens of jewellery store robberies and a bank hold-up for which he has never been charged, refused to co-operate with police except by his plea of guilty and later agreement to give testimony. Part of his evidence was to deny that he had anything to do with the prison stabbing of Joseph Reginald Pitre, originally co-accused in the murder until a stay of proceedings was entered on the indictment.

On September 21, 1982, John MacKenzie was sentenced: "Imprisonment for life, without eligibility for parole until you have served at least 20 years."

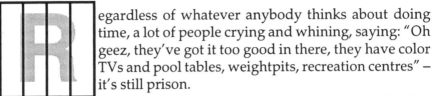egardless of whatever anybody thinks about doing time, a lot of people crying and whining, saying: "Oh geez, they've got it too good in there, they have color TVs and pool tables, weightpits, recreation centres" – it's still prison.

The day to day drudgery and stress involved in doing time is something a lot of people don't realize. It's a political game, and you make friends and you make enemies. And there's always the constant possibility of violence happening, not only to yourself, but to people you care about. Even if you aren't involved in anything at all. Your friends may be involved in something, somebody may think your friends are involved in something, and the reality of the situation is not nearly as important as the perception. It may very well be that people are targeting a friend of yours, for whatever reason: drug debts; looked at the guy the wrong way at breakfast; whatever it is. And they figure in order to take him out, they may have to take you out first to prevent you from backing him up. That's something that is in the back of the minds of everybody daily.

The worst part of being in prison is the knowledge of the loss of freedom. It's the fact that you know that you can't get up and leave when you want to. The actual physical loss of freedom is one thing to deal with; it's the knowledge that the confinement is there that is the biggest stress. If there's a dispute, you can't get up and take off out of the building and go to a different location. Nope. You're going to see that guy tomorrow, and you're going to see him the next day, and the next day, and the next day, and the next day. And if it's not resolved, it may very well be over in some other method that you're not looking forward to. It's sort of like a constant self-vigilance on what you say, how you act, what you do. You hesitate. You know somebody's been stabbed or something. You don't want to walk in the office and ask for a request form. Why? Because somebody's going to say: "What's he doing in the office?" You know, you don't want to talk to a bull unless you've got two or three guys there with you to witness what's being said. That applies to everybody. It's a constant vigilance of your own actions and how those actions are perceived by other people. Most people on the street don't pay a whole lot of attention to that.

Most people can be reasoned with, but there are times when there's no point in it. There's gonna be times where action will be taken against you or your friends. Want a friend? Buy a dog. It's [a human] characteristic; people want to fit in, really bad. You know, even a situation like this, people want to be sociable. They need other people around them to communicate with, talk to. What happens far too often is that people start hanging around with the wrong people. They do not realize the duplicitous nature of most individuals in the Pen. I'll be the first person to tell you, "Hey, Pens house dangerous people. That's their nature. That's what they're there for." And a lot of people seem to forget that when they show up here. Everybody operates differently when they first enter prison. People are individuals, and there's no set pattern. Probably the best thing, if somebody wants to come in and stay out of shit, is talk with as few people as you can and don't try to fit in with the shooters (high-profile people), because the shooters are the guys that are going to create misery for yourself and themselves. You try to avoid them. Find one or two people that seem to have their shit together, for themselves, and stick with that crowd. That is usually the best. Prison gangs are not like they used to be. A gang now is usually probably like four or five guys. People have realized in the last few years, that in almost any joint you go to, if you've got a gang of 10 guys, you've clued-in the man to your gang. Because the odds are, somebody not saying something on purpose about inmate activity, is saying something out of stupidity. When that happens, the guards are tipped off.

A lot of people aren't aware of the technology behind the intelligence system in the institution. The telephones, every phone in this joint, are all hooked up in such a way that they don't have to be off the hook, you don't have to be talking into them. If you're having a conversation 10 feet from that bloody phone, they can pick up every

John Mackenzie —"I don't believe there's one cataclysmic event that all of a sudden the person wakes up and says, 'Well, that's it. I'm becoming a crook today.' It's a series of things. Personality plays a big part of it. Environment is a key factor as well."

bloody word. On the hook, off the hook, it don't matter, they'll hear you. And you get guys all the time figure they're being just the coolest people in the world, doing their little deals, left, right, for dope, whatever it is, two feet from the phone. I've had guys approach me about stuff right in the vestibule, where there's literally what we call hot boxes. They're little microphone boxes designed to talk to the officer in the sub-control. Who's running that? It doesn't even cross their minds. They'll come in and say: "Hey Freddy, Harry. Any hash around? Any of this around? Any of that around?" The screws standing six feet away in the glass bubble listening to every word. They don't even think about it, right? Ninety percent of the time, the guys are ratting themselves out, out of carelessness and that's why they get themselves in shit all the time. They don't realize the constant surveillance.

The biggest problem as far as the cons go, is that cons, as people, tend to downgrade things they despise. If you don't like something, or you hate something, or somebody, you tend not to give them credit for anything. "I don't like the guy, he's stupid. I don't like the screws, they're dumb." They're not all dumb. Yeah, a lot of the line screws are stupid, they can't get a job anywhere else, they can't get hired at Dairy Queen, and that's why they've been correctional officer 2s for 20 years. But the guy that's done 20 years with the RCMP, worked on police intelligence, well, he's not an idiot. Might be nice if he was, but unfortunately he's not. They specialize in gathering intelligence. Very few people keep a counter-intelligence attitude about them, not realizing that the goal of these individuals is to gather information. That's what they live for. That's what they're paid to do. You have to be aware, you have to take the attitude that my actions are being watched and judged by another individual who is not my friend.

Starting at the beginning, I was born in Victoria, British Columbia. My father was also a career criminal and my mother married him so she couldn't testify against him in a possession of stolen property trial. They went down to Seattle and had a wedding, and when they came back and she was subpoenaed as a hostile witness against him, she said:

"Oh, I cannot be compelled to testify against Mr. MacKenzie."

"Well, why is that?"

"Well, we're married. I can't be compelled to testify against my husband."

My father did end up getting busted on another charge and he ended up doing a bunch of time in BC Pen. My mother took off to

Toronto when I was 14 months old, and I was basically adopted by a foster family there, and grew up there until I was 11.

They had four of their own kids. I would best describe them probably as a Victorian mentality. Everything was very proper: nobody swore; nobody yelled; acted up. But times were changing. This was in the late '60s to early '70s. People were changing, society was changing, and they weren't. Their own kids were rebelling against them. I certainly wasn't helping the situation any. Most of their own kids, the youngest is 10 years older than I am, formed an in-house gang almost. It was sort of like the kids against the parents. It was always a game of cat and mouse in the house.

My foster father was basically a weak individual. The mother, to a small extent, ran the household, and was very forceful, but also a bitch.

Even as a kid, I was always conscious that these were not my parents. It's funny. It was kind of like being aware that these are not my parents, but these are my brothers and sisters. You know, Pauline, Ross, Doug and Marilyn, who were their own kids, we thought of each other as family. Those were my brothers and sisters, however, those were not my parents. It's a difficult thing to try and rationalize. I guess you don't. It's more of just a feeling, an emotive response. So you know, you can't really think like that.

I don't believe there's one cataclysmic event, that all of a sudden the person wakes up and says, "Well, that's it. I'm becoming a crook today." It's a series of things. Personality plays a big part of it. Environment is a key factor as well. There's a whole lot of people who go through exactly the same type of situations that don't become crooks. I don't think anybody could ever nail it down, and say "this caused it." It's one of those things that happened. I mean, what is the event that caused somebody to become a lawyer? What is the thing that causes somebody to become a doctor?

I started running into trouble with the law when I was about six. I think that was the time I threw a snowball through the police car window and hit the cop in the head. The cop was sitting on the side of the road with his radar gun, trying to get guys for speeding. I just thought he made a rather nice target. Six or seven years old with a snowball, and I immediately got ratted out by four or five friends that were standing around and couldn't believe I'd just done that. By the time I got home, the cop car was parked in the driveway. Nothing happened. It was just basically try to scare the shit out of the little demon.

By the time I was 11, there was an incident with the cops, and I can't even remember what the hell it was. Anyways, the cops got involved and the Children's Aid Society got involved. I think initially they gave me this ultimatum, to try and scare the shit out of me, but it just didn't work. They made a line like, "You can either stay here with this family or you can go live in a group home, and you have that decision to make." And, clearly, I said:

"I'll wait in the car."

I got up and I left and I walked out to the white Volkswagen and sat there while everybody stared out the window:

"Shit! He is in the car!"

Until I was 16, I got tossed around to various homes. Nobody cares. I think I was 13 years old when I got my hands on my first handgun and was out practising with that thing. I remember sitting up in the bedroom, stripping that thing down, hunting through the shag carpet for the return springs which bounced out either side of the slide when I took it apart, because I never stripped one down before.

One time in the group home, I think I was about 14 years old, we'd get kids talking about weapons, about hunting and shit, and on more than one occasion the kid would say,

"Well, my dad's got some guns."

"Oh really! Your dad got any handguns?"

"Yeah, I think he's got a few. I think he's got like a revolver thing . . ."

"Oh really! Why don't we go to the park and play around with it tonight?"

"Oh no, we're busy, we're going to a movie."

"Well, after you get back from the movie?"

"Well, we won't be back until 9 or 10, it'll be too late."

"Oh, OK."

Next day it would be: "Did you know somebody broke into my house last night and stole my dad's guns?"

"Geez, you're kidding! It's a tragedy!"

Sixteen years old, I robbed my first bank. At that point, it was a career for armed robbery for sure. I did that on a bet. There were four of us who lived in the group home sitting in McDonalds, on Yonge Street, right across from a bank. We were just talking. My partner knew I had the piece on me, and guys were talking about it, because we'd been doing some B&Es and stuff like that, getting not too bad money. But still it wasn't anything impressive right? And somebody made a crack about, "Robbing that bank would be a good way."

And, I said, "Actually that's not such a bad idea."

One of the other guys said, "You don't have the parts to rob the bank."

And my partner threw me into it and said, "John will rob the bank, no problem at all. I'll bet you $50 he'll rob the bank."

I walked about, walked a little ways away, and there was a drugstore there and I picked up a pair of nylons, and walked back to McDonald's. Walked into the McDonald's, I had a toque, had the jacket which I borrowed – I borrowed my partner's jacket because I had my jacket on underneath it. Had the toque on, had the nylon just under the toque-line, just walked into the bank, basically with the nylon just rolled down. Just kept my head down, walked in and pulled the gun, empty the tills, got three of the tills, out the other door of the bank, and gone. Got about $3800. Never got pinched for it.

I decided $3800 wasn't enough money for armed robbery. As far as I was concerned, it was a pretty high risk for not enough money. Three of us, the one guy bowed out of it – he just wasn't comfortable with that type of action at all – started doing ARs regularly in the city.

I was motivated by boredom, pure excitement. I personally believe that anybody that's a crook professionally, that's what they consider they do for a living. It's more than just the money. There's lots of ways to make money. It's also, you become an adrenalin addict. It's like an adrenalin junkie. You live for the excitement.

The first time I ever had to fire a gun was during an AR. I was about 17 and we hit a jewellery store. I had a Remington .870, 12-gauge, sawed-off front and back, about 18, 20 inches long. My other partner also had a shotgun, and the other partner had a handgun. We walked in, pulled the pieces, had masks on, and the guy just looked at me and said:

"I ain't giving you nothing, you f—ing punks. I'm calling the cops."

And he reached for the phone. I blew the phone off the wall with the 12-gauge.

"Get on the ground or you're next."

He was on the ground in a hurry, more than co-operative.

The police took a key interest in us on another armed robbery, which they never proved we did. The story goes that the individuals that committed the robbery – it was a home-invasion of a guy that owned a jewellery store – entered the house by force, when they were sitting down at the dining-room table. Masks on, shotguns, and apparently they taped the family to the chairs.

We never were officially picked up for it, just word got out that our little gang was responsible for it. It was the sort of thing where the sheriff told you to be out of town by sundown and we left.

Off to Vancouver. I travelled alone. That was my personal decision. I really believe that once the cops are onto you, and they decide to get you, they will get you one way or the other. And once they're onto you like that, it's time to pack up shop and move. They don't have to be smart, they don't have to be quick, all they have to do is be patient.

This time [in Vancouver] – don't shit in your own backyard – we're travelling to Edmonton and Calgary to do our ARs. Do our scores and we're out of town usually within 40 minutes afterwards. Never take a plane. Always bus or train.

The last one that we did in Calgary was a night deposit for a restaurant where I'd actually had dinner one night and I looked around and estimated seating capacity to be about 50, 75. I figured your average person at the meal would probably drop anywhere between $50 and $100, and we worked it out at the time, it was somewhere around 30 or 40 grand we were supposed to get. And we came out pretty close. I think we got 26 grand, in cash, out of that. But it was just two of us which made it not too bad of a score.

Every Sunday, they'd do their receipts for the week. This time, we didn't get the whole week's receipts. I think we only got like half. They must have done a double deposit because I remember we were actually supposed to get more than we did. Anyway, the guy was doing the money-drop to a night deposit. I just stood maybe 10 feet from the night deposit looking in a store window, with a 12-gauge strapped around one shoulder, hanging down my side, under a jacket, waiting for him to walk over. Just as he was getting the key in the night deposit box, I walked in. I wondered if he'd been robbed before because when I racked the 12, he just jumped a straight three feet in the air, like he was on a f——ing trampoline. He jumped straight up in the air, came down, and I said:

"All right, drop the bag! Drop the bag, turn around, go back into the restaurant, call the police and tell them you've been robbed!"

And it was, "I won't call the police! I swear I'm not going to call the police! I won't call anybody!"

And I said, "Listen! I'm telling you: drop the bag, go back in and tell them you've been robbed. No big deal, no muss, no fuss, just get the f—- out of here."

"I'm not going to call the police, I swear! I won't tell anybody!"

This went on for a little while and it got to the point where I said,

"Listen! Drop the bag, get the f—- back in the restaurant or I'm going to blow you away right here!"

And he walked away like Tin Man. I just picked up the bag, walked out, gone.

Twenty-six thousand dollars is not a helluva lot. If, and, no shit, we did this a couple of times, we tried to account for our money, we could account for maybe 10 maybe 25 percent of it and the rest of it would just be gone. I was never into the dope very much. I didn't have a fancy car or anything. I just drove an MGB. I'd see something, like a painting I liked. I remember one time there was a set of swords, like a Cottana and a Makazishi, like the Samurai swords. Together in a really nice dragonfly stand. Dragonflies have two sets of wings. The top pair of wings held the Cottana and the bottom pair of wings held the Makazishi. I think it was made of Mongolian wood and it was just a beautiful set-up. The thing was like four-and-a-half grand or something, and I just said: "Oh well, that's nice," walked in and took that back to the apartment. You know, just go down and see: "Oh yeah, nice brass bed." Stopped in at Dunn's Tailors. Get a set of clothing, suits. Lot of money on ammunition and firearms.

Eventually what happened, and I never did find out to this day how anybody found out, but we were staying at the Carriage House in Calgary. We were coming out of the Coach House, which is the dining lounge they've got there. My partner was already upstairs, because I was paying the bill. I didn't have any guns on me or anything, no pieces. Everything was up in the apartment getting cleaned.

I was waiting for the elevator to show up and I looked in the mirror behind me, and I could see the desk clerk talking to two cops. They were plainclothed, but obviously cops, suffering bad neck twitches in my direction. Then the cop, sort of looking, one of them being sly, pulled out his walkie-talkie and then walked around to the far corner where I couldn't see him talking into it. Real swift one, that boy. And I said:

"Oh boy, we're f—-ing had. Time to get the hell out of here."

Took the elevator back up to the room, told Brad,

"Pack up the goodies, we're gone."

Grabbed two shotguns, two handguns, a .357, a .45. The .45 was stripped down at the time because Brad was cleaning it. But we loaded up the two shotguns, Remington .870 Wingmaster again, sort of a trademark for me. If I can get a shotgun, that's what I'll use. The other one was a Sabre Stevens .820B chromed riot gun which I had bought off a guy in the Okanagan for something like eight bucks. He'd stolen it somewhere. This thing, I didn't like using. It was a really nice, really nice shotgun. Fourteen-inch barrel on it, chromed right from the front, a gold bead side on the front. A trademark weapon if ever there was. If you ever wanted to get pegged for every job you ever did, this was the thing to use. Unfortunately, my partner took a liking to it, so he was using that.

The hallways in the Carriage House are sort of like a split-L. If you are looking down one hallway, you can see one elevator door but it's like a little anteroom there and the hallway continues down in the opposite corner. You can only ever see down half. So we opened the door. I had the 12-gauge, I was in front. I gave her a peek around the corner and the hallway was clear, and we knew that the stairwell down at the far end went down into the parking lot around the back of the Carriage House. And the other one, we'd gone down and checked it out but it was one of those panic bars that trip the fire alarm, or whatever, when you whack it, so we never opened it. So we're going down the hallway into the anteroom. I'd just turned the corner and the cops are clearing the people out of their rooms. There's like five or six cops on the floor and they're just standing there. Everybody gives you an, "Oh my God."

"Down on the ground! Nobody move!"

One cop tried to go for his gun and the other cop stopped him. Grabbed his hand, because they were in the hallway like three feet wide, and I had a 12-gauge. The one cop said,

"Uh-uh, that's dumb."

So they all laid down on the ground. My partner left the other way and I just held there for a second. Then I just backed up and ran down the hall, ran down the stairs. Yelled on the way down that I was coming down so that my partner didn't shoot me. He was waiting at the bottom of the stairs by the door, his shotgun pointed up behind me. I came up to him, boom, gave that door a flying dropkick and landed in the middle of the kitchen with a 12-gauge. People just looked and of course were diving for cover and shit. We just flew through that kitchen, out the other door. So, boom, we kicked that out, we just go out in the field. We lie down in the field now, because we know we're not going to get away, but we got the shotguns pointing back towards the door handle. The door opens and about six inches of a .38 comes out and that cops flies out of the door and lands face first into the snow. And he gets up and he's yelling at his partner,

"You f——ing asshole, you trying to get me killed? They've got f——ing shotguns! Let them get away!"

His partner pushed him out the door!

We got away. We crawled through the scrub brush field, while they were busy arguing with each other, and then ran across this open parking lot that was lit. I've got a shotgun in one hand and an attache case in the other, and I got a 12-gauge. We both ran across this open parking lot, about six cars cruising by 40 feet away from us in plain view and I guess nobody decided to look out their passenger window. They were just concentrating on heading to the Carriage House, which suited us just fine, because we were concentrating on heading away from the Carriage House. We ran across a school parking lot, rested beside there for a second, then realized that we'd be hashed if we stayed there because they'd be getting the dogs, right, so took the chance, ran right across Macleod Trail. Nobody called the cops, I assume, because we never got pinched. Went into one of those two-storey apartment complexes, almost like a little condo outfit. I had a bootknife on me and I used that just to slip the latch on one of the doors. Run underneath the stairs, put the handgun together, loaded up the .357. I put the .45 together, loaded that up, and I just let the slide go. Then I heard,

"Oh!"

There's a broad peeking under the stairs. There's two guys huffing and puffing with 12-gauges laying against the wall, attache case open, assembling a handgun. She f——ed off. I said,

"Well, it's about time to get out of here."

And we booted it. Called a guy that I knew in Calgary, he got us a room at the Calgary Inn and we decided to lay low for three or four days, just hide out there. We paid for the room a week in advance and that was it. Ordered room service, big meals for one person, and whenever room service showed up the shower was on, the washroom door was closed, nobody was visible. Money was left on the table.

"Yeah, just leave it on the table and get out."

And we did that.

Now, one of the guy's girls that had booked the room for us got picked up. She thought it was a drug deal or something. She had no idea in the world who she was ratting out or what she was ratting out. The morning we decided it was time to get the hell out of here, maybe go from Calgary to Edmonton, dump the guns, then book a flight from Edmonton to Van. Brad got up to change the channel. The door was open a few inches and it was a TAC team there. You could just see the guy with the shotgun, the M16, peeking through the door. The guy saw me, Brad saw me going "f——," and the door goes boom. I was laying on the bed and I had the Remington right there. One was off the stove, he was ready to go, all you had to do was go take the safety off, pull the trigger.

The guy ran right in front of me. I'm laying on the bed. He ran, stands right in front of me. Brad and I are at, like 90-degree angles to each other in the room, and he stands there going:

"You get on the ground! Don't you move! You get on the ground, you stay on the bed, don't you move, you just stay there," pointing his gun back and forth. And I said, well, we could take him, right, you know, the 12-gauge at that range. I don't care if he's got a vest on or not, the guy's going down and that's the end of that story. But where there's one TAC team guy, there's 10 more and you're usually sur-rounded. So we said f—— it, right, just give up, no big deal. But then the rest of the TAC team, I couldn't believe the Calgary TAC team, what a bunch of clowns. The rest of them, as a group, like they'd been crazy glued together, came down this little hallway all in a bundle.

Later on, one of the sergeants or somebody said what did I think of the TAC team, because I'd been hit by a couple of others before. I said,

"You guys are a bunch of clowns here. One kick could have killed you all."

They came down this little hall in a bundle and if I had been a nut bar, I could have gone boom, got the guy in front of me, he would have been out, jumped out of the bed, and as soon as I hear them coming down the hall, just stick a 12-gauge around the corner. I got four more rounds, just go bang, bang, bang, bang, right? They're down. Now I got an M16 lying at my feet from the guy that's down in the first place, picked that thing up and it would have been toast. If I hada' been convinced that using the gun would have prevented me from being arrested, I would have used it. At that point in my life, I wouldn't have lost any more sleep than over the poor escargot that I just ate.

Didn't even think about it, not for one second. When you're that age, 17, 18, 19, you view yourself as immortal, where you don't consider loss of life. That's not something that's thought about, not for one second. There's no animosity, no hatred or anything. It's like a cat and mouse game. I'm a crook, and I'm an armed robber. I got a gun. He's a cop, he knows he's a cop, that's his job. If he wants a safe job, and makes sure he comes home to the wife and kids every night, well go work at McDonald's for f— sakes.

This was the first time we were actually looking at any type of real time. They had me down at that point: two counts of pointing a firearm; two counts possession of a prohibited weapon; two counts possession of a restricted weapon; a count of possession of house breaking instruments – I had a complete set of lock picks with me. They tried to charge us with a couple of armed robberies which didn't go anywhere. Yeah, we started looking at some real time and I decided that I really didn't feel like staying in the Calgary Remand Centre anymore.

We rigged the security elevator to take it down to the floor we needed to go to, forced the door to the courtroom, looked up, and we could see one guy buffing the floor. We had to force the door, which sort of f—-ed up the whole plan. My idea was to just sort of like vanish, fall off the face of the earth and have them crashing their melons as to where the hell somebody went. That didn't work when we had to force the courtroom door.

I drove to New Brunswick. They were tapping somebody else's phone. We had a meeting with this person, they knew the meeting involved illegal activities, just from the conversation on the phone, they knew who the individual was, and that was that. They followed into the site, in order to pick him up. They didn't have a clue in the world who the hell I was until I was actually in the police station and they were asking me who I was. I assumed they were after me right from the word go. It wasn't until they started addressing me as Mr. Vankeer, who was on the name on the ID that I was using at the time, that I realized, these guys don't know who I am. And I almost made it, I almost got bail. It took them 72 hours to get my fingerprints back and I was almost gone. If they had been a day slower on retrieving those prints, too bad, damn. They didn't have a clue about the Calgary charges, it was a murder charge they got me on. The individual that was driving the car at the time when the murder went down, basically turned evidence against me and got me a life bit. He got air-conditioned, by way of a knife. Died twice. Once in the joint hospital at Dorchester Penitentiary and once on the way down. But the ambulance resuscitators brought him back both times.

With the earlier killing, the victim attempted to get the shotgun off me. It was sort of robbery and he decided that he could get the gun. He was wrong. I pulled the trigger, he went back against the wall, put his arms to his chest, looked up, and said "You bastard" – and died. And that one second I thought, this motherf—er is wearing a bullet proof vest and I better reload. It was just the shock of the reaction hadn't quite sunk in yet, for him, and he had that two seconds.

When you kill somebody, there's usually not very much blood if you've given the kill shot. There ain't much blood because the heart has stopped and once the heart stops there's not a whole lot of bleeding. That's how I knew he was dead for sure, he wasn't bleeding very much. The shot took about a 30-degree angle from the front left side. One ounce Remington slug hit him almost square on the sternum, number four buckshot right underneath it, blew out four inches of his spinal column, half his heart and a quarter of one lung.

As far as going to sleep that night, I didn't even think about it. I tend to try and look forward. The only time you're looking back, is if you look back to plan the future. To say, OK, these are the possible actions that people are going to take because of what I've done in the past, and these are the things that I have to do in order to plan or prepare for them. In the last few years, this is sort of really neat, you spend more time realizing what it is to take a life. A lot of that deals with the fact I've seen a lot of people that I love die. And that sort of hits home. But when you're 18, 19, you don't think about that. It's very methodical, very mechanical, very almost TV-like. It's very two-dimensional.

While I was picking up some ID, that's when I got picked up. At that time, after being sentenced, it was Dorchester. For me anyways, and other people that I've talked to, it's much the same thing. There's always the fear there, but it's not something you can draw on. If you draw on it you're f—ed. I guess the best way to put it is, out of a few of the novels, fear is the mind killer. Fear is what stops you from thinking, and if you let fear take control, you can no longer plan and you've lost. Fear is the little death that leads to the big one.

Initially, what happened is the guy that was rolling over on me figured that he could do a lot better, probably because he was in there with me at the time, and he didn't know that I had a clue the whole thing was rolling over. He hired somebody else for $2500 to kill me. And then he had second thoughts about it, and he himself told me that this guy was planning on killing me, expecting me to go out and do him immediately. Instead of that, I went over, approached the individual, told him point-blank that I had a weapon on me, was fully prepared to use it and said:

"I hear you have a contract on me."

And he sort of looked at me and said, "Well, who told you this?"

And I told him. "Reggie told me that you have a contract on me."

He said "Yeah."

I said: "Do you want to fill it?"

He goes, "Well, he's the guy that hired me."

And I said, "What?"

He says, "Well, yeah. He's the guy that's paid me. Promised me $2500 if I'd kill you."

I said, "Really!"

And we sat down. We had a long talk about that. After we had the talk, he said,

"You know, really, why would he?" He was sort of shocked. Here's a 19-year-old kid, with a good size guy, right? He says, "Why the f—— did you ever come up to me?"

I said, "Because I was pretty confident that if I came down here that I could kill you." And I was. If you don't want to play, don't step on the field.

Dorchester's an old, old place. It's the second or third oldest joint in Canada. It's made of hewn limestone blocks about 36 inches long and 24 inches high. The wall, I think, is 12-and-a-half or 13-and-a-half feet thick at the base and two feet thick at the top. There's cracks in it so big in some places you can literally step into them and disappear. Guys have physically climbed the wall, just free-climbing right to the top.

We had one excellent, excellent, plan to escape which I knew would have worked perfectly. Unfortunately, some guys from segregation tried a similar thing, so similar, like it was so close to what we had planned, that it f——ed up our plans completely. The difference between our two plans was going up in between the cell blocks, out to the roof, and pry the roof up, which had tar and sheet metal on top of it. Because they were in Seg, they didn't have access to anything they could sharpen – a bar or anything. All they had was a weightlifting bar and they tried to hammer their way through the roof. In the process of hammering their way through the roof with this bar, they made so much noise that guys down on the far cell block could hear them clear as day. Like what the hell is that? Bang, bang, bang! And it went on for 20 minutes, half-an-hour, and eventually the screws must have said "What the hell is that?" and ran up to the roof and got the guys while they were busy trying to hammer their way through. Our plan was almost identical except that we had stuff that had been sharpened down to wedges, which we could have just stuck in there. That would have got the roof, that would have got the stuff off nice and quiet. No noise, no muss, no fuss.

This wasn't ours, friend. So we were never charged with anything. It was some other guys that tried it and f——ed up our plan. In the course of events some other shit went down. We ended up getting locked up. Farce. Bit of a gang war, right in the joint. And we got segregation for another year and a half or so.

Segregation is 23 hours a day lock-up. You read lots. That's basically it. You read lots. People think that's a joke. I'm banging off a novel a day, 400, 500-page novel, no problem. I read *Shogun* in one sitting.

I used to work out occasionally, but I never put a whole lot of faith in muscle masses saving your buns. It ain't happening. If you're going to be in a fight, it's going to be your head and speed that's going to take over rather than just sheer power.

They have psychologists that are supposed to interview you once a week and write a report on your psychological condition. Instead, they sit up in their office once a week and say, "Um . . . MacKenzie's fine. Next."

Guys do stuff, and you know, they do right. They do go stir crazy. They slash up and that. I can't say that I understand it, but I sympathize with them.

You try to shut out life removed from prison. It depends on the amount of time you get and how you do it. Now, for myself, at this point and time in my bit, I don't think about it hardly at all. The world that I think about is the joint. I've learned that you can't do time in the street, or in the joint and on the street at the same time. It doesn't work like that. You will f—— yourself up.

After segregation at Dorchester, the Saskatchewan Penitentiary in Prince Albert, also known as PA, turned over to population, where inmates who had previously been separated from each other were now mixed together. We were given the options of A: staying locked up; or B: getting shipped out of the region. We said, f—— it. We'll get shipped out of the region. It's done fast. They've got a plane there, she's warmed up and ready to go. Bus pulls up, they've got a video camera there just so nobody can say, "I was beaten, dragged, gassed, and then tossed on the plane." Video camera, boom, you're on the plane, doors shut, props are wound up, you're up. Same thing land-ing. Lands, boom, off the plane, into a bus, into the Pen.

Shithole full of creeps. The administration there ran it like their own little kingdom. Jimmy O [former warden Jim O'Sullivan] was God. That's sort of the end of that story. Whole lot of guys there that have serious problems. And when I say serious problems, I'm talking guys that are in on skin beefs, rape crimes, right, and they're just f——ing in the melon as far as I'm concerned. I do not understand what the hell is going through their heads, and I doubt if there will ever be a treatment for them. I can understand the motivation for somebody that does an armed robbery, B&E, it's a combination of excitement by putting your own skin on the line, and the monetary reward at the end.

I was locked up constantly. The skinhounds are so paranoid that if you were looking at them the wrong way, or even if, you know, "What the f—— are you looking at?" Guy walks by and he's staring in your house. You don't do that. You don't look in the guy's house when you're walking by. That's his world and keep your head facing the other way – unless you know the guy. These guys walk by.

"You f——ing window shopping or what?"

"Oh, I'm sorry."

"Don't be sorry, be gone."

And the next thing you know there's a kite in, saying that you threatened to cut their melon off with a chainsaw. Then security would interview you and say,

"Geez, what happened?"

You'd say, "What happened with what?"

"Well, you threatened somebody the other day."

"No, I never threatened anybody."

"Well, we got it from a reliable source."

"Who? Kreston?"

I don't mind the hole. It's actually Seg in f——ing PA. Seg sort of sucks because it's open, all open bars. People are yelling. Half the guys sleep during the day, the other half sleep during the night. They're yelling back and forth constantly. It's really hard to get any rest or anything. When you go in the hole, the hole is built in the newer part of the joint and it's all solid doors. It's quiet all the time. They bring you your meals, 350 personal servants. There to see to your every need.

PA gets classified as officially medium security, and I get a little thing in the mail which says due to an identified knowledge of weapons, explosives and lock pickings, you are rated as maximum security. Also, on the following incidents: two suspicions of stabbings; getting caught with a handcuff key once; set of blueprints to the joint another time; what else do they have down there? I can't remember.

It wasn't bad when I first got here, October 6, 1992, at the Edmonton Institution, which is known as the Edmonton Max. Wasn't too bad as far as a max goes. It was pretty good. And then, couple of more killings went down in the joint just after we got here and the place just turned into a shithole at that point. A lot of the beefs that go down: two guys with a bad temper; wrong time; wrong day; wrong place; wrong move. It's not premeditated, it ain't planned. It's just a sudden flare of tempers and buff, it's off.

I'm vice-president of the lifers' group. We try and deal with the factors that affect people doing life specifically. Anybody that ain't doing a life bit has a date of release. You know that on this date your sentence expires and you're gone. That's it, period. Society, everybody, the parole board, they can all jump up and down and cry and whine all they like, date of expiry signed by that judge, you're gone, history. Bye-bye. Somebody that's doing life doesn't have that. There is no release date. There's nothing anywhere that says they ever have to let you go. All life sentences are just that. Life 20 means I'm going to do minimum 20 before I'll be able to apply for parole. Doesn't mean you're getting out. All it means is that you'll do 20 before we even consider letting you out.

As far as being eligible to apply for parole in six years, having now served about 14 years, right now the way things are in this country, I refuse to concern myself with that. I've got my immediate goals in front of me that I know that I want to do and that's what I concentrate on. I'm doing my damndest to get published as a science fiction writer and I'm breeding my fish left, right and centre. Other than that, the rest of the world can flush itself down the great shitter of existence.

When I talk about violent incidents in the past and the present, it may sound like I have a very cavalier attitude toward things, like so-and-so died. It's not the real attitude, but it's sort of the way you have to look at it because it's such an omnipresent thing when you're doing time. You can't get into this big headspace of, "Oh my God, it's a tragedy." It's something that's constantly there. To some extent you become inert to it, to where it's sort of like: "Oh really. So-and-so got the shit beat out of him. Oh that's nice. What's on channel 12, right?"

Because it's not a big thing anymore, right? That doesn't mean when you sit back and reflect on that, it's not a big thing. It is. And the person that I was, even five years ago or six years ago, it's not the person that I am today. And I've had even friends of mine, that knew me then, ask me about the change.

"Like what caused you to change?"

And I go, "I don't know." I really don't. It's beyond me. But you reach a point, you realize that the game you're playing, the big cat and mouse game, it's not a winning game for yourself or anybody else. People are getting hurt over bullshit.

When I was 19 years old, I was a dangerous, dangerous individual because I just didn't give a shit. And if the positions had been reversed, as a judge, I would have done the same thing. Honestly, looking at me, I would have said:

"No. Out of here. Next."

It's not that different in here than it is anywhere else. Life is what you make of it. Not only out there, but also in here. Only thing is, in here it's harder. I have had a bitch of a time, for the longest time, to get any books in on computer programming because there were visions of financial empires worldwide collapsing. John MacKenzie getting infinitely wealthy transferring hoards and hoards of money into an account, mysteriously. Somehow or other accessing it. Who knows, maybe buying the country. The feds see that security and can come up with things that just can't happen.

You say, "This is just not possible. It will not occur."

They say, "Well, you're an awful clever character."

You know I ain't that f——ing clever, I'll tell you that. But that's the sort of mentality you have to deal with. And it takes patience, and it takes practice to be able to stick with it. So many people, they just get frustrated with the shit, of dealing with the people on a day to day basis that they, in the long run, end up f——ing themselves.

We're hurting big time in here due to a lack of industrial training. For a lot of the time I've been involved in committee type stuff, try to make things better for everybody. And one of the things: a lot of people are in jail simply because they don't have a marketable skill. They don't have anything that they can go out with and earn a living. And at the same time, they've got pride, and they will not beg, and they will not go down to welfare, and they won't do these things, but they will rob. And unless you give them a marketable skill, something that they can compete in the workplace to earn a wage with, they will rob. They will be crooks. And CSC still doesn't seem to have this quite through their melon yet. They seem to think that if you throw people in jail for X number of years, they'll go out and all of a sudden they'll magically get a career and realize how futile they've been. It don't work like that. They're going to go out and they're going to say:

"Jesus Christ, I need this, this, this, this, this, and this. I don't have any marketable skill. Let's go steal."

There is no vocational shop in here right now at all.

The focus for education is from Grade 3 to Grade 9. Once you go past Grade 10, you're screwed. Until I got to this joint here, there was nobody that could teach Grade 11 or 12 chem. The one guy, a good friend of mine, actually wasn't a good friend of mine until I got a job down at the school as a cleaner, because it was the only thing that was available, was taking Grade 12 chem at the time. He was stuck because there was no teacher down there that could teach Grade 12 chem. He was working some shit on the blackboard, trying to balance chemical equations, and he was having a nightmare with it due to the fact that some of it involved gas equations. So I go through the process of explaining how to balance these equations.

One of the teachers walked in, looked at me: "You know how to do that?"

I said, "Well yeah. I took chemistry years ago."

"Oh, really."

Next thing I knew I was hired as a tutor. No more cleaning. But that was like an exception. He was one of the few guys that has taken Grade 11 or 12. Grade 10 today in the workplace ain't shit. It ain't going to get you nothing. It'll get you in the door.

"You got Grade 10? Yeah. So do these 80 other guys. What do you got for experience or higher qualifications?"

I entered prison with Grade 13 Ontario. Today, second year university. Information systems major out of Athabasca correspondence university. The most important thing I've learned in the last 14 years is probably, if you got to get goldfish to breed properly, you got to make sure you're feeding them high protein.

I broke off family contact years ago. It's too much of a strain, for me anyways. Some guys seem to be able to deal with it, but I question that too, because I see them go off all the time. When you got people you care about on the street, you're paralysed in the joint. If somebody's going through a really hard time in their life, there's a responsibility as a friend or a husband, or a father, to be there for that person. But you can't do that in here.

"Yes, honey. I'd like to talk to you but I have to go lock up now, click."

Any relationship, there are good times, there will be bad times. You can't pack it in every time things get a little rough. But it's very hard to meet those responsibilities, those expectations that I have of myself in a relationship, when you are locked up in here. You can't do it. I don't feel good about myself half the time, because I say I should be there and I should be dealing with the situation, and you can't.

I think the biggest thing a lot of people tend to forget is that anybody's capable of committing crimes, especially murder more than anything else. And people have the knee-jerk reaction,

"Oh my God, he committed murder. How is that possible?"

My case is not the typical case. It was during an armed robbery. Eighty percent of the murders that go down occurred between family and friends, people that know each other, and what happens is a momentary loss of restraint. The person loses his cool. Snaps out.

There's no such thing as a deterrent. It doesn't work. When a murder goes down, it's either premeditated or it's emotional. We could even include under emotional, mind-altering substances, alcohol, drugs. In the case of premeditated murder, I go and plan a murder. I'm not going to commit that murder until I'm satisfied that my plan is going to let me get away with it. The moment I believe that I'm getting caught, I ain't going to do it. I'll just change the plan until such a time as I believe I'm getting away with it. And the other cases, where the guy's high or he's drunk or it's an emotional situation, you're not thinking 10 seconds in advance let alone 20 years in advance. You're thinking, right now. You're not thinking at all, gone. You're out to lunch, yet you acted. You don't even realize what you've done until after it's over. In most cases – I know a lot of the people like that – you often find that they make better friends than the other kind. My kind of murderer usually. They were just as horrified by what they've done as anybody else, if not more so than people on the street. The only difference is they have to live with it.

As far as a deterrent, there are as many answers to that as there are people in jail for murder. Everybody's an individual. I hate to use clichés, but it's like a crossroads, where you realize there's a few ways you could go. Even doing time. I've seen guys that they do five years, 10 years, whatever. And there's sort of a time where you see they're bouncing either way, and they could go down one road where they just become really embittered towards the system and life and everybody else. Where, you know, the whole world has f——ed me over forever and ever and ever and ever, and poor me, I'm going to make everybody pay. Or they go the other way and say this is the situation I'm in and I'm going to make the best of it that I can. And unfortunately a lot more guys had to go down the whole world has f——ed me over path, than the other one. The reason for it is the system does not work as far as treating anybody goes.

The goal of the justice system is not to keep people in jail, it is not to get people locked up. The goal of the justice system should be to reduce the crime rate. Longer sentences and tough prisons don't do that. The United States proves it. If you want to look at a model that doesn't work, go look at the USA. And here we are in Canada like a bunch of boneheads copying a broken machine.

You have to fit the punishment to the crime. You can't say these 10 guys all shot somebody with a shotgun, so they should all get the exact same thing. In my case, I would have said something like: "This individual is sentenced to life imprisonment until such time as he shows signs to re-enter society." That could be five years, could be two years, could be 20 years. And what those signs are and how you gauge them is going to be something that is beyond me. That is complex, big time. But a system has to be worked out there. I've seen guys that are doing life bits that six months after they're in you could let them go tomorrow and you know they're not coming back. Other guys, they've got 15, 18, 23 years, and if you let them out tomorrow there'd be a body there within a week.

In my case I think it took about 12 years. I'm pretty confident that I could get a job somewhere in the computer industry. An ability to do the job is becoming more and more important. And I know that I've got the ability. I've proven that.

I Was Nervous

Dwight Greg

"I was scared. The fact of being in a maximum institution. Hearing stories about guys getting killed when you're in. There's a lot of lifers."

ot everyone in a maximum security federal prison slit someone's throat, blew them away with a shotgun, or as you will read later, torched another human. Dwight Greg (not his real name) did none of those things. What he did was drink and drive too many times to count. And he got caught – again, again, again, again, again, again, again, again and again.

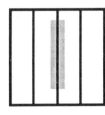was born in an old town in Saskatchewan. I don't know anything about that place. All I know is that I was born there and haven't really went back there. It's called Paradise Hill, Saskatchewan, the nearest hospital from a reserve called Onion Lake – 30 miles north of Lloydminster. That's where I grew up till I was about 14.

I came from a large family. There were five brothers and five sisters. I'm the only one that gets into trouble. I'm the only one that is always in jail.

We used to live in a little log house. There was no bedroom in there. It's just a log house itself. And we lived there 'til 1975 when the band gave us a new house.

We had no running water, no furnace. We used to chop wood for heat in the wintertime. Melt the snow for water or try to get water. This is about three, four miles away, the nearest well.

Crowded, yes it was. I don't really remember that much about it, all I know is that my family's been travelling around. My father was working all over Saskatchewan and Alberta in order for us to survive.

Sometimes we'd go with my father, and my father would work for some farmers.

I got into a lot of sports back at the reserve. I played hockey, I played baseball, fastball, got into all kinds of sports the reserve had to offer. I went through my ups and downs. Sometimes I'd get hit if I didn't listen to my father. He hit pretty bad, used to get hit with a stick or get kicked around by his boots. I remember when he'd use a long, long tool. He'd hit pretty good with that.

I done some stuff back home and sort of got into trouble, when my parents were still together.

I broke into the school, and made a mess of the school. We ransacked it. We got caught, you know, a few times. And when we got caught by the cops, they just usually took us to the police station they have up there, and sort of scared us. Tried to throw us in jail for a little while.

We weren't drinking. We were only 12, 13 at the time when me and my friends did it. And I wanted to fit in and I heard these other guys were talking about what they were planning on doing and I wanted to see how it's like once they got caught and they was going to take me to the police station. I didn't stay in jail because they had a social worker sitting there and they wanted to know what I did, and why I did it. The social worker was only there to observe I guess. He didn't say anything much. I didn't tell them anything. I just lied my way through.

There wasn't any parental drinking involved until they split up. I was 15 when they split up. I felt a lot of resentment, lot of hate, anger. I didn't understand why they broke up. Some of my other family members were living on their own, and my mother took the youngest ones with her. We moved to Lloyd (Lloydminster). I lived there, at my mother's place, off and on.

I left school after Grade 9, yeah. I was doing odd jobs around that area. I started getting into trouble when I turned 18, when the legal age to enter the bar in Alberta was 18. I'd been to bars, started drinking a lot, partying around, borrowing my mother's car. I just couldn't sit in one place, sit still in one place and drink. I had to move around.

I never served, I didn't start going to jail until I was 19 going on 20. I was living in Lloyd and another reserve not too far from there, Brown Lake. The first time I got an impaired was in '85. I got just a fine. I was scared to go to jail. I'd heard all these stories about jail. After I got done with the court, I'd say about six to eight months before I got caught again. I kept on driving around with no licence, they charged me for driving while disqualified. I received fines.

I'd been working on farms, or working for some farmers, or living off welfare. I left to do more drinking, more depressed, nowhere to turn, no one to turn to.

Again, an impaired driving. They were all traffic violations: speeding, no insurance, littering, towed my car in, that's what I can remember. When I went to court, I had 17 charges. I walked away with a $1100 fine and seven days in jail.

Taken out by RCs, they drag you down there. Drove me from Lloydminster through Vermilion, Vermilion to St. Paul. I wasn't shackled. I wasn't handcuffed or anything. Seven days, first time in jail, seven days, seemed like a long time. Seemed forever for me. I didn't know what I'd be facing, or what's in store for me.

When I got there, I knew some guys from the street, I thought it's not all that bad because I knew somebody in there. They showed me around, showed me about this inmate code. Their code: not to rat out on one another; not to steal things from one another; things like that.

From the reserve, I didn't know anything about racism until I went to start getting in trouble with the law, the police. And people I was hanging around with, they didn't like the police too much. They taught me to hate the police. Natives kind of stick together, and I haven't really experienced any racism.

I worked off the fine while I was in jail, correctional centre in St. Paul. I served four days. I started drinking again as soon as I walked out. I had to find my way back, back home by hitchhiking. I had a few dollars on me, but it wasn't enough to buy myself a bus ticket.

Not too long to break the law again. As soon as I start drinking, I don't think twice about what I'm going to do when I'm drunk. I just go ahead and do it. I don't think about the consequences. I got picked up for mischief. I got charged for assault, which I don't even know about. I got thrown in. I had some warrants on the Saskatchewan side. I had another impaired charge waiting for me in Saskatchewan.

They gave me a fine, and I walked out. I don't remember how long I stayed out before I started getting into trouble. It was impaired or assault, mischief.

I didn't really start going to jail until '88, then I got sentenced to a year in jail. I didn't stay for very long. I stayed in for about four months and I went to Poundmakers substance abuse treatment centre in

Edmonton. I did my 28 days there. I was out on temporary absence for the remainder of my sentence.

Around Christmas, I got stopped twice, four hours apart. They picked me up in Lloyd. They stopped me, they pulled me over, they took me to the cop station and did a breathalyser, they released me. I figured they released me. I went back to my vehicle, started driving again. Four hours later I got picked up. Got sentenced to 14 months. They shipped me to Edmonton Remand, from Edmonton to Grande Cache, and from Grande Cache I transferred to St. Paul. I didn't really think anything, didn't really think about that much. I was planning for my release date.

As soon as I got back to Lloyd, I started drinking again, or getting into trouble. When I get in trouble, I end up getting in trouble in some other little town. Mostly all drinking and driving.

Late '89, I got picked up in Red Deer for driving while disqualified. Sentenced to four months. They sent me down to Spy Hill in Calgary.

Every time I get into trouble, knowing that they're going to use my name and they're going to hold me and I get a longer sentence, I make up different names. So, I had a warrant out for me in Bonnyville when I got released from Spy Hill. I went to court there in '90. Between '88 and '92, I didn't stay out very long. The longest I stayed out was a couple months.

In '92, resulting in a federal sentence, I got charged for an impaired driving while disqualified. My eighth impaired there, but I wasn't drinking, I was high on pills. I didn't like the way I was living, I didn't want to live any longer, I wanted to end it. I just got out of Fort Saskatchewan that time, I was only out for a couple days. When I was in Fort Saskatchewan I planned my suicide. There was so much hurt and anger in me that I didn't know how to get rid of. And that's the only way I could think of was to commit suicide. I didn't want to talk about my problems because I wasn't shown how to talk about my problems.

I took some sleeping pills, not too sure what kind of sleeping pills they were, but I asked my wife what kind of pills, what are they? And she said they're sleeping pills. Her grandfather left some pills there too, and I just read the labels. I knew that if I took these I would end my life. I'd take a bunch of them, sit around have some coffee, and then take some more until they started kicking in. Maybe I'll fall asleep and never wake up.

I don't really remember what happened that night. All I know is, my wife was trying to phone the ambulance. She tried to phone 911, this was when I was living in Edmonton, and I didn't want her to phone the ambulance. I took the phone away from her, ripped those cords off, went downstairs and did the same to the other one. And sat down and had some more coffee, and sat there for a while, and then I heard the door open. By this time, the pills were starting to kick in, and that's when I realized that she went running out and used a phone booth to phone 911. So I found that out. I didn't want to go to a hospital. I didn't want to be saved. I wanted to end it all. I remember getting on my shoes and my jacket, and getting truck keys and my money. That's it. Next thing, I was blacking out, some parts I remember, and some parts I wouldn't. But I blacked out. After I got the keys, next thing I woke up I was at a 7-11 store. I didn't know what I was doing there and I blacked out again. When I came to, I was sitting on steps there, and a city cop was beside me, talking to me, trying to keep me awake. As soon as I came to, the ambulance were there and I was being strapped down on the stretcher. Took me to the hospital, and they pumped my stomach out.

I was in custody for a couple of months, fighting this charge, eventually lost, and I don't know what kind of charges they were. I got tired of sitting around the remand doing dead time. So I sat and sat in the remand, and all this anger is going through me. I wanted to end it all, because my relationship wasn't going good. I started reading the Bible. Met a few Christians in jail, helped me out.

In court, they were trying to give me provincial time, and I told them I wanted to go federal. All my crimes are alcohol related. I get into trouble every time I drink. The only way to stay away from trouble is to abstain from alcohol and to learn how to talk about my problems. I wanted to take some programs to help me release all this anger. The judge agreed with my request. He gave me two years on each charge. Two years for impaired, and two years for driving while disqualified. Two years concurrent.

I felt kind of satisfied, knowing that I can take some programs for my alcoholism. I thought I would have a better lifestyle on the streets, stay out of trouble.

I asked to go to Bowden. I spent eight months of a two year sentence there, then I was released, they paroled me. I went to Poundmakers again. From Poundmakers, I went to a halfway house for 30 days, to do my day parole. After my 30 days was up, I was granted full parole. I stayed out for about eight-and-a-half months, started drinking again, and picked up my ninth impaired. The judge gave me three years for impaired and one year for driving while disqualified. That's consecutive.

They were trying to send me back to Bowden, but I didn't want to go back there. I didn't like the people that were in there. I wouldn't call them fellow inmates. The majority of them – there's some good people in there that aren't in for bad beefs – are in for rape, molesting children, rats.

I had some troubles with them, these guys that were raping children, killing children. They weren't coming on to me. I didn't like them. I didn't want to be near them. I don't want them to be near me, sort of told them straight out.

I thought I was going to be staying in the Edmonton Max waiting to be transferred out to PA. I was nervous. I was scared. The fact of being in a maximum institution. Hearing stories about guys getting killed when you're in. There's a lot of lifers. I kept to myself. I wouldn't look at people, I'd look down. I didn't bother anybody. At night, guys called me over, asked me who I was, and how much time I was doing. I found some of the guys in here, the natives, made me feel comfortable, letting me know things, how this joint, how this jail operates. I don't think natives really hang around in big groups. The whites and the natives, they get along OK in here.

I'm the front hallway cleaner and keep myself busy by reading the Bible. It helps me out a lot. Been praying a lot, and going to church. My family were Christians, for a while, and I don't know what happened, they stopped going to church. I enjoyed going to church when I was younger.

Being in here – there's a lot of lifers – they consider me a short-timer, them doing life and me only doing four years. Still, for me, I think four years is too long.

I miss being with my wife and six children. I haven't seen my baby yet. My wife plans on moving to wherever I'm sent so she can visit. I phone them once or twice a week from here. She gives me encouragement that I need to stay strong and not to worry about anything. I do a lot of praying in here. I pray when I'm feeling down. If I'm angry, I pray. It helps quite a lot.

That Big Yard

Allen Jensen

"I'm thinking 17 years, and just wondering: I can't do it, I cannot do it . . . I'm going to go crazy if I don't get out now. And I planned and I watched. And I escaped. I succeeded. I escaped out of there."

his chapter could just as easily have been entitled *All In The Family*. Allen, 35, is one of four Jensen sons who have spent a lot of years in federal penitentiaries. He's lived behind bars most of his life – a life that he tried unsuccessfully to snuff out. His years have not always meant prison, but they've been about as close as humanly possible. His life story, one of love and violence, has been troubled from the start.

was born in Innisfail, Alberta. My mother was French and Native. I'm not too sure what that would make her. My dad came from Denmark in the Second World War, he was just a kid. They met later on, and that's basically where I came from.

I remember when I was real small, and we lived on a farm. My dad, I guess he used to farm, I never really asked him about that, due to the fact that I've been in prison all my life. But from what I remember, he was a grain farmer. I grew up pretty normal, I thought, compared to other kids. Now, when I look back, I guess it wasn't normal.

I have three brothers and three sisters. I have one brother that was in here doing a 25-year sentence for murder. He's since been transferred to Regional Psychiatric Centre. I guess he couldn't handle it, being in jail for 25 years.

When I was young, I used to look up to him because he was very active in sports, he was a good athlete. He probably would have played in the NHL had he not become an alcoholic.

Allen Jensen –"*I remember when I was real small, and we lived on a farm. My dad, I guess he used to farm, I never really asked him about that, due to the fact that I've been in prison all my life. But from what I remember, he was a grain farmer. I grew up pretty normal, I thought, compared to other kids. Now, when I look back, I guess it wasn't normal.*"

I did time with two other brothers that were in the penitentiary too. One was co-accused with me when I first came to the penitentiary when I was 21. He's since got out, and been on the street now almost seven years. He's doing well.

My sisters grew up wild too, and they're on the street. One is a born again Christian, one was adopted when she was six, I've never talked to her since, and one had two children, and I haven't talked to her in over 10 years. I don't know what happened to her. The one I know, the born again Christian, comes to visit me periodically.

My parents were alcoholics. My mother died in fact of a heart attack, induced by alcoholism. I seen a lot of things when I was young that bothered me.

My father was not violent but aggressive. If something was bothering him, you knew about it. No abuse, he wouldn't beat the living daylights out of you or nothing like that. Just a cuff across the head, or a slap. Maybe that's why I ended up in prison, because I didn't get a beating when I was a kid. I don't know.

He was a law-abiding person, but I can remember numerous occasions where the police come, and he would be mad, and he would chase them away. He was very protective.

I remember a time when my dad took me to a hotel, and he bought me ice cream. I remember the first time I had ice cream, it was chocolate. And to this day, I don't like chocolate ice cream. I don't know if dad had any bearing on it or not. I remember that vividly, him buying me ice cream and I was happy. And a lot of times when I was in jail I'd think back on my life and I would think I never really had it too bad, and I often wondered why I ended up here.

I played hockey, baseball, all kinds of sports, football. I never really became good until I came to prison. I can remember playing ringette and hockey in youth detention centres and they used to always say I was the best. But I never thought that I was good. I always aspired to do good at whatever I did, be it crime or whatever. I always gave my best effort. I had a lot of opportunity to better myself, but never took advantage of that.

I didn't do that well in school. I was always skipping and always into something wrong. I used to get my brothers and sisters to steal. I remember them in foster homes saying, "That one, something's wrong with him. He's not like the other ones." I was kind of a leader, yet being in prison all my life they categorized me as being a follower. I can't understand that one.

I was taken away from my mother and father when I was five, and put in Bethany Homes for Children near Gwynn, Alberta. It was a big farm and a big four-storey building, the biggest building I'd ever seen. I remember being scared of heights. I would go up to the top floor and look down and I used to always hold onto the window ledge real tight, and be scared, and make sure no one was around me because I was afraid they'd push me closer.

Being removed from the family home was a very traumatic experience. I remember vividly when I turned six years old and they tried to put me on the school bus to go to school. There were three adults trying to get me on there, they couldn't. I was six years old, they could not put me on that bus. Because of that I didn't start school until I was seven, already a year behind the other children.

They let me go back home sometime later. I believe I was about eight, about the time I first had a run-in with the police. I was in a Safeway shopping centre, in Wetaskiwin, shoplifting, and I got caught. They called the police. That was my first brush with the law.

They took me to family court and made me a ward of the government. They investigated my family, thought my parents were neglecting us children, and we were all placed in different homes.

They placed me under the care of these Hungarian people that were foster parents in Warburg. I was there until I was in Grade 5.

When I was at Bethany Homes, they were very caring. As for the one in Warburg, they were very mean. I remember years later my brothers asking me if I wanted to go there and do things that I won't mention now, but I talked them out of it and I straightened them on it, because it was a very hateful experience for them as well as my other family members.

We had to pick weeds when it was 80-above. My youngest sister was six years old and she got sun stroke. I knew something was wrong. Other kids would be viciously hit, and I knew that wasn't right. Most of the kids would turn away, but when they went to hit me I would look them in the eye, and I remember them saying, "Don't hit that one, he's not right." So I ran away from there, went back to Wetaskiwin. I walked all the way, it was about 70 miles. It took me about three or four days, as an eight-year-old.

I went in the house, nobody was home. I remember feeling like – I ran away, but why did I run away and come back here? There was no one there. I never felt so alone. My parents come home, they were drunk and they called the welfare, and they come, and they took me back to that home.

The welfare officials asked me why I ran away, and I told them how they would hit us, make us work, the abuse. They didn't believe me, they thought I was lying and they thought I was just a bad apple. Finally, someone read some report or something and went there and investigated. As a result, all the kids were taken from that home.

I went to another foster home in the rural community and went to school in Ponoka.

They were farmers, they had cows and horses. They were good people, they treated me better than their own children. I guess they thought no one ever loved me, and that was why I was the way I was. They heard a lot of things from welfare people that they disbelieved. They treated me very well, but I still ran away. I wanted my own parents even though things weren't right there.

As a result of running away, I went to another foster home. They treated me better than the last, yet I ran away. They couldn't understand why, they also treated me better than their own kids. I remember them telling me if I passed Grade 6 they would buy me a 10-speed bike. I passed and they took me down to the store and I got to pick out a bicycle. Their daughter and son were very jealous of me because of that. They used to do things and blame it on me.

I ran home again, and my parents were still drinking. I was 14 years of age when I ran away from the last foster home. I was hoping it would be like when we were really small, my brothers and sisters, playing, doing something, having fun, be wrestling with each other, or just as kids played. I wanted it to be like that, but it wasn't. We were all split-up and it was unstable. I always ran home hoping that it would be better, but it never did get better.

When I ran away, I started stealing things that were a necessity. It was cold at night and I would break in someplace for shelter and food. It was always for a need, because I didn't have that and wanted it, or I needed it to survive.

They would handcuff me, put me in the police car, take me, lock me in a room and then the interrogation process would start. Some of them would be rough, some of them would yell. Maybe because they had children and they wanted to scare me. I remember them telling me that I would spend the rest of my life in jail, and I used to laugh. I never believed that would happen. Yet, years later, the prophecy is true, so to speak.

I was 13 years old in YDC in Edmonton and I was scared. I was there because I ran away. I'd been stealing up until that time. They finally came to terms that there was nothing else to do but put me in youth detention centre.

When I ended up in YDC, it was scary. I was very small, I was shy, I wouldn't talk. I remember them thinking that I was retarded or something because I was different than other kids of my age who committed similar offences. I was there for about a year and I escaped three times.

One day I ran, just bolted. They chased me. They chased me for a long ways but they couldn't catch me. I got away. I went home and then I finally realized I was running to nowhere. I was caught some time later after breaking in places. I remember stealing my first car at that age, not knowing how to drive. I did it. I learned on my own, no one told me how or anything.

I stole a car, drove to Calgary, stole another car, and drove to Vancouver because I had an older sister in Victoria. I thought if I went there, somehow things would be better. But I never made it, they arrested me in Vancouver. They caught me there and placed me in jail, in New Westminster. There was guys in the other cells yelling to put me in their cell, and I remember being really scared, taking the blanket, hanging it across the bars, so they couldn't look at me.

When they found out I was only 15, they got in touch with welfare. They came down, took me to the airport, pushed me through a door and said: "Go that way." I looked around and I was all alone. I ran back out, stole a car, drove to Calgary and was caught. I went to provincial court and received 60 days in jail. I remember thinking 60 days was long, it seemed very long to me. I couldn't believe 60 days in jail. I remember saying that in my mind, over and over.

It was the old Fort Saskatchewan. It was a frightening experience. I learned that you go to jail when you break the law, when they've had enough of you. And I learned how to defend myself real quick. Be it physically or verbally.

They used to bug me because I was so young and tiny. Guys would tease me and as a result I would end up in fights. I remember being punched in the head and just looking at the guy, and the guy was shocked that I would look at him, that I didn't cower.

After serving the jail term, they gave me a bus ticket and I went back home again. Same old story. I went home and I was in trouble just as fast as I'd gotten out. I'd broken in to a place, and received a one-year sentence. I did that year, got out, did it again, received two years less a day.

When I got out of there, I went to Leduc. I had just turned 18. I was drinking in the bar and they came over and they said I was cut off. I got in a big fight with the proprietors and ended up in jail the first day I got out, the same day I got out after doing two years less a day. I was charged and in prison that night for assault.

They felt sorry for me, they'd let me out if I promised to appear. I took off to Medicine Hat to my cousin's place. I received a 21-month sentence there, and did it in Lethbridge provincial jail.

It was the same old trip that I had been through a thousand times. It was just a hopeless feeling, wondering if anything good would ever come of my life. Upon release I would be sent to my older brother's girlfriend's place in Calgary.

It was the most important part of my life now that I think back. One night, I went out to the Black Bow lounge. I was sitting in this lounge in Calgary, feeling really hopeless. Like I said, I was staying at my brother's girlfriend's place, and I just felt I didn't belong there, like I was an intruder. So I went out this one night, I only had seven or eight dollars, and at that time I think a beer cost two dollars. I had just turned 20. Anyways, I was just sitting there, wallowing in it, thinking, where am I going to go, what am I going to do? And this lady come over, the waiter, and said,

"This girl over there would like you to go to her table."

I looked over there and she's really pretty, dressed real nice. I was feeling real bad about myself, and I remember thinking, why would she want to know me? Why would she want to talk to me? I just sat there looking at her. Finally I went over. She was sitting there with three other girls, and she asked if she could buy me a drink. I remember saying,

"Why do you want to buy me a drink?"

She was looking at me like maybe she had made a mistake calling me over. But I sat down and we talked. She just came right out and said, would I come home with her. And I thought, wow, why didn't this ever happen to me before? I went home to her place and we had sex and she brought me some beer. She was the first person I think that ever treated me like I was special. And that's when I had a job. The first time in my life I ever went out and got a job.

I was working at Totem Lumber. And I woke up and I remember she was smiling, looking at me, and I said:

"I got to go. I got to go to work."

And she asked me where and what time I had to be there. I told her I worked at the lumber yard and that I had to be there at 2. She said,

"It's only 9," and I told her,

"Well, I have to walk all the way to work, and it's about 15 miles."

I don't think she believed me, but she gave me her phone number on a book of matches and away I went. I went to work, went back to where I was staying, took out that match pack and thought, should I call her? I was really undecided because I wasn't feeling good about myself at all. Finally I called and she was real happy to hear me. She told me to get over there right now, not to worry. I told her I'd have to walk, it would take me about three hours because she was on the other side of the city. She told me to take a cab and not worry about the money. That was the only time in my life where I really thought I had it great. I was living life like I wanted to.

Anything I wanted, she bought me. If I wanted new clothes, she would go buy them. She had a good job, she was a straight person. She had a lot of bad experiences too. Child abuse, she told me about. She was an honest person, and she really loved me. At least when I look back I think she did, or I like to think that.

This lasted very briefly, about a month. That's when I was walking by this building, the Alberta Report where they print that news magazine. I remember seeing a camera sitting on a tripod in the window. I was really drunk. I remember looking at that camera and thinking, I want to take some pictures of her, although I'd never seen a camera up until that time, other than from a distance. So I broke in, stole that camera, and passed out. The police came there in the morning because the janitor come to clean. He was the first person at work and he found me laying there passed out with that camera around my neck.

I got charged and received 18 months in Spy Hill Correctional Centre in Calgary. One time, out of all the time I was ever in prison, I broke the law when I was drunk. Every other time, it was always after the crime, not before.

My girlfriend got me this lawyer, and I got time served. I was out in six months. I went to her place, and I'd never been so happy in my life. She just treated me like I had never been treated. She couldn't do enough for me.

My brother came there – he was on parole at that time, it was his first or second penitentiary bit – trying to convince her to let me go out with him to steal. He wouldn't leave us alone. We would have to sneak off, we would have to story him, make up a story, to get away from him, get our time together. When I was young I was afraid of my older brother because we always used to fight. I remember finally standing up to him, he ran and got a butcher knife and he threatened to kill me. My girlfriend was really shook up by that experience. She would go to sleep, afraid he was going to kill us both. Eventually my other brother showed up, he had escaped out of a bush camp up at Fort Saskatchewan. He had a gun. That was when I first really, really cracked. We went out and robbed a store.

I didn't want to do it. I remember him egging me on, and me telling him I don't have to steal.

"Look what I have. I have a beautiful woman. We have a home, we have a bed."

She had things I never had until that point in my life. And they were mine. What was hers was mine, she made that perfectly clear. I didn't want to do it. I really think at that point in my life, had he not have come there, I never would have broken the law. I firmly believe that.

I took a loaded .22 handgun. Then we went to this gas station and I walked in. I had a jean jacket on and a down filled parka. There were two young kids there at the gas station, they were younger than me.

I reached into my coat to pull out the gun and the hammer got caught in the button of the jean jacket. I couldn't get it out and I was looking them right in the eye. They didn't have a clue they were being robbed. There was a clock behind them, and I said,

"What time is it?"

When they turned around to look at the time, I looked down, undid my button and got the gun out of there. When they turned around, they were staring into the gun. They just stared, they went blank. It was like they couldn't believe that would happen. I told them to take all the money out and hand it to him, my brother. They set it on the counter and I told them:

"I told you, hand it to him."

He picked it up, handed it to my brother. He asked if he wanted the change, and I turned to my brother and I told him:

"Get out of here. Go."

When I figured he was far enough ahead, I ran out. We went back to my girlfriend's apartment, and my older brother and his friend were still sitting there. I said,

"Did you call the cab?"

He said, "No."

I told him: "Hurry up! Call the cab!"

They called, the cab got there, we drove right by that gas station. I remember laughing, saying to the taxi driver:

"I wonder what happened there? Look there's police there, and there was dogs." The cab driver didn't have any idea that I was the one that had just robbed that gas station. We didn't get nothing, really. I think it was $200 and change.

We went downtown, started drinking, and me and my older brother started fighting. My younger brother couldn't believe that he was on the run, that there we were, me and my older brother, fist fighting it out in the middle of the street in Calgary, after we robbed a gas station, and him being on the run from jail.

We went back to my girlfriend's place. She had no idea what had happened. I was ashamed to tell her. But the police dogs, they tracked our footprints, because the gas station was 400 feet away from her apartment. They come the next day, knocked on the door real late at night. My girlfriend opened the door, come back up the stairs, and there was two detectives with her. I knew I was in trouble.

They took all five of us down to Calgary city police headquarters, placed us all in different rooms and took our pictures. The standard interrogation. When they come to my brother they said,

"Who's this?"

I said, "I don't know who that is."

He asked me where I met him. I said I met him in the bar, he had no place to go, so I invited him to come to stay at my place. They didn't know that he was my brother and that he had escaped from Fort Saskatchewan bush camp. Subsequently, they let us all go. They did not have any idea they had the right guys. They drove us all back to my girlfriend's place. I told my girlfriend,

"I did this, I robbed this gas station."

We sold everything she had, her TV, her waterbed, everything in her house, and we packed up what was left, and we sent it on the train to her mother's in Victoria.

Me and my girlfriend, and I took my younger brother, went and lived at her mom's place for a month before I was caught.

Her family really liked me, they just thought I was the greatest. They had no idea of where I came from, or who I was, because when I'm around people I act normal although some of the things I did were probably considered abnormal. They really took a shine to me. They lent me their cars, they treated me real good, like I was family. I got caught because I was driving her mom's car and I didn't have a licence. I ran a red light, they pulled me over, took me in and they give me a $35 fine for driving without a licence. My brother got picked up, the older one that stayed in Calgary. I wouldn't take him with us because he just wasn't smart when it came to crime. He didn't care. He was bound to get caught. My younger brother and me, I knew we could get away and we did for a short while. But my older brother, for whatever reason, caved in, wrote a statement against us.

So there I was in the Calgary Remand Centre all alone again, and the only real person that I cared for was living in Victoria. I remember feeling so hopeless, like so many times before.

In court, I really believed that I was getting home. I really believed that, until it come time to go, and they said "last witness for the Crown," and in walked my older brother. I remember sitting in the prisoner's box, looking at my girlfriend, telling my younger brother,

"Everything's going to be OK. Today we go home."

And then, I knew that wasn't the case. I wasn't going home. I was caught, and I was going to be made to pay.

When he walked in, I stood up and they grabbed me. He seen my reaction, and immediately started acting irrational. He was yelling:

"I didn't say anything, they said it. They made me sign it."

To this day, I don't think I forgive him for that. Although some days I think I do.

As that day ends, it was a judge and jury and I was charged for nine offences including four robbery and four armed while committing. I remember sitting there, the woman I loved was sitting there with my sister, and one by one the 12 jurors got up and they said guilty, nine times each. It took them a long time to find me guilty. While I stood there, my knees shaking, they started to sentence me. My girlfriend started to scream, loud, and she ran out of the courtroom. It was packed. All eyes were on me. I remember listening to that song by Pink Floyd, and I could really relate to that, when that guy says, "You little shit, you really did it now, they're going to throw away the key." I remember that going through my mind and just sinking. I felt like I was sinking into the floor. I never felt so small in my life.

My girlfriend thought I had got 100 years because they sentenced me to one year for this, four years for this, like nine times. But she didn't know how court worked. She just added up the four years, eight times, and the one year, eight times, and she just freaked. She must have thought, he's never getting out. He just got sentenced to 100 years, or something. She didn't know what concurrent meant.

I received a five-year sentence and they marched me out of the courtroom. I don't know why they did that, they usually take you through the back. They took me out in the lobby, handcuffed, and my girlfriend come running with my sister. They were both crying and I told her,

"I only got five years, that's all I got."

She was still screaming and crying. I didn't know what to say.

My older brother was free. He wasn't there. I didn't see him again, until he received a 25-year sentence and he was in the next cell to me. He was scared. For the first time in my life, he was scared of me.

They appealed it, we both got three years added on for a total of eight years each in the penitentiary, me and my younger brother. They sent my brother to Drumheller. I went to PA. It was bad, the worst criminals in Canada, deviants, like Clifford Olson.

I grew up real quick. I remember walking in there, into a big dome. There were 200 people, and all their eyes were looking at me. I looked right back at them, like I didn't care. I had to stand up for myself and

I did. At that time, I had already been in a lot of fights. I knew what I was capable of. I wasn't scared to die. As a result, I got in a lot of fist fights, broke my hands, had my teeth knocked out. I even believed that my nose was broken, but I can't really tell now. I never did see the doctor.

The first time in jail, when I got in a fight, I beat up the guy bad. His buddy come, and he started threatening me, but that's all he did, because that guy was beat up. In prison, it's like this: If they think you'll kill them or you'll fight, they won't mess with you. They'll be snakes and wait until you're sleeping or until you're pilled up. If they know you won't fight, they will take advantage of that too, but if they think you will fight, they approach you more cautiously. Lots of times, guys came on to me. That was the first time I ever really got into a fight. When I fought with my brothers, I didn't consider it a fight, it wasn't serious. But when I got in a fight in prison, it was. I tried to win. I don't believe I ever lost.

The noises drive you crazy. People would cry. They would be crying, some slashed up. Weird sounds. It would put me in a weird head space, when you're just laying there and you can't sleep. I don't believe I had a good night's sleep in years. I'd be laying there and I'd hear these sounds and it would be maddening, almost drive you where you were ready to crack. The guys that did crack, they would do things that they normally wouldn't do. They would either get in fights or they would slash their wrists or some would hang themselves. Weird things. People would do weird things.

I remember coming out of my cell in the morning, just screaming on a range, where there's 50 on my range and 50 on the above one, calling every person off. I called them goofs, skinners, rats. One would have the spine to come up and say, "I hate that." I'd tell him to get in the f——ing cell. They would go, and they were scared of me, and I was just a skinny little man, but I didn't care. I looked them in the eye, it was probably the first time they ever seen the hate. They could have killed me, but they didn't.

My girlfriend would come to visit me every month. She'd write me, sometimes every day. I saved every letter. Sometimes I would write her every day, for months at a time, because I really loved her. I would phone her and they would listen, they would record it. When you first got on the phone you couldn't be yourself because you knew they were listening. Then I would just think, well, what do I care? I love her, she loves me. We would just be ourselves. I think they thought something was wrong. When I remember back, some of the things we would talk about, it was kind of funny now.

I would worry that somebody else was sleeping with her, and those kinds of things would be maddening. I would hate if I would phone and she wouldn't be there right away. I would think bad things towards her, and then I would go back to my cell. I would think, that's wrong, you shouldn't be thinking like that. That's how your dad was. When he'd catch your mom fooling around, he'd bust her arms, blacken her eyes. I would go, I'm not like that, I seen that when I was young and I said to myself, "No matter what my wife is like I would never treat her like that." But I would think bad things, it would almost make me snap. It would drive me to do things that I wouldn't normally do. I'd get up in the morning, if somebody looked at me wrong or said something, I would quickly judge whether I could beat him up or not. If I could beat him up, he got beat up. Sometimes I misjudged people and I'd get rocked. I'd get knocked around, but I would always win because I never gave up and they'd tire out and that's when I'd get them. I had a girl I loved very much and she was very pretty, she was really attractive. I never lost hope. Once you get a taste of the good life, you don't give up, you dream that you'll make it back to that place. I was there until I received parole in 1984, four whole years. I went back to my girlfriend. It was not the same. I was given parole in Calgary. I didn't even go to the parole centre, I went right to her apartment. It was a culture shock to say the least. One minute I was in another world and now I was here at her home. It was a weird feeling, even though I loved her very much. I felt like I didn't belong. It was a strange, strange feeling.

She felt really good. She was all smiling at me for the things I'd been through, because I was jealous, because many nights I couldn't sleep. I wondered where she was, how she was doing.

I wasn't thinking right, I expected things to be more than what they were. And when they weren't, I reverted back to my old ways.

I was at her place feeling really jealous. I was verbally abusive. After about a week, she couldn't take it any more. She would say, "Get out."

I'm on my own and right away I pulled an armed robbery, a whole bunch. I was convicted of one, got nine more years, and was placed in Drumheller Penitentiary. I was doing this sentence now 17 years long.

It was the same feeling. Scared, just scared, because you know that once you're through that gate you may never leave. You could die in there, or just may be there forever. Even though you have confidence in yourself when you walk through that gate again, you're alone. You know you're alone. You're walking through that gate, and you know there's 200, 300 or how many other people in there. You know you're just one more guy, and now you're alone, you're walking through that gate alone. So it's you against them, and right away you see somebody you know, and you go right up to them, just go right up to them, "Hi, how you doing?" And it's like you never left.

It's a new experience, then all of a sudden you wake up one day and you go, nothing's changed. It's the same. The buildings are a different shape or the cells a different shape, but the rules are the same, and you go through the same trips: fights, or sports, or confrontations with the guards or other convicts.

You see visitors come and go and if no one's visiting you, you would wish someone would. When you see them leave and get in their car from the hole at night, you wish you were getting in that car and driving away. You just dream, dream of better things.

I phoned my girlfriend and she was hurt. She said, "Just don't call me any more." And I remember feeling real bad, realizing that I made a mistake. For the first time in my life, I really felt that what I had done was wrong. I lost the one person I really cared about. And that was the only thing that kept me going all the years after, was wanting that again.

I'm there about a year in Drumheller, and I remember going to work out and play hockey. Then I would go sit in that big yard and I would think, here I am. Here I am. I have to be here for 17 years. I'm thinking 17 years, and just wondering: I can't do it, I cannot do it. I've been away from home since I was five. This is it, I can't take it any more. I'm going to go crazy if I don't get out now. And I planned and I watched. And I escaped. I succeeded, I escaped out of there.

A friend of mine, I shouldn't say friend because I don't think I ever had a real friend in jail, this guy I knew, asked me to come and work in the gym. They were renovating the gym. We used to talk with the contractors and joke. They couldn't believe I was in jail for 17 years, just because of the way I was. I was polite, treated them with respect. They couldn't believe, here's a young guy in prison for 17 years and he never hurt anybody. Just couldn't believe that. And I remember them saying, "Load that truck up with garbage." That was six years ago. And I loaded that truck up with garbage, then asked where he's taking it. He said, "To the dump." Right away, my mind just spun, and I went, I'm getting out. Now I know how I'm getting out. So the next day – or a week later, I forget how much time elapsed – I hid in the back of that truck and it drove out to the dump. There I was, in the back. They didn't even search it. It just drove right through the gates. The guard was tapping on the back tailgate of this half-ton Ford truck, with a standard transmission. He was asking the driver, the worker, "What's in there?" He said, "Just garbage." He tapped the tailgate and didn't even look in. He said, "OK, go ahead." He closed the door, the gate closed, they opened the other one, and there I was. I had a strong urge to laugh, really laugh. I had to cover my mouth because I was so happy that I would have laughed out loud and they would have heard me. He got to the dump, opened the back door and started unloading it. I had a knife that I had made in my cell, and he had me uncovered. I was looking at his leg, right next to mine. I don't know how he didn't see, but he didn't, and I remember thinking, if you're going to do something, do it now. I was kind of hesitant because I heard other voices, but I didn't know who they were. So I jumped up. He was shocked. He couldn't believe. His exact words were: "Al, I never thought you would do this." He couldn't believe there I was with a knife at his body, out of prison, escaped. And he was scared. He was fearful.

I said, "Do I have to kill you?" But I never would have killed him. I knew what you had to say. Even though you wouldn't follow through with it, you had to say it. He was a prison employee. He had dealings with inmates every day. He wasn't armed.

The other voices were employees from the city of Drumheller sanitation department. There was two of them. One was on the caterpillar at the landfill, one was in a city garbage truck. I just looked and said, "How are you today?"

He said, "Fine. How are you?"

"Wonderful." Got in the truck and I drove away.

I went toward Calgary with that guy in the back. I pulled off to the side of the road after about five miles. I was thinking, if cops drove by they would see that it was a government penitentiary truck, because of the color and the markings, and if they seen this guy in the back they would wonder, why is the guy in the crew cab driving and there's a guy in the back under the canopy? So I pulled over, tied him up, put him behind the front seat of the crew cab.

He was scared. He kept asking me what I was going to do to him. Then I would joke with him. I would say, "I don't know yet." He was very scared, very scared. I drove all the way to Calgary, untied him, drove by the police station. I told him that's where he'd go to rat me out and I told him to make sure that he lets them know that I didn't endanger his life, and that at one point he was in danger of losing his life. He did just that.

I ditched the truck in Calgary. Then I ran down to the river and shaved – which was a mistake. Once I shaved every hair on my face, I looked exactly like the day they arrested me. They had my picture in the paper. I was caught, one day, almost to the minute, later.

I was back in jail. I knew that was the last straw. I knew that I had been given 17 years and now I escaped, kidnapped a guy, pulled an armed robbery. I remember thinking, I'm never getting out, this is it, this is home. Sitting in f—ing Calgary thinking, that's it man, this is where you're going to be the rest of your life so get used to it. And I just said, I'll have the last laugh. When they call me for court tomorrow morning, they're going to have to say "He's dead. He hung himself."

I waited until the lights went out and I hung a blanket in the back of the cell so they wouldn't see the shadow in the next cell. I was really bitter, and I remember thinking, I won't make a sound, they won't hear a peep or a cry or nothing. I'll just hang myself. It'll be real quiet, and that'll be it. When they find me, I'll be dead. But I didn't know about hanging. I tied myself up, lowered myself real slowly, started gagging, making real idiot sounds, and all the other inmates started banging and yelling for the guards. I had the cell lock plugged with matches so they couldn't save me, couldn't get their key in, I'd be dead. I thought it all out but it didn't work. They saved me and I come to on the floor. They just cut me down, let me drop. I smashed my head off the table, almost took my eye out. I would have really felt bad if I would have lost an eye. I remember looking in the mirror, big bruise, I could have lost my eye. And I'm thinking, geez, what would be worse, being dead or walking around with one eye?

I pleaded guilty and they jumped up and said, they're not accepting that. "This is very serious. This man is doing a 17-year sentence. He escaped out of prison, kidnapped a prison employee. This is very serious. We will not accept a guilty plea." The judge looked at me like I wasn't coherent, like I didn't know where I was. He asked me if I know what I did, if I want a lawyer. I told him, "I do not need a lawyer." I had already decided that as soon as they didn't watch me again, I was going to kill myself. It didn't matter how long they gave me, because I wasn't doing it. I firmly believed I would not do another day.

They put me in the rubber room, so to speak, under observation. They wouldn't give me a cigarette until I talked to this psychiatrist, and this psychiatrist had to come from the region, because I was under the Federal Penitentiary Act. This guy had to come from Saskatoon to interview me, and nobody came near me until he interviewed me, because now I was a serious threat to myself, or maybe to the guards or other inmates or however they come to terms for what they do.

I sat in that cell, and I thought, f——, I can't even do that right. Man, I'm a real loser. Some time later, I don't know how long, they sent me in to see this guy, and I don't know if I was hallucinating or what, but I swear he looked just like that psychiatrist in *One Flew Over the Cuckoo's Nest*. I had a real funny feeling, I laughed. I laughed at him. It was like, I've been here before. And he said, "Are you going to do it again?"

I looked him right in the eye and I said, "No. I won't do that again."

He said, "What do you mean? You'll do it again a different way?"

And I told him, the first chance I get I'll cut my head half off. I said, "We'll see you try to save me then."

He freaked. He said, "Get him out, interview terminated." They put me in that room again with a camera, little thick thing on that you can't rip up and hang yourself, really heavy sewn garment like a dress. They put me in that, left me, and there I stayed. Then they come and they said, "Will you take this medication?"

I told them, "Yeah when you drive it down my throat." They left. I would never take medication because I'd seen so many other guys on that, and messed up. I knew that if I took that, I might never come out of there. They got rid of me. They got in touch with the penitentiary and said, "We can't deal with this guy. We're not prepared to deal with this kind."

They sent me back to Drumheller and I was placed in the hole, and there I was in observation. Now I know this is it. This is where I am. This is where I stay. This is what I've got to look forward to. Nobody would say nothing to me. They all looked at me like they were scared of me. I was just a skinny little guy, I couldn't understand it. I could see that when they come to bring my meal, they looked fearful, like they had something to worry from me. They didn't know that I was harmless. If anything, I was just a threat to myself. They sent a committee member down to the hole. It just so happened that I knew this guy. And he come in and asked me if I wanted a cigarette. I said, "Yeah, I haven't had a cigarette for a week."

He just gave me all these cigarettes and he said, "I'll do you some canteen; some pop, chips, cigarettes, books." Then he said, "They said you tried to kill yourself." He started laughing. He said, "You wouldn't do that. I know you, you wouldn't do that." He seen me play sports, and he seen how much heart I had when we played hockey. I wouldn't shy away from bigger guys. I'd get hit, and hit back. He just couldn't believe that I was the kind of guy that would kill myself. I showed him the marks, his mouth dropped open. He didn't know what to say. He knew it was true, what they told him. He wanted to get out of there because he didn't know how to deal with that. He liked me as a friend and here I was, I tried to kill myself. He didn't know what to say or do.

I spent a year in the hole, went to court, and they wanted to give me a life sentence. This well-respected lawyer just happened to be at the remand centre. He seen me down there, come over, and said, "Allen, I was reading about you in the paper. You need a lawyer. I'll represent you. Let me represent you."

And I told him, "I don't know if they will let you. I got no money."

He said, "Don't worry about that. I'll be your lawyer." He said, "I'll come and see you tomorrow," and he came the next day and he asked me what happened, what's that on my neck? Right away he said, "Did the police beat you up?" He thought they forced me to confess or something.

I told him, "No. I hung myself."

He asked me why and I told him. He said, "I'll get you off, don't worry. I'll get you the least amount of time that you can get, just don't give up." He said, "I know lots of guys that are in jail, you can't give up." I thought about that. I would think about giving up, or going on, back and forth. It was maddening. In the end, I was doing 23 years, three months and seven days.

When I got sentenced, they sent three people: Jim O'Sullivan, he was the head of the wardens' association of North America, and two others. The first question he said was, "Did you kill anybody?"

I looked at him and said, "Do I look psychotic?"

His exact words were: "If I thought you were psychotic I wouldn't have told them to take the handcuffs off." And he said, "I would like to know what happened, how you escaped?" He accused me of having somebody help me. I told him exactly what happened and he said, "Well, you did it. I suggest to you to put in an application to a transfer to maximum security anywhere in Canada and I'll see that you get there. I thank you for being so candid with me." They took me away and I went back to my cell. And I thought, anywhere in Canada eh? I didn't give it any more thought. It doesn't matter. Wherever I am, there I am. It's all the same. So I just stayed there and one day they come, handcuffed me, put me on the bus, and I was in

PA. Again in the hole, thinking, here I am, 23 years, three months, seven days. At that time, I had six years in, I think, so until I could be released that left me with about 12 years, 12 years to go.

The hole, at that time in PA, was just a cement bed with wood slapped together, strips of wood that were laminated, different colors like you see a butcher block. A light in the centre of the cell. A heater in the floor that's covered by cement so you can't smash it. And bare, a steel sink. The door was closed, no window, and it had a little slot they slid open when they stick your food in. They'd give you a book, you'd just lay there and read. Or if you have a paper and pen you would write a letter. You were just there. I was there all alone, with nothing, feeling hopeless. A bad feeling, a really, really bad, sorry feeling.

They come and see me, the head of security, and said if I promised not to kill anybody they would let me out. I said, "I promise. I'm not going to kill anybody."

He said, "OK." He left. It seemed like five minutes later the door opened and they said, "Go!" They put me down in a cell and there was my younger brother. Not in the same cell, but in the same block. A few hours later when I went to the gym, there he was. I was sitting outside and he come walking right up to me, "How you doing Al?"

I said, "Oh, all right."

He said, "What happened to your teeth? You got two teeth missing."

I said, "Somebody knocked them out." We talked about what was happening to him, how I escaped, just stuff brothers would talk about. He asked me about our older brother who had testified against us and we had long conversations about him. I didn't like what he did. I didn't do nothing to him. But I remember telling him one day, one day he'd be in jail and he'll know how I feel. And then he's going to know. He's going to feel the pain. He's going to know what he did to me was wrong, and he's going to feel the same hopelessness I did. It was like I put a jinx on him, six years later he was in the next cell doing a 25-year sentence.

It was movement, time to go to work or meals, or something. It was about 100 guys out of their cells, the new admitting guys were coming in. My older brother was walking up the stairs to the range he was on. I seen him. He didn't see me. I ran over there, came up to him, and said, "Hey Ernie."

He looked and was just shocked. I guess it had been about six or seven years since he seen me and he said, "Oh, you got muscles and everything!" He grabbed me, he was scared, because of what he did in the past. Going to court against me, my brother. When we were young, he was always in control. Now it was reversed. He was just scared, he was really scared of me. I could see it in his eyes. I had seen fear in a lot of people's eyes. You can tell when you look in another man's eyes if he's angry or scared, and he was scared.

I just grabbed him, give him a hug, and told him, "Don't worry about it, everything will be OK." But he was never the same.

Eventually, they moved us. He was acting weird and stuff so I told him to try and get on my range, and he got on my range. Then one day he come and he asked me for a cigarette. I was mad, kind of bitter over the years. I snapped at him. I told him, "You're asking me for a cigarette? You should be giving me cigarettes." And he went back to his cell. A few days later he cut his throat. Ever since then he hasn't been the same.

In terms of witnessing violence, everything that could happen in prison. Guys getting killed, guys getting muscled for whatever reason. When you're in here, if you're weak you're preyed upon. It never used to be like that in the old days. If you bothered people, and you had problems, guys seen that and you'd get it. Now, it's like a new generation of criminals with no morals. A guy could have a nice watch, somebody could see it and just say, "I want that watch." And if that guy was the kind of person that couldn't fight, or wouldn't stand up for himself, that person would have the watch. You're only respected in here if people know: don't mess with that guy, if you f— with that guy he's going to fight, he's going to stab you or whatever. In here people are looked upon, like, that guy's weak, so he has a hard go. I've seen everything. They've asked me on a number of occasions about a number of things, and I told them, "No, I never seen it. I know nothing about it." It's less problems.

When it's a serious situation, where you know something bad's going to happen, I just turn and walk away. You don't see, you don't let that affect you, you become detached from that.

I've seen guys come in, that were just the nicest guys, never swear or nothing, well mannered. It's virtually overnight they change. They're just full of hate and it wears you down. You could be the strongest guy you ever seen and then after 15 years you'll see him, look at him, his hair is falling out, it's turning grey, just because of how he does his time. A lot of people on the street, they have stress because of making payments and stuff like that. But here there's no stress like that. Me, I'm 35 years old. I don't look 35, but inside I'm much older. It wears on you. There comes a time when you've just had enough and you don't want nothing to do with nothing. You just want to get out and live the rest of your life.

I used to always think of the street when I first came in. I met all kinds of guys that been in for a long time, and they always used to tell me, "Forget about the street."

I always used to say, "I'll never forget. I want out of here," because for the short time I was out there I had a good time and I threw it away. I always wanted to remember what it was like. In the last 10 years, I've forgotten about the street. I don't know when it comes Easter time or Mother's Day. I don't even think about that until someone reminds me. I don't get any visits hardly. I hardly ever phone. I never write, very seldom will I write a letter. The best way to do it is, just do it, just do it. Find something you enjoy. For me, it's been working out. Every day I go and work out. If I miss a day, if you were to observe me, and you seen that I wasn't working out, right away that would be an indication of the mood, that something's wrong, that guy's having a bad day.

I've been in prison since I was 16. In that time, I've probably been out maybe 14, 15 months. Just one of my brothers, doing a life sentence, remains in prison, besides me. The other two got out. I'm eligible for every type of release now, but so many things are happening in this prison, I don't believe I'll be released until mandatory, 1998. Nobody wants to go to bat for you because guys got out of here and went to Edmonton and killed people for no reason. I've met guys like that, were friends with them actually, that got out on parole and did that. I never gave it much thought, even to this day. "He's got his own problems." But now, the people that work here, they don't want to be involved with anybody. Some of them lost their jobs. So, no one wants to say, "Yeah, let that person out." They're afraid you'll get out and kill somebody and it's going to come back at them.

My father's still alive. He's quit drinking. If I phoned him up tonight and asked him to come visit tomorrow, he'd be there. I don't bother, because he doesn't have a lot of money and I think he thinks a lot of my problems are his fault. I told him that my being here had nothing to do with him. The last time I talked to my ex-girlfriend was in 1984. I don't have any idea what became of her. I often thought about that, where she is and what she's doing, but I have no idea.

My present girlfriend lives in Regina. She comes whenever she can, but it's a long ways to drive to the Edmonton Institution and she works.

In prison, you meet girls a lot of different ways, usually through a friend. If you have a friend in here and he's got a girlfriend, you just send a picture of yourself with him, she'll show it to her friends, and some girl might think, that guy's good looking, or whatever, and ask if she can write. Myself, I met this girl because she was a friend of my sister's. She seen a picture of me, asked if she could come visit me, and my sister told her, "Well, write him, ask him." She wrote me a letter and asked if she could come visit me and I said sure. She's been visiting ever since. That's been a couple years now.

I don't know what I'm going to do when I walk out of these gates. I've never really given that thought, that could be why I'm still sitting here. Nobody gave me much hope for the future, and I never gave that much thought. I guess I'd like to have a good night's sleep. I'd like to sleep peacefully. When you're in jail and you see a lot of violent things happening, you try your hardest not to let that bother you. A guy got in a fight the other day, and that's all you heard them talking about. I come onto the range and right away, a guy approached me, that's the first thing he said, "A guy got beat up."

And I said, "I don't want to hear it, I don't care about it. It doesn't interest me." Even on the news, I see horrible things that would just shock normal people, but to me, I don't even think about that. When I get out, the first thing I want to do is to be able to lay down and relax. I can't remember the last time where I relaxed. So I'd like to have a good sleep.

Slashed Up

Mika Piilila

"They knew I'd be quiet for a month if they said, 'Next month you're leaving'. . . . I got pretty frustrated and I slashed with a disposable razor. I lost so much blood that when they were putting the gauze pads on me, it was just going right through them. "

erge Kujawa, former head of prosecutions in Saskatchewan, once said with great conviction: "It's interesting to see how little psychiatry knows about humanity." Mr. Kujawa, who handled the courtroom drama that followed Canada's worst random mass murder, the Shell Lake Massacre, maintained "More than 95 percent of those charged with horrible crimes have had involvement with the psychiatric system before the fact."

Mika Piilila, 23, mentally unstable, did not commit a horrible crime. Yet, somewhere, something went terribly wrong.

He thought this chapter could be entitled, Society's Waste: The true story of a young man sent to one of Canada's toughest prisons because he was guilty of what is commonly known as dine and dash.

His crime, quite simply, was eating and running from a restaurant without paying the tab.

was just reading this thing in the paper. They had a drama play, and they had a little article; you know, how this place is and stuff. A writer in the Edmonton Journal made a comment that you could be quite sure there's nobody with misdemeanors in a place like this, which is a false fabrication. Society doesn't know what goes on in these places. They've never lived in here, they don't know, they can't say they know. Society can't say they know how it feels to fly like a bird. They can't say that because they never were a bird, so they don't know how it's like to fly. And they don't know what it's like in here. They have misconceptions. These people here, the officials, put misconceptions into society's minds that all the people here are dangerous, just animals. Society doesn't know what's going on.

I was born in Burnaby and I stayed there until I was four years old, when I moved to Edmonton with my mother and father. I lived in Edmonton until I was 15, then we moved to Toronto. There was a big boom in the construction trade, my dad was a unionized carpenter. They had their boom, it seemed like things were getting too expensive and downhill, so we moved back to Edmonton. I was about 19.

When I was born, I had the umbilical cord wrapped around my neck and lost a lot of oxygen to my brain. It led me to be hyperactive. I always had trouble concentrating in school and keeping a focus on what I was supposed to be doing. I made it pretty apparent to make it on hot dog days, and ice cream days, but other than that I wasn't too good at school.

I was about 13, started on trouble with the law, stealing sweaters and stuff. You know, try to make a buck. Ten bucks for stealing a sweater. But nothing hard core, just a youth getting into mischief, just how a youth does, gets in trouble when he's young. Kind of went through that phase, but nothing serious. Just petty shit.

I had one job as a janitor in a pharmaceutical factory in Toronto. I seemed to work there for about two weeks, then I screwed up. I didn't have the concentration level, the attention span to do something like that, to stick to something for a long time. I got a mental illness too, schizophrenia.

I was living with my mother and father. My father passed away in '92. Stomach hemorrhage, too much drinking. Guess the liver was bleeding and his stomach hemorrhaged. He passed away and it hit me pretty hard. Still does hit me hard.

Drinking was a problem for me because I figure that drinking's hereditary. You know, you see it all your life, a lot of drinking, so you kind of take that role. I think that's part of life. I could consider myself an alcoholic.

I broke into Beaver Lumber, just trashed it. The police came to arrest me. I didn't know what I was doing at all. I was incoherent. They took blood and alcohol samples, nothing in my system, nothing. I kind of lost my mind there. I went to Alberta Hospital for a month, got on medication, stabilized myself, went back to court about a month later, and got a two-year suspended sentence, a probationary period.

My psychiatrist had prescribed medication. When this incident happened, I was kind of on a trip, saying, "Hey, I can go without medication. I'll be normal, just like anybody else." But that proved to be wrong.

I think it was a Pizza Hut. I was drinking, kind of intoxicated. I went in there, I must have lost some money, or whatever the situation was, didn't have the money to pay for the bill. I think it was one of them mediums with everything on it, or whatever kind of pizzas they have at Pizza Hut.

Mike Piilila – *"One of the things I think about is, what's the next day going to bring? Is something going to happen? Is someone going to get killed? Are you going to bump into somebody? . . . I could get killed, just like that. You don't know what's coming. You have to watch what you do at all times."*

It wasn't bad, it wasn't bad. It was pretty good. Thirty days, 18 months probation.

I know I did wrong, it wasn't such a horrendous sentence or nothing. It's nothing compared to the Pen, when you go to a provincial jail. The atmosphere is nothing like here. It's a different head space altogether. So, it really didn't have an effect on me, like it does now.

I stayed with my mother and brother between that sentence and what I'm in for now. Just stayed at home, collecting welfare, taking my medication. I was doing pretty well until this current offence happened, the dine and dash and throwing a boulder through a window.

I had some extra pocket change, a few hundred bucks, and I wanted to go to Vancouver to visit some people. I was off my medication at the time. It was more of a spontaneous thing than anything. I jumped on a train, I was getting sick of the ride, 16, 17 hours. I got off in Kamloops, had enough money to get a hotel for the night, had a couple hundred dollars. The next day, I was drinking. The day after, I didn't have any money whatsoever. I was hungry, didn't know there was any Sally Ann or soup kitchens, so I thought I'd go and eat a meal and maybe do 30 days over it. But I was quite wrong on that one.

I went to Oriental Garden and ordered some kind of Chinese buffet or something. I don't know what the hell I was eating. It wasn't even that good.

I consumed three beers and 12 rye and cokes, quite a bit of alcohol. Then it came time for me to pay my bill. I zoomed out of there and that's when I threw the rock through the window. Just kind of in that head space. The police stopped me, I gave them a wrong name, went to court the next day.

I wasn't wasting the court's time or nothing. I wanted to get this over with. They didn't even take into account my first chance to plead guilty, which I did. I got two years.

I think I appeared in front of a judge that doesn't like transients in his town, and I think I got two years because he wants to set an example that if transients want to come to his town, in Kamloops, and not pay for their meals, they're not welcome. I think that's pretty well what happened to me. I was just a transient and he wanted to set an example to all other transients who don't pay their meals.

There's no justice in that decision at all. I just can't see how two years warrants not paying a restaurant bill and throwing a rock through a window. It's just crazy. A blind person can see this clearly. It's just wrong.

They didn't take my previous record into account when they sentenced me. I was very unstable. I wasn't on my medication or nothing. To give a guy two years for a restaurant bill, they should at least do some kind of PDR (pre-disposition report) or some kind of assessment or something. You don't just send a guy that has no violence, no drug convictions, no nothing on his record, to a penitentiary.

I did have a lawyer, not a very good one, a legal aid lawyer. I thought of appealing but when you get sentenced to the Kamloops Regional Correctional Centre, waiting to go to the Pen, they tell me to sign this piece of paper and I'll get to the Pen faster. If I sign this, I won't have to wait 30 days. Apparently that was my appeal papers I was signing away. They didn't even tell me. They just said, "Sign here and it'll get you out of here faster," waiving my rights to appeal.

I never talked to my lawyer, just signed the thing for legal aid after I got sentenced, that he represented me. I shouldn't have even signed that, but I did so he could get his money. I went to Matsqui Penitentiary about two weeks later.

I was kind of in a daze during the four, five hour van ride to the prison. One day I'm eating, not paying the restaurant, next, I'm going to the penitentiary. I was kind of stunned. I didn't really have a good comprehension of what was going on. I was just dumbfounded.

We were partitioned, two to a seat. We were shackled and hand-cuffed together, guns and everything. I didn't really know what to think, if it was a dream, or what was going on. There was no conversation.

It was daylight when we arrived there, about 11, just before lunch rolled around. I was very nervous. I never experienced penitentiary life, and you hear stories about it and stuff. I felt very scared, very confused. I kind of felt betrayed by the justice system.

I was treated like any other inmate, just like a piece of garbage. They found out the extent of my psychiatric history and thought it would be a good idea for me to go to RPC (Regional Psychiatric Centre) just next door. Very high security. I was there six months. I felt terrible, they treated me like I was a piece of shit. They were changing my medication every other day, they weren't telling me what was going on. They didn't tell me first time federal offenders could get accelerated paroles. They didn't clue me in, they just kind of, "This guy's just an inmate, just like everybody else," which I am, and just kind of forgot about me. I shouldn't even have been there in the first place. Most first federal inmates have a choice of signing over and going to provincial, to do a federal exchange program, if their crime ain't too serious, or no extensive violence. They never even told me. They promised me about four months in a row that I was going to get a transfer back to Alberta region. They kept falling through there. They'd give me a story every month. They knew I'd be quiet for a month if they said, "Next month you're leaving." They kept playing head games with me. I didn't want to be in that situation any more. I just thought of a different alternative. At that point I was so confused, so sick, that I thought that would be the best ultimatum, to do that. I got pretty frustrated and I slashed with a disposable razor. I lost so much blood that when they were putting the gauze pads on me, it was just going right through them. I was very serious about it. I knew what the extent could be, I could die. That option seemed a little bit more promising than having to sit in the penitentiary for nothing.

I was bleeding, very dizzy, very nauseated, 'cause I lost so much blood. Pint and a half at least. They didn't even take me to the hospital. They waited 35 minutes until the institution doctor came. He gave me 250 stitches, worked for about four and a half hours on my arm and then threw me in the screen room, a segregation kind of cell. You don't get no clothes, nothing. I was awake throughout the procedure. They inserted some kind of anaesthetic which didn't even numb my arm. I was in such a bad mental health state that I didn't even care. The pain didn't bother me. It was like watching someone do this to another person. It was like, it wasn't me. It was just a daze, confusion.

The next morning, my arm, very sore, very raw, looked like a bunch of hamburger, raw meat. They wouldn't give me any antipsychotic medication, which I was supposed to have. Matter of fact, they didn't even wrap my arm up. I had these big, thick stitches. I told them my arm was very sore, they didn't give me as much as an aspirin, for pain. They just let me sit there.

I stayed there for about three weeks and they let me out. They said, "We're pretty sure we're going to get your transfer." It was kind of unfortunate that something to this extent would have had to get me a transfer, even possibly lose my life.

At RPC, it was kind of a joke, "Oh, two years for a dine and dash," but I felt very nervous. First time in a federal institution, gun towers, trucks roaming around all the time. I didn't feel too comfortable. I think a person that comes into a penitentiary should have to at least warrant his stay. Just don't throw people in penitentiaries like that, unless it's totally necessary. It's just not right. I mean, you're putting somebody's life at risk for nothing. For peanuts, you're putting somebody's life at risk.

Had about two fights when I was there. You know, just kind of protecting myself. They thought my tobacco was their tobacco. I got into altercations for that. I went to warden's court a couple times for telling the guards to f— off. They charged me with threatening behavior.

I was the only one that came up to Edmonton, and they had about seven guards. It was like a big Greyhound, says charter on the front. What they do is lock you in your seat. They had a full arsenal. I think they had semi-automatics, full-automatics. For me! What's the tax-payers paying for? Seven guards take you all the way from there to Edmonton. A $94 restaurant bill to pay a thousand times more. It cost a couple hundred thousand, I think, to keep an inmate in a peniten-tiary, to feed them and everything else. I think it would have been much more cost efficient for them just to make me do some dishes, give me a month to pay for the restaurant bill, do some restitution, some community work or something.

I went to admittance and discharge (A&D). They gave me a shower, gave me some stuff to wash my hair, and gave me some institution clothes. Then I just waited in a cell. They said, "Are you population or are you PC (protective custody)?"

"I'm population," I said. I was very nervous, very nervous.

When you walk into a setting like that, they don't say nothing to you basically. That's what makes it even more nerve-racking. They won't say nothing to you. This is a very serious penitentiary, and I knew this before I even came. I couldn't even believe that I was even coming here. Because, you know, I'm at risk if someone gets in a fight or something and they have the tear gas out. Maybe they have to shoot someone, maybe one of the pellets is going to hit me in the eye or something. This is geared for maximum security. All the f—ups that can't make it in other penitentiaries come here, and that's basically what it is, and I couldn't believe I was here. I didn't really know what to comprehend, what's going to happen next? Am I going to get killed?

One of the things I think about is what's the next day going to bring? Is something going to happen? Is someone going to get killed? Are you going to get hurt for doing a mistake? Are you going to bump into somebody? What's going to happen? In an environment like this, you don't know what's going to happen. I could walk outside and I could get killed, just like that. You don't know what's coming. You have to watch what you do at all times. Not just some time, but all times. The prices of a mistake in here are very costly. You're putting your life in jeopardy when you make a mistake.

There's a lot of bullshit that goes on in these places. Guards give you a little shove, just to make you screw up. I can see that the officials go out of their way to make you screw up. I think they're more corrupt than we are really. For myself, I made a mistake in my life, and I believe they make mistakes too, but they just never got caught and they think they're better than us.

A lot of guys take me under their wing, look after me. They understand my situation. They don't think I should be here either. I haven't really had no trouble with inmates. But it's a very intense environment, very intense. You just got to wake up in the morning, and you know, survive another day.

I'm double bunked. Bunking up with two people is not humanitarian. The whole cell's probably about 9' by 4', so you've only got a very little space. You've got to smell the other guy's shit. Guys who do life sentences, I don't understand how they could double bunk.

My cell mate, in for armed robbery, took me under his wing. I've been admitted to health care a few times, because I have some psychiatric problems, hallucinate and stuff. I had those troubles when I first came here. They did get me stabilized on my medication, which was good.

The first thing I'm going to do when I get out, I'm going to get my brother to bring me a Big Mac. That's for sure. A Big Mac and a big chocolate milkshake.

I'm going to take as many programs as I can, life skills. Maybe get into some kind of AADAC (Alberta Alcoholism and Drug Abuse Commission) course, an anger management course, anything to stay out of here. Whatever restrictions they have for me, I want to fill, because I don't want to come back here. Nothing's worth coming back to this place.

Surviving is the Key

Claude Robinson

"There's times when people will step out and get involved in a fist fight or whatever, and settle scores. That's natural even outside, just like in here. But, in here you can't leave. You know, you can't go away and go home."

nce one of Calgary's most wanted fugitives, Claude Joseph Robinson, born in a small Prairie town, January 19, 1955, continues to spend his life behind the high walls of one of Canada's hardest prisons.

He's bilingual, clean cut, a non-smoker, someone who lived in the same neighborhood and went to the same high school as me.

Before, during and since those years, Claude Robinson has known a lot of trouble and even less freedom. It started off petty, escalating along the way.

Convicted, among other things, of murder, and blowing up an armored car, the words of this federal inmate should be required reading for every young offender who believes that crime pays.

he laws have got a lot stricter because people are fed up with crime, although there's too much media hype put on it. The media have a definite tendency to hype things up that they hear in court. An example was when I was accused of trying to kidnap hockey star Wayne Gretzky. That story come out at a conspiracy trial in Calgary. An American who turned evidence on me, more of a liar than anything else, was at a meeting with myself and two other people in Edmonton. As a matter of fact, one of the others was the one that brought up the Gretzky story about a kidnap plot during the playoffs. It was just talked over, hashed over, but no agreement was ever made. It was just another idea passed around.

Claude Robinson – *"What a waste of time it's been. All the time I've wasted being in prison that I could have had with my family, friends, and what I could have done, what I could have had today. Instead of getting involved in this ridiculous bullshit with crime." He was unsuccessful in appealing his second-degree murder conviction. It involved the death of a 23-year-old man who was beaten with a baseball bat and blasted with a shotgun.*

I wanted to maintain a certain level of lifestyle, just stepped out and committed crimes. It never got me anywhere, just always in more trouble, more time. It's not hard to find people who are willing to participate in break and enters or thieving. A lot of people are hurting for money. It seems like a friendship at the time, but when something goes wrong there's no more friendship. It's betrayal and the trust factor is gone. You just can't trust anybody in this business whatsoever. Not at all.

At 7 a.m. there's a count, the first of the day. We get up. The doors break open some time around 7:30. We go out, have our breakfast in the dining-hall, or stay in our cage and try and get some more rest. We're cracked open again after we get back from breakfast. If we have a work assignment we go to that, or school, or whatever the situation might be, otherwise we're locked up in our cage all day. We come back around 11, then we're locked up for count again. They break us open for dinner about 12:15 to 12:30. They have two lines. The first three units go, come back, they'll be all locked up. Then the next three units go. When that's over, some time between 1:30 and 2, the way the routine is now, they'll crack the people open again, only the cells that people have work, school, some kind of program or whatever. Then we come back at 4. There's another count at 4:15. Then there's the meal line situation again, and it alternates day by day. The first three units today will be the second three units the next day. Then at 6 there's visits, for whoever's got visits. At 6:30 all the doors are cracked open and whoever wants to go to the gymnasium and the outside yard goes. There's an upper level and a lower level in each unit and on alternate days, it'll be either the upper level that stays out or the lower level. Then 10 minutes later all the doors are locked, there's no more movement. At 8 everything's opened again, we get movement from the gym, for 10 minutes, to the units, come back, and there's a 10-minute movement to the gym. The other ranges are out until 9:30. At 9:30 we're all out for jug-up. That's when we make toast and peanut butter and jam sandwiches or whatever, and cook up popcorn from our canteen, or we open up a can of tuna. At 10 we're locked up again. There's a count in the unit. At 11 there's a another final count, the shift change. Then there's a count at 3:30 in the morning.

Overnight, you might hear some yelling, because of the guards turning on the night lights for their count on their walk every hour. In the summertime, sometimes we hear airplanes going by, with our window open. We might hear a loud TV or stereo once in a while, but we just tell the guy to turn it down. Most people have headphones.

The noise starts at 7 when the day shift comes on, the constant opening and closing of doors, yelling on the speakers, everybody yelling back and forth and talking. It's gotten really bad with all the racket, really stressful. The overcrowding is getting on everybody's nerves. The constant lock-up. The place stinks all the time, the air is putrid. All the cigarette smoke, it's unhealthy. The potential for spreading disease and sickness is overwhelming. A lot of people are fearful of what might be going on, if somebody comes in with something that might be contagious, it'll be an epidemic, and we shouldn't be susceptible to that, or exposed to that.

I was born in St. Paul, Alberta. That's where I was raised, on a small acreage right in town. There was four brothers and my mother and father. On the acreage there was two houses, my grandparents and cousins lived next door. I had quite a few friends and we used to always hang around together. There was quite a bit of trees, we lived right on the edge of the lake, so we had a lot of land to play on. We had clubhouses, the barn, the gardens, and all the animals, the horses and cows. It was unlimited, the things we used to do.

I remember every weekend we'd all scrounge our money together. We'd go collecting empty beer bottles in ditches and we'd get enough to go to the movies. I remember a couple of years in a row, every weekend we'd be gone to the movies. Either that or we'd be at the lake trying to make rafts to go out to the islands on the lake. We'd be trucking around the forest, cutting down trees, hauling logs and making forts, or riding horses, riding our bikes. It was incredible. I went to school there until Grade 4. Then we moved to Edmonton. It was different. I had to take the buses to school and all that, so it was tough getting used to. It took a while.

I was 10 years old when I moved to the city in 1965. I went to Sacred Heart School, lived in what was known as the Highlands district for about a year. Then we moved to the Glenora district, that was quite the place. That's where my parents started keeping boarders, like a foster home, kids from broken homes. There was two of them there and that's where I first got into stealing. They taught me how to cut the lining of the jacket and different little tricks in shoplifting. I was 12 years old then.

The first week was quite an adventure 'cause I ended up having a box full of stuff – pens, toys, firecrackers – from a couple of drugstores in the neighborhood. I gave all the pens away for Christmas presents. It was quite the trick.

Then we moved into another district, Wellington, on the edge of town. There was a lot of trees, horseback riding, Speedway Park (a raceway), a lot of activity. They had better community leagues then, so things went pretty well. There was an older fellow that lived just up the alley from us that used to do taxidermy. He got crippled in a hunting accident and was in a wheelchair all the time, and was he good at taxidermy. I used to spend a lot of time in his garage workshop, mounting birds and preparing hides. He taught me quite a few things about taxidermy. But after we moved away, I never touched it again.

When I was about 14, that was the first time I ever got caught. I got caught stealing school supplies at Eaton's shopping centre with my cousin and another friend. We were getting them for ourselves for school. A detective caught us putting stuff in a bag, so we got quite a tongue-lashing and quite the scare. We got a warning and sent home. They phoned our parents. They were pretty upset, so we had a long talk and that was about the end of it. I never went to Eaton's again for about three or four years, although they only banned me for one year. I didn't want to set foot in that place again.

Then we moved to Gold Bar on the southside and lived there for about five or six years. I was doing pretty well in Grade 7, 8 and 9. Most of the people I used to hang around with were a pretty popular group. We were always helping out the neighborhood, pretty active, there was about eight or nine of us. I met a really wonderful girl. She had just moved to our district, and at the local school, Hardisty junior high, they used to hold dances every weekend. That's where I met her and started a good relationship that lasted about six months. I went to College St. Jean in Edmonton, a French school. I have a French background, so I maintained that. Those were really exciting times, playing all the sports and activities. I was involved in a lot, plus I had to bus it back to the community we were living in at that time.

I got into trouble early on in my Grade 10 year. I dropped out, ended up going to Austin O'Brien high school, and then myself and two other fellows got rapped pretty heavily for B&E in the school. I got 15 months probation. I was the prime mover all the time. Most of my friends, especially in that district in Gold Bar, their parents were alcoholics. They never had anything, they were stealing already too.

In the wintertime, we used to snowmobile. We used to have a couple boarders that brought snowmobiles. Those boarders, after the foster kids we used to keep, well, they were kind of shit-disturbers too. So I got another negative influence in my life. I used to go partying, 15 years of age, and I'm partying with people 20, 21, all the time. There was never any drugs. I never did experiment, or touch drugs until I was about 17. I didn't even know drugs existed when I went to jail the first time. And booze, I've always hated the taste and what it done to people because I've seen too much of it around me. I stayed away from booze.

That same year, I got caught with some other fellows in our neighborhood with a bunch of stolen bicycles. We took them from other neighborhoods, just to take the parts for our bikes. I got a year's probation for that.

My father, a carpenter, was always out of town. My parents were always working hard and were never around. They separated when I was 16, which traumatized the whole family.

Shortly after that bike crime, I got tied up with another group of fellows. We got caught for breaking into a couple of gun shops in Wetaskiwin and Vegreville and I got 16 months in Fort Saskatchewan jail.

It was scary. It was incredibly scary and lonely, because it was the first time I had been exposed to drugs, people fixing drugs in their arms. It was tough, trying to deal with that and not get involved. There was a lot of other people in there, older people, pretty smart, and they took me under their wing, guided me, looked after me.

My girlfriend died while I was in my first six weeks of that sentence. It was tough doing the rest of the time, trying to cope. I was really in love and we were really good for each other. She was bright, really active in school politics.

It was a Friday evening. I remember that evening really well, because I couldn't sleep at all. I knew something was wrong. Around midnight, a friend of mine was driving Louise to a girlfriend's place. A vehicle with two women coming from a bar apparently crossed the centre line and smacked head on. She was killed, with a broken neck, and our friend was seriously injured.

Louise was quite an achiever in school, very popular. We developed quite a strong relationship. Being in jail, having her come visit me once a week with my parents and her parents, we were all very close. So it had a profound effect on me. It still does, I still think about it. As a matter of fact, I named my daughter after her.

I was released and went back to school at St. Mary's in Edmonton for a month or two. I couldn't adapt because of my jailhouse experience. I couldn't relate to the kids any more. I just felt totally different. I ended up dropping out and getting a job at a service station. That experience lasted for about two months and I swore I'd never work mechanics again.

My next appearance with the law happened in 1974 when some other fellows broke into some places. I was sharing a basement suite with one of them, the police came the next day and arrested everybody. I ended up going to jail on that one along with some other charges. I ended up getting a total of about 33 months. I went to Drumheller Penitentiary where I finished my high school and read a lot of books.

I didn't have a girlfriend when I went to Drumheller, so that made the time easier. It's really tough doing time when you have somebody you love out on the street. People should realize when you do time, the heartbreak and everything else, the loneliness, is so intense. The party on the street will do everything they can to help you and try to cope, but for some reason it's three or four months, and if it goes past that, it should last for a while. But usually that first three or four months, that's when relationships either make it or break it.

That was a hell of a lonely place, as any prison is at any time, miserable, lonely. But with the self-help books and some of the guidance from more experienced prisoners, the ones that have done a lot of time, I made the most use of that sentence. One of our teachers was a pretty good guy. He helped me cope a lot, same as the principal of the school at the time. I just studied, studied, and studied and exercised and worked out. Played a lot of baseball, ran, did a lot of gymnastics, played tennis. I was involved in a lot of things, anything that I could learn.

I straightened my attitude out, my thoughts on life, and I was sure I was going to make it, try everything I could to go straight. I did for a number of years, but I could never fully adapt. I always felt out of place. I never had a good mentor, somebody to guide me, give me options. Everything I've had to do, I've had to learn on my own, from my mistakes. I just had that problem.

After spending all that time, 23 months inside, and I only had one visit a month, if that, from my family, and in those days there was no phone calls, I felt pretty alienated from people around me. You feel like people know where you came from. But I was determined. I was in excellent shape, thought I knew everything, that I could handle myself and move forward, because of all the business courses I took, all the self-help books that I read. Dozens and dozens of books in those days. I must have read, in that whole time I spent in Drumheller, over 100 books. That's all we did. There was no TV in our cells in those days. I didn't have a radio. The only TV was on the range in the evening. That was it.

I got back out and phoned up an old friend. The whole family, the brothers, the mother, wouldn't talk to me. I was wondering, what's going on? They were all messed up, and I couldn't understand what was going on with them. They wouldn't explain what was the matter. I phoned again early in the morning and they told me what had happened. The oldest boy had been murdered at the Kingsway hotel. So that kind of threw me for a loop. I went and visited them the next day. That started off my life on the street again.

The parole officer I had wasn't too bad at all. He gave me time to get back on my feet, get my "land legs" as he called it. He gave me three or four months to get a place, get settled down, try and get myself together, see where I want to go. I ended up working for a produce company, a clothing manufacturer delivering their garments, and then I worked for Census Canada for a while, doing the 1976 Census. I went to school for eight weeks taking a program in heavy duty diesel mechanics. I learned a lot. I had a really good instructor, although I never did apply any of that knowledge. I tried, but I don't know what happened. I tried various jobs. I couldn't find the niche that I wanted to fall into.

When I look back on it, I wish I would have got married, it would have changed me around a lot and settled me down. I always got involved with the wrong crowd or the wrong group of people. I ended up doing more crime, to try to make that extra buck 'cause I didn't know what I was going to do for a job or a career. I didn't know what I was going to do in school or training. I never did have anybody, or any help deciding.

I ended up finishing that parole. The next time I went to jail was for possession of pot, I think a couple B&Es or something, possession of stolen property, 'cause I ended up getting 15 months. That was a long dreary bit.

My daughter Louise was born in 1981. Her mother abandoned the relationship when I went to jail in 1982. I got charged with possession of stolen vehicles in Calgary and ended up getting two years less a day. Five months into that, I escaped from a work gang. I used to go and visit my daughter, take her for two or three weeks at a time to my place in Calgary, where I lived when I was on the run from the law.

I got caught in '85 for armed robbery of the Northwest Drug Company in Calgary. A pharmaceutical drug is the easiest thing there is to sell. It turns over quite quickly. There's never any complaints 'cause its quality is always there. The police estimate in the street value of the narcotics and all the drugs that were taken was $1.25 million. But their prices are embellished somewhat.

I needed $25,000 because I wanted out. I was tired of doing crime, all this nickel and diming all the time – selling travel trailers, 4 x 4s, industrial equipment. There was so many people involved, everybody wanted something. Never mind all the expense of the gas, travelling to Winnipeg, Edmonton, Calgary, to all the auctions selling this equipment.

A couple of people that I worked with were fed up because they never had any money, they were always broke. They ended up going out to grab a delivery truck at 1:30 in the morning that made a route around the interior of B.C. They were going to grab all the narcotics and pills. But 45 minutes after they left, I felt uncomfortable. I was sitting with my girlfriend at the time, so we went to have a look to see what was going on. We finally spotted them hiding in the back of another stolen van and they were waiting for the truck. I ended up leaving with her, and came back about half an hour later and they were still there and they said they were going to do an armed robbery of the whole place, hold everybody at bay, hit the vault. Nobody knew anything about the inside of the building or anything. It was completely unplanned. I ended up participating, watching out for them. My girlfriend was watching in the car on the other side. The robbery was done, everybody left, and because of a foul up with the walkie-talkies, people talking at the same time cut off communication, she couldn't get the message to get out of there. We're trying to tell her to get out, she started to come, but the police were already there. People had set the alarm. She got caught, and because of papers found in her purse, they came to the house and grabbed the other two fellows about two or three days later. Got the fourth fellow, on the fifth day, I believe. I just took off to the States. I lived there for about eight months, came back to Canada, and got caught in a high speed chase near Vulcan, Alberta. I got charged for that armed robbery. I also got charged for bombing an empty Brinks truck in Calgary with another fellow.

It was an experimental bombing and I got talked into going along on the ride and ended up getting convicted of planning the whole thing, which to this day I'm still trying to get straightened out. There was three trucks at the back of Brinks in Calgary going to the scrap yard. The fellow that was with me was an American who was supposed to have been some ranger, some military superman – quite experienced – which turned out to be all bullshit. He was nothing but a cook and a map reader, as it turned out, but I'd been lied to by the whole group of people I'd gotten involved with. He wanted to blow up the first truck, but it was 1:30 in the morning and it was only a couple of blocks from one of the police stations in Calgary. I insisted if we're going to blow out a window, we're going to blow out the one in the middle truck in case any shrapnel or anything comes flying about. I didn't know what might happen. We applied this thing to the window, put the long fuse on it, took off down the street, and waited and waited and waited. Finally the thing blew up and we came back to look at the damage. When we were driving by, there was a whole bunch of guards with guns all over the place. I just couldn't believe it. I guess they'd been waiting for somebody to pull something off at their headquarters 'cause the week before, one of their other trucks, the windows had been shot out with a small calibre handgun or something.

When the bomb went off, the two-inch windows just completely went in, blasted the back wall out, pushed the steering down, the seat, everything. It was fairly loud.

I didn't get arrested until May 29, about three weeks later. It was a fluke actually. Some of the people I was involved with were smuggling cocaine and this supposed expert was one of the smugglers. Apparently, the police were watching them out of Lethbridge and they came to meet me twice in Calgary and the police followed them. They had a monitor on the phone, came up with my real name, and all the bells started ringing.

We ended up deciding to meet at Vulcan. That's where the police set the trap and we ended up in a high-speed chase outside of town. They were following, even in an airplane, and I ended up high-ending the car.

There were all kinds of stories being made up by a couple of the accused. Most of them ended up co-operating with the police and I'm the only one that got the big time, because of all my activities and involvements with different things.

I got 20 years. I got 10 years for the one armed robbery at that drug warehouse and I got 10 years consecutive for the bombing of the Brinks truck. The police tactical team took me right out of the courtroom and flew me straight to Edmonton Max. Within an hour and a half after being sentenced, I was sitting in prison. December 19, 1986. I've been here ever since that day.

It's been a miserable, miserable time that's for sure. The whole concept of prison has changed so much. It's so negative now, trying

The Brinks armored truck blown up by Claude Robinson.

to get things to try and improve yourself. Years ago, I realized what I needed, what I should have done, what I need now, and what I need to do. I'm trying to achieve that but there's so many barriers to it.

I'm getting some mentors, some community support. My whole base for my community support is here. I've got lots of really excellent friends, people in the community that support me. I've started different groups, the Family Interaction Network Society, for prisoners, to bring in families, wives, children and parents. That lasted for several months until there was a realignment of policies with the new warden and they cancelled all the groups. I think only two or three groups survived that realignment. Since then my interest has been into maintaining and going forward with my education, trying to get more resources in the community to help myself out with my release.

In 1989 here, I was arrested for first-degree murder. I ended up getting charged out of Wetaskiwin, went to Red Deer for trial, got convicted in 1990 of second-degree murder, and I'm still appealing that.

A fellow I used to steal travel trailers and industrial equipment with in 1981, got caught in Regina stealing a trailer with a stolen van and he ended up getting six months. He escaped and he came back to our acreage in Calgary. He only had another month left, his wife and kids were there, so we had to get him out of there because naturally the police are going to come looking where your family is. They never came, but everybody was all just a bag of nerves. We took him to try and keep him at some friends' places in Calgary. Nobody wanted to keep this guy because he was too much of a bullshit artist and nobody liked his attitude, so I ended up driving him to Red Deer, dropping him off there, and I went back to Calgary. A few days later, I went back to Red Deer to pick him up, but he was already gone. They had kicked him out of the house. They couldn't take him any more, the friends that I had left him with. I seen him again one more time in Calgary. He came back to visit the acreage with some hippie looking guy that I thought was a cop, about a week to 10 days after I'd dropped him off. That was the last time I seen him. In 1989, they came and arrested me and charged me with murdering some individual that had been killed during that time span. He ended up testifying against me, this fellow, and I ended up getting convicted under a jury. There was a tactical team in the courtroom all the time, so I had to fight the impression that I was some kind of dangerous criminal. There was about a dozen police always fully armed, tactical unit, metal detectors. I had to fight a negative impression.

This all goes back to 1985 when I was first arrested. They wanted my co-operation because they insisted I was internationally connected with organized crime and possibly involved in terrorist activity. Totally off the wall, unrealistic stuff that there's no truth to it whatsoever. There were allegations about mass murders, they wanted my co-operation, to clear up whatever they suspected. There was nothing to co-operate about and it was the last thing I was going to do anyway. So I kind of told them to shove it and they kept coming and coming and coming and coming every couple of days, grinding on me, grinding on me for hours and hours, trying to break me, and I just told them to drive it. They told me that one way or another I will eventually co-operate. Both teams from the RCMP and the city police in Calgary, one team told me they would "two-bit-me," meaning they would give me a life 25 sentence one way or another. Another team came in and said they would nickel and dime me and I would never hit the street again. Now, I'm doing life 15 on the second-degree conviction.

There's been quite a few incidents, all the time I've been in different prisons. Especially with people that rip other prisoners off, cell thieves, guys that steal tobacco or stuff like that. I've seen hands broken in door frames, big metal doors being slammed against the fingers. People have a tendency to protect their groups, maintain a certain level. There's times when people will step out and get involved in a fist fight or whatever, and settle scores. That's natural even outside, just like in here. But in here, you can't leave. You know, you can't go away and go home. You live here so you got to deal with different situations. I've been involved in a few fist fights in here over the years. I'm still here. Surviving is the key thing. It's like I tell a lot of people who had their own situations over the many years that they've been in, just to look at the whole situation, you're still alive. You're still winning.

My first few years here, it seemed every time I went to court on my hearings, while I was gone, something would happen. There would be a ball bat incident, a knifing, something. I was kind of glad to not be here during most of the incidents although there's been quite a few violent incidents and a few deaths. I think December 1992 was the first death just after they cut off the programs. I believe cutting off the programs, self-help groups, had a direct effect on the increase in violence because there was nothing to do any more, there was nothing to lose.

There are a lot of convicts who try to avoid violence, most of them do a lot of cell time and stick to themselves. There's a lot of people who have never been involved in ongoing criminal activity, armed robberies, B&Es or drug dealing. A lot of people are in here for the first time, for murder, manslaughter or fraud. The first time they ever did anything, they got caught, they got their time, and that's the only sentence they're going to have. Sometimes it's life 25. They don't know nothing about crime, they just killed somebody out of rage or whatever it might be. A lot of them keep to themselves, they do their studies, they go to work, and they don't get involved in a lot of things, which is unfortunate in some ways, because there's ball teams and sports that they could get involved in. But because they don't want to have anything to do with anybody, they just keep to themselves.

There's a sense of fear among prisoners, some more so than others. There's a lot of people that have done things to other prisoners in other sentences or in other prisons and they get transferred here. There's sex offenders who really fear for their lives. There's the informants, they're all hated, nobody likes any of them. Then there's people that are active informers in the institutions. Eventually, they all get found out. Once you done enough time you get suspicious of certain people. You're always suspicious. And because of the betrayals that I've gone through over the years, with the people betraying me and testifying against me, and turning me in to the police, I don't trust anyone. I'm careful what I say and who I hang around with. I try to pick my friends out of experience. People with good backgrounds to begin with. People who have a clear goal, a clear vision of life, people with integrity and honor and respect for one another, and they try to maintain that at all costs. There's loyalty above everything else. Honor is one of the big rules in prison. If you lose your honor, you lose your respect and that goes without saying anywhere in society. When you got no respect for yourself, nobody is going to have respect for you either.

Some people will put on a mask when they come into population, come out of your cage or your unit. You got to present an image a lot of times, so more people leave you alone. There's a tendency for some individuals to try and make a name for themselves by attacking certain people, putting other people down. That goes on for awhile, then they eventually end up getting taken out and hurt themselves, so it doesn't last very long. There's a standard and a code that's still the old code from the '60s and '70s. It's still there because a lot of the old-timers try to hang on to that. The system is falling apart, unity among the guys is having a hard time maintaining itself because of all the betrayal that's been happening inside the prisons.

CSC (Correctional Service of Canada) is to blame for a lot of this violence. They nurse along prison informers, give them all kinds of privileges, then they end up getting an early release because of all the informing they've done. They get out in the community and as you read the papers over the years, you'll see all the people they have killed. They come out, they come back in, and it's come out that they were prison informers, part of the dark side. These people consistently have been doing that for a lot of years. It's the fault of the administrations in different prisons, it's the correctional service itself for letting this stuff go on. It's the same outside on the street. You have the informers that work for the police and they are given tickets to commit crimes, sell drugs, and these people somehow get thoughts in their mind that they're untouchable. They go out and they end up committing murders, serious crimes, believing that they're going to be protected by their police friends.

It's really sad to see that happening. There never was a code as far as honor among thieves, there never has been. In almost every case, every time a group of people get busted, there will always be one part of the group that turns over and ends up testifying and betraying the rest. The others, because of their honor and their integrity, will end up doing big time. There's a lot of people doing big time because their honor and integrity just will not let them become stool-pigeons or rats. I fall in that category, where I wouldn't crack and I wouldn't give it up, save my life by giving somebody else's life up. Unfortunately, I'm now doing a life 15 bit because of it, and hated by the authorities and the police.

As far as being preyed upon by homosexuals, there's a certain percentage in the population that are, and don't hide it. There's been incidents of people muscling younger offenders to have sex. But that's been dealt with because the general population frowns upon that. Sex offenders are the worst scum of the earth. They're just looked on as dirt, garbage. Anybody that does that, even in prison, they're dealt with harshly. If they don't check into protection, they'll either be killed or injured.

As far as drug use is concerned, it's minimal, very hard to come by in this prison. Around here, it's very rare. Alcohol, that's the history of prisons. You always have your brews and your brewmasters. But there's even less and less of that as time goes on, because of security and all the cameras. You can only hide the brew in a spot so many times before it's checked. You run out of hiding places.

I see my daughter almost every week. We also have private family visits together, with my parents, my brothers and one of my friends. I have a lot of support in the community, and I have all kinds of ideas. I'm phoning, making contacts, and learning new things about business or family I want to get involved in when I get out.

Sometime within the next six years or so, I'm hoping to get out, get my life started. I will have parole at least to the year 2006, so I won't be free. I'll still have the controls imposed upon me by the parole board and my parole officer. I'll be restricted.

I'm 40 years old. They say life starts at 40, so hopefully I'll be out soon and be able to start with all the support I have, and all the knowledge I've gained now. What a waste of time it's been. All the time I've wasted being in prison that I could have had with my family, friends, and what I could have done, what I could have had today. Instead of getting involved in this ridiculous bullshit with crime.

There's no winning in crime. It's so much work for nothing, it's incredible. Some of the things I used to do, going out and break into safes, travelling around looking for trailers, industrial equipment, finding buyers, making deals, this and that. The work that I put in and what I gained, I could have been putting all that energy into a legal aspect. There's no shortage of drive for me to achieve my goals and desires. I've got lots of ambition, I've got lots of drive. I'm going to get involved in business. I'm not going to go on a grandiose scale, I'm going to do several little things. That way, if I lose out on one thing, I don't lose everything. This is it. I'm burnt out of doing time right now. Coping with the misery of doing time. Not being able to move forward to have a life is unbearable.

I think society should get realistic with what's going on in the criminal justice system, from the courts to the sentencing, and what's going on in the prisons and the whole cycle of people coming in through the revolving door. That's all got to be looked at. So many people have the attitude, lock them up, throw away the key, be done with them. That's not what happens. You put people in prison and you mistreat them, just like animals. We're humans, not animals. You mistreat a dog or a cat or any animal, that animal gets out and remembers what happened. It hasn't had any training to be useful, to get along with the rest of nature or the rest of society. It's going to hit back. And every time you lock that animal up or that person up, every time they get out, they will become worse and worse and worse. The headlines over the years attest to that. You keep locking people up, they get more time, they come out, they do a worse crime.

When I was 18 and I did all that self-help stuff, I thought I was on top of the world, because of all the awareness. I was aware to a certain extent, but I still didn't have the training. It's fine to have motivation programs like they do right now. But it's no sense motivating a person if they don't have a skill to apply it. It's fine to have treatment programs, but you also got to have skills training.

As far as giving advice to young offenders, what I've gone through, what other people have gone through, and what kids are going through these days, I know, despite all the news, the doom and gloom that's always put on television, the world is still going to be here 50 or 500 years from now. Try and do what you can to improve yourself. Get an education. I know school is boring, it hasn't changed. The thing to do is to try and make the best of it, take some time at home, try to learn what you can. As far as education, try and find some mentors to help you get advice in your life, at whatever age you are, whether you're 10 years old, 15, 20 or 25. Try to get guidance from family, friends or whoever. I strongly recommend that anybody who's having troubles at home, there's help for everything in this day and age. We live in the best times of mankind because there's so many people and agencies willing to help, and there to help.

Find something you're good at, something you like to do, and stick with that one thing. Don't think you'll know it all, too many people think they do. Stay away from drug and substance abuse. There is use and then there is abuse. And try to help other people. As much as you help yourself, make sure that everything you do for yourself you pass on to other people less fortunate. That whole cycle will just keep on going. Plant that seed, nurture it and watch it grow.

I think more parents should take more responsibility in their own families with their own kids and help them along and help themselves. People despair and give up too easy. It's the people you associate with. And if you hang around with people that have no goals in life, want to waste their life, that's the way you're going to go, naturally. You're a product of your environment. Everybody wants to succeed, I don't care who you are, how bad you feel today, how rough things are, how your family life is, whatever experiences you've had in your family, or at school or whatever. Pick new friends, get your life focused and get some help to get it focused. Keep on going, because life is great, it's enjoyable. It's what you make of it, it's the people you associate with. It's that simple.

That Last Step

Doug Bailey

"I lost a lot of friends in the 10 years I've been in. Hangings, setting themselves up to get killed, like bad drug deals or something like that. I'm really glad that I made it."

A prison term, for many, is a death sentence. In 1995-96, 48 federal prisoners never got out alive. The previous year, 56 left this world from behind bars. Suicide took the greatest toll, about 35 percent, illness and murder claimed others.

Douglas George Bailey, 27, is a powerful man with a record of violence and a feared reputation. He was tested on the streets of Winnipeg and his opponent, with a knife slicing into his stomach, was lucky to survive. In prison, there's been fights, knifings, the night a fellow prisoner was thrown off a tier, and the time yet another inmate barely escaped with his life from the wrath of this very, very tough Manitoba-born convict.

You certainly would not want to encounter this convicted felon in a street fight, most definitely would not want to cross him in a place where you could not leave. Those who have, forever carry the scars.

I'm past the point of worrying about a reputation. All that does is get you in trouble. I spent the first five, six years of my life in prisons trying to build up a reputation and the only place it got me was super maximum security. If that's what having a reputation meant, well I didn't want it. When I came out to population, there was a number of fights where before I wouldn't have walked away. A reputation doesn't really impress me anymore. There's a point in my incarceration where that really meant everything, and I had to learn the hard way that that's not the only thing about doing time. The idea of doing time is just to try and get it

Doug Bailey –
"I remember one time watching my mom run away from my dad, around in a circle, going from the kitchen to the bedrooms to the back of the living room. It was just a circle that she was going, there was just a little piece of wall separating all these rooms, and her leaving blood trails on the wall and floor."

done, in one piece, with no stab wounds, no humiliation. When I say humiliation, I mean by getting thunked out by five or six guys.

There was a sex offender really putting down everybody in the max range. We got one of the cleaners to pour some boiling hot water on this guy. They dragged the cleaner off, put him in the hole. There was guys that didn't like that so we all rioted. We broke our sinks, smashed our toilets, our light fixtures. Most of the guys had enough respect for the guys that were going to be coming in to the max range, so we didn't smash the TVs. We burnt anything we could burn, toilet paper, towels, threw them outside the bars. Tried to smash the windows outside the bars.

I got beaten up a couple times, but it's nothing I didn't ask for. I had a big mouth when I was growing up. Thinking I was untouchable, thinking that it wouldn't happen to me, but I was proven wrong. It happens to almost everybody at one time or another in their incarceration.

Some guys will really hate guards, but I just found that if you leave them alone they'll leave you alone. That's my policy now. I don't lip off to them, unless they start playing with me, not opening a door when I press the button, or being pricks on pat downs. Then you got no choice but to let them know I don't appreciate being treated like that. I'm not going to stand for it either. Now, I can deal with it in a more civilized way, not swear, not put them on their guard, but let them know I'm not going to take the shit.

I was born in Norway House, a reserve 500 miles north of Winnipeg. My parents were both full-blooded Cree and we lived in a little yellow house. Every winter the basement would flood. It made the whole house cold, killed the furnace. I remember it really being cold. There were days when the whole family would stay in bed. It was the only warmth we could get. Those were fun times, because I remember a lot of talking going on, a lot of attention being given to me; because I was the youngest, trying to keep me warm, you know. My other brothers would go running to the washroom and come running back all cold, really, really, cold. I remember some good parts but the bad times sort of really killed the good times. There was a lot of family togetherness there, until the age of four and my mother and dad were having problems.

The bad times, when they did come, came in really disturbing images. I remember one time watching my mom run away from my dad, around in a circle, going from the kitchen to the bedrooms to the back to the living-room. It was just a circle that she was going, there was just a little piece of wall separating all these rooms, and her leaving blood trails on the walls and the floor. It had a really bad effect on me when I slept. Gave me nightmares. Just something I had to try to deal with in growing up.

It was to the point where she couldn't take it no more, where she was getting beaten so badly that it was having a really bad effect on us kids. Where we would smash bottles over my dad's head to try and keep him away from my mother, or try to get him to chase one of us just to give her a break from getting beaten. Four of us boys were really protective of her. It was to the point where my mother couldn't deal with us doing that for her, putting us on the line like that. She separated from my dad.

Alcohol was a part of that. And I guess my mom had a part of it too, because I confronted my dad when I was 14 years old – I got into a fight with my dad when I was 14 years old – and he broke down crying and told me my mom was cheating on him, he would catch her, and that was why she would get all these beatings. I never really did believe that. That's just his word against my mom's. I'd like to believe my mom, because she was the one who raised me. She was the one who tried to give me everything that I had, everything she could. She'd go hungry for most of us kids, make sure we eat first. She was a really good woman.

My father stayed in Norway House. I never really seen him until I was nine years old. Two brothers stayed with my mother, they were the oldest brothers, so they stayed with her in Norway House. Two of us, me and my second youngest brother, moved to a foster home in the community. The foster father was a school teacher, a Christian. He forbid me and my brother to speak our language, which I've lost because of that. It was the only language we knew. We didn't understand English because we were straight off the reserve, and so we had to learn English or be punished severely. It was kind of scary. I didn't want to be there.

I ran away a number of times, because I really wanted to be home. My mother had to bring me back to these white foster parents because she was having a hard enough time supporting two kids. I guess it was for my own good that I stayed there. But I couldn't understand why I couldn't go live with one of my aunties or one of my uncles. My mother had a number of brothers and sisters I thought might have taken care of me. Instead they got some stranger to take care of me and my brother. I just couldn't understand this. I was wondering who's doing this to us, and I was trying to run away all the time, trying to get back to the family I wanted, I needed.

He was my stepmonster for two years, until the age of six. My mother moved to Winnipeg, and I met up with her there. I used to go play in the forest with my brothers and with my cousins. We would go hunting for whatever our slingshots could bring down. We had woods to go hunting, a big lake to swim, rocks to go climbing, bonfires, a lot of things we liked. Coming to the city we didn't have these things. We had to go hunting under bridges, if we wanted to go shoot at some birds.

It was my mother's girlfriend's house, she was helping us out, so we stayed there for a little while. I couldn't remember any father figure. I couldn't even understand why we were living there, whose house this was. All I knew was that I was there. I guess there must have been some drinking going on, because I got drunk there when I was just a kid. I found a bottle of whiskey and drank it up. My brothers came looking for me, they called me, and I came down the stairs head first. I passed out on the bottom of the stairs. My brothers, I guess they got concerned about me, phoned my mom. I remember waking up sober and sick from the alcohol that I drank. That was my first real taste of alcohol.

It wasn't long until I started getting in trouble, with my brothers. Going out, climbing on trains, breaking windows, stealing, raiding gardens, just getting into the city life. Exploring, and getting into trouble along the way.

My mom was pregnant at the time, my little brother was on the way, and so she was basically at home, taking trips to the hospital, or just visiting other people, making friends. I was usually left in the charge of my brothers, who were a lot older than me.

I just can't remember going to school at that time, because I was really fascinated with the city. I'd never been in an elevator before. And when I first came into the city, I cried when I went into an elevator, got on one floor and ended up on another floor, and I was freaked out. A little kid not knowing what was happening. I was scared the first time I was in the city. All the traffic and so many people walking around at one time. I went into the Richardson Building when I was a kid, and that's a pretty tall building. Just the amazement of being able to see so far, and all the little people down there on the ground, and all the toy trucks, toy cars, toy buses, and all this. It was really fascinating to me.

I didn't stay at home for too long. I got into trouble and with my mom being pregnant and all, she felt that I wasn't really controlled. I guess you could say, I was really in trouble. I always wanted to go out and get in trouble. I wanted to go out and stay out for long periods of time. Just to run around and have fun. On the reserve that's common, but in the cities I guess that's not really acceptable. When I was six I went into a group home.

It was a learning experience for me. It was all new. Other kids in there with me were there for being troublemakers or because their family couldn't support them, and they had a hard time. I learned how to fight. We'd sneak out windows and run away, do almost everything we could just to get out. It was a challenge. It was an experience. Staying out with other kids, breaking windows, throwing eggs at cars. It was fun, but I missed my family too. I stayed in the group home for about six months.

After my mother had her kid, I came back, and took my place back in my family. We moved into a house after my brother was born. I really cared for this new member of the family, because I was youngest and now he was the youngest. I basically spent a lot of time with him.

My mother had problems with drinking all through my childhood, and after she had the baby, she still had problems drinking. We stayed near the train tracks pretty far from town. The lure of the city would get the better of her. She'd always want to go out there, get out of the house. Usually I'd be the one stuck looking after my little brother. My other brothers would go looking for her. I remember one time I told my brothers I wasn't going to stay home, I wasn't going to look after him. I remember staying away from the house for maybe 10 minutes, because they went to town on the train. They jumped a train, a boxcar, going into town. And I was just under the bridge, just waiting for these guys to come back. I was hiding, seeing if they were going to jump off the train and go back to the house, but they didn't. So I ended up going back and crying to my little brother. I told him, we didn't need those guys, I'd look after him, and no one was going to hurt him and nothing was going to happen to him. I was scared myself. I was sort of trying to convince myself that nothing was going to happen. These were pretty screwy, vivid times in my life. I can recall that very easily.

When I was seven years old I got caught breaking windows, shooting slingshots at cars, killing pigeons. I went to group homes, 'cause my mom had a hard enough time looking after a little baby, and four other kids. I remember always running away from these foster homes. Always trying to get home to my family, and rebelling in the foster homes, trying to get other kids to get in trouble with me. I just wanted to do my own thing. I didn't want anybody telling me what to do. I didn't feel like I should have been where I was. I was really hating life. I was really hating the people that put me where I was, and why couldn't they just leave me alone? I couldn't understand this, so I did what I wanted to do, ran away, got drunk. I didn't care too much.

I didn't really think about being anything then. I just wanted to have fun. I basically had nobody telling me what to do because I was really unmanageable due to the fact that I was in group homes for two years and I lost my mom's authority, so I didn't really listen too good to her. Like the way I would have, before, if I would have stayed there.

I had some pretty fun times. Went to school with three of my brothers. It was about an eight-block-walk, and some times we'd go bowling after school. One winter, when we were at school, my brother told me to lick a piece of metal. He wanted me to see what it tasted like. I put my tongue on the metal, and I was just crying, waiting for somebody to get my tongue off. It was winter and my tongue was stuck. I thought that was a really cruel joke.

I can't remember any discrimination, any racism. I didn't distinguish one race to another. I was basically a kid trying to grow up in a different setting, whether there's a lot of long haired Indians, or there was other kids. I remember feeling ashamed a couple of times, because I had to go to school dirty. My pants would be torn or something, because when we played, we played near the tracks or under bridges, and I had to see other kids dressed nicer, you know, sort of made me jealous. But that didn't really hinder me in my schooling or anything like that.

My schooling wasn't that good. I remember being a slow learner. I sort of picked up with the attitude of being the tough guy. I was always pushing everybody away that was trying to help me. There would be some really sincere staff that were trying to look out for my best interests, but if I felt someone caring for me I'd do whatever I could to get out of that situation. School wasn't very good for me, because I didn't really want to learn. I didn't want to sit down. I was really hyper when I was a kid. Sitting down in a classroom was really hard for me, so I'd skip, I'd go stealing in department stores, stuff like that.

I went into the Manitoba Youth Centre. I was in there 31 times: for stealing cars; breaking into houses; running away from group homes; running away from wilderness camps; stealing group home vehicles. I was pretty much into trouble then. There's 10 units in this centre. They've got a unit for 10 to 12 year olds, 12 to 14 year olds, 14 to 16 year olds, and 16 to 18 year olds. There's two girl cottages, and the rest are boys, 'cause I guess the girls didn't get in trouble that much. I was in all those cottages ever since the age of nine when I started going there. I was a little too young to be in there, so they usually just kept me overnight and tried to get someone to come and pick me up and take me to the boys' home or something.

Security was pretty tight. I'd say about a 15 foot wall surrounding the whole place, and plexiglas. It was really tight. If you went over the wall it was a real feat. Not too many kids did that. I didn't. I got away once on a TA (temporary absence). I just didn't return. It was my 13th birthday, so I decided to extend my leave.

I felt that I should have been free. I was really into the outdoors. I remember nights where, they had a little speaker on the ceiling, and there's one main control up at the front gate, and they'd play a station where a lot of songs were sad. They'd really be depressing. And you'd be looking out your window and just saying, "That's it, I'm never coming back here. I don't like this, I don't want to be locked up like this." I knew that the Red River Exhibition would be on and all my friends would be enjoying the rides, walking with girls. Here I am, locked up behind plexiglas, hating life. I felt a lot of loneliness and a lot of self-pitying there. I was always fighting other kids, because I was really trying to establish a reputation. After my last time there, I was known for being one of the toughest kids.

My 31st time there, I got transferred to adult court and sent to prison. I was charged for break and enter and attempted murder. I was 16 years old. Grade 10 was the last grade I went to.

I was drinking with my brothers, my girlfriend, my girlfriend's sister, and my neighbors. We were all at the bar, and I already had a lot to drink that night. I have to tell you that I'm really possessive 'cause I have a lot of insecurities. I had a really good-looking girlfriend and I was really jealous if she talked to anybody else. That night I seen her dancing with another guy, and I just couldn't deal with that. I went bar hopping, and I ran into a guy who had pills, and I started doing pills and drinking at the same time. On the main drag in Winnipeg there's about six bars, and while I was bar hopping I blacked out in the last bar. When I woke up I had blood on my jeans, and I couldn't remember what happened that night. When I went to my brother's place, where I was staying, I was already on the run from the youth centre. He told me that someone across the hall got stabbed.

If I stabbed you four times – in the arm, leg, shoulder, abdomen – there's going to be a 90 percent chance that I'm going to get blood on me. I had no blood, nobody else's blood than my own. That night, I had my knife, I pulled it out and I cut my finger, my thumb. I wiped it on my pants. When they brought those pants to court, it was my own blood that was on them. I can't remember doing it, so I can't really take responsibility for it. I still have a hard time believing it. I had blood on me, but going to trial, the victim's blood was not on me at all, even my clothes. They never had a weapon, they never had fingerprints, they had nothing, nothing at all. No solid evidence, but I got made for this.

I went through eight lawyers. At the age of 16 you don't want to hear your lawyer telling you, "You're looking at eight to 14 years." I didn't want to hear that. I was 16 years old, I expected to get a couple years. I got eight. They dropped a year off 'cause I did a year dead time in the remand centre in Winnipeg waiting to go to trial.

That was really hell for me. I never saw the sunshine for 10 months. I never set foot outside that building. I was always in a cell block where I couldn't look out the windows. Where the only sunshine would be coming from down the hall. There'd be bars separating me from that sunshine. I already had bad experiences with lawyers, so I went to appeal on my own. I handled my own case. And I got two years knocked off. I was doing five years. They sent me to Stony Mountain.

It was really scary for me, 'cause I was just a kid when I went in there, so naturally I had a lot of guys wanting to get to know me better. There was a lot of homos. I'd have to fight. I'd take a lot of beatings while I was there, but you know, I'd never let anything happen to me. I'd take a beating rather than do anything else. I always stood my ground. It wasn't until 1986, when I almost killed a guy in Stony, because of remarks he made, I earned some respect.

He wasn't coming on to me for anything. Him and 10 buddies beat up a friend of mine on the street. He came to prison, and I sort of, being a good friend of the guy, took things into my own hands. I almost killed him for what he did.

I knocked the guy out by putting him in a sleeper, and throwing him on his head, in the gym. When you go for canteen, they give you big brown bags to put your canteen in. It took six of those paper bags to cover this pool of blood that was coming from his head. I tried taking him to the washroom where I could clean him up, and not get caught. That's what I was thinking anyways. Dragging this guy across the gym floor while he's screaming, I didn't hear too much, in my excitement. I drew a lot of heat on me from other inmates.

The investigator called me to the warden's office and asked what happened. I told him, "Nothing happened." They told me this guy told, said everything that happened, but he wasn't going to press charges, because he was scared. They couldn't press charges for that reason. But they told me they'd be keeping an eye on me, and I'd have to watch what I was doing. They kept me in the hole for a day. The next day they come in and they dragged me to the max range, and I was really confused. The warden's office told me they weren't going to do anything, I was thinking I got away with something, and here they sent five guards to take me to the max range. I was written up for the SHU, but the special handling unit sent word back to Stony that I was too young.

In the max range, you're locked up 23 hours a day. You only get an hour to exercise and shower. I was there for six months. You do a lot of thinking about what you want to do when you get out in population. All the freedom that you took for granted. There's no contact. You miss the company of being able to talk and laugh with your friends. You do a lot of reminiscing, a lot of thinking of future. There's only so much you can think about and boredom kicks in.

While I was in the hole in Stony, I tried to swallow some pills, so they wanted to send me to the Regional Psychiatric Centre to help me deal with some problems. I had a lot of anger in me. I had a lot of resentment for authority that I had to get out, a lot of shit that I had to deal with. So I spent nine months in RPC in Saskatoon.

I kept in contact with my mom and some of my brothers while I was in there. But in the first five years that I did, I never got a visit from my family. I got one or two letters from them, telling me what was going on. That's as far as I ever got with them.

I got a lot of help at RPC. I took an anger management program, assertiveness training, stress management, drug and alcohol, Children of Dysfunctional Families, AA, money management, all kinds of programs to try and better myself. They thought I could have gotten more. They didn't think I really committed myself to that program. I think they were right. I didn't really deal with everything that was inside. They recommended I come back, before I got out of prison, and I did go back for 13 months. I did really good then. I dealt with a lot of my childhood, my upbringing, and all the resentments I had towards authority.

I wanted to start over again. Go to a place where I didn't know anybody and no one knew me. I went to a little reserve in Saskatchewan called Standing Buffalo. I did pretty good for two months, no drinking, no getting in trouble. I went to Winnipeg for a three-day visit. I arrived in Winnipeg about 10 at night. My brothers threw a getting out party for me. And Sunday morning I was at the wrong place at the wrong time. Somebody mistook me, thought I was the one that robbed this certain individual, and I got blamed for it.

This guy was fairly big, 6'4", 280 pounds. He was scary, homely looking. I didn't run from people in the Pen, so why would I run from people outside? That was my attitude. I wasn't going to let anybody walk over me, but then again, in the same breath, I was trying to stay clean out of trouble, trying to keep from going back to prison. I wasn't supposed to be in Winnipeg. I had a travelling permit, but it wasn't for a couple of days, so I was trying to stay clear of the cops before I reported in, saying that I was in town.

I tried running away from this guy for a couple blocks, just to stay away from trouble. I ran to the back part of the parking lot. He was chasing me, and I pulled out my knife. I told him that he would get hurt if he kept chasing me. My words were: "Get the f— away from me or you're getting it. You got the wrong guy. I didn't do f— all."

He ran to his car and I ran behind Main Street. I went a couple of blocks. After drinking all night, drinking in the morning, I had a hangover. I didn't feel much like running. I stopped. He had a crowbar in his hand. I was tired, I was sick, and he came after me with this crowbar.

He hit me on the head, and I stabbed him after he swung at me. It was a buck knife, about a four-inch blade on it. I hit him right in the abdomen, and he lost a piece of his kidney. I go for the lower part of the body, near the pelvis or the abdomen, 'cause that kind of wound can stop anybody, and that's what I was trying to do, stop this guy from chasing me. I was going to go in for another poke at him, I was going to stab him again, but my brother stopped me, pulled me off. I took off. I went to an old girlfriend's house, stayed there one night, and left for Saskatchewan. Picked up a paper before we left. What happened on Main street was in the paper. I was worried that I was going back to prison again. But it wasn't for a while, a month and a couple weeks.

I came back to Winnipeg 'cause I just wanted to come back. I knew I was in trouble already, so what's the use of trying to do good when you know you're going back to prison. I partied, got in trouble, just did what I usually did. Walking through a bar, two undercover cops picked me up and took me to the station. I had my day in court, and I got eight years, consecutive on my five years.

I said: "F— it. F— with my freedom." I started turning really bad. I was in fights a lot in Stony when I came back. Beating up skinners, rats, child molesters, anybody that was a goof. I had two knife incidents where I chased guys around the range with a knife. I threw another guy off the top tier of Stony, and I sent another guy to hospital because I split his eye open. This last sex-offender, the one I threw off the tier, was the last straw for that pull over at Stony. They sent me to the SHU for two years. Two years doing basically nothing, 'cause there it's a 23 hour lock-up. You can get a little more freedom there, but you have to go in stages. You go from a waiting period to population. There you get, maybe, six hours free time, and the rest is all lock-up. That really straightened me out. That really gave me a chance to look at where I want to go in life, what I want to do. I've been out of the SHU for 10 months now. I haven't been charged for three years for any fighting, and I haven't been to the hole for three years. I received one charge for not having my name tag on my clothes. In there that's a big scene, if you don't have a name tag on your clothes.

I basically turned my life around since I've been there, because it's really a sobering thought, that place. There's no drugs. I guess you can't say there's no alcohol, because I made brew there. It's really an eye-opener, 'cause you got guys doing five life bits, nothing to lose.

They're really easy to get along with, but piss them off and you know they can kill you, and what are they going to do? Throw them in jail? In the hole? That's the bottom of the line. I hit bottom. There's no place else they could have sent me if I would have got in trouble there. That's where they send Canada's most dangerous criminals, people like serial killer Clifford Olson.

Olson threatened me. He told me he was going to take my life whenever he came out, into population, but I think everybody knows that this guy is never going to come into population again. He's not going to see population. He was just shooting his mouth off, because I used to piss on his window, spit on his window, call him all sorts of names. I had some real dislike for this guy, he had a whole tier to himself, a whole wing to himself, where no one else was on that side with him.

I'm laughing, trying to make his life hell, going outside every night, in freezing cold weather, just to tease this guy, sit there and spit on his window or call him names. Sometimes I'd be the only one out there, spending whole periods. And he'd be pressing his button, whining to the guards, "Get this little Indian away."

When I did come back in, the guards would say, "I hear you're bugging Clifford Olson."

Really hating these guys for sticking up for this guy, I'd say, "Yeah, what's it to you?"

And they'd say: "Well, keep up the good work." They'd hate this guy just as much as most of the guys would too.

I met some really good friends in there. It wasn't all bad. It really changed around my outlook on life and what I want to do with it. It gave me purpose to my life again.

After two years, I came to the Edmonton Max. This place was locked down, after the murders that happened earlier. I guess this place went to the dogs. It's still really bad. People that they're bringing in here, double bunking that they're doing. In 10 years, I've never had to double bunk with anybody. I'm not going to start now.

For a while, they were giving us a little exercise, maybe half an hour. The SHU had more freedom. I was really pissed off, leaving the highest maximum security prison to come to another place where it's even tighter. I wanted to go back to the SHU, but I figured I'd ride it out.

Things are starting to get a little better. I enjoy walking the yard at night. In the SHU, it's all pavement. At least here, I can touch grass, go to a sweat, where in the SHU, you can't do it, you have very restricted movements.

A sweat lodge is a ceremony for people who want to take all your problems, all the hell that's going on in your life, and you come out stronger. The concept of a sweat is going into your mother's womb again. You go in there on your hands and knees, you're humbled when you're going in, when you come out you're humbled again, on your hands and knees. You come out with no problems. I've seen guys wanting to kill each other go into a sweat and come out and hug each other. That's a pretty potent place. It's helped me out lots.

I've taken a lot of courses in money management and electrical work. I have a lot of experience working in painting shops. I've got a lot of options. It's all been in prison that I learned painting, electrical work. I do weightlifting. I play a lot of sports. I go to church, attend the native brotherhood. I spend time in the yard with a couple of friends. I've been a range cleaner now for nine months. I haven't been in trouble for the better part of three years, so I guess I paid my dues. Going to a medium security prison is not too far from my future. I guess you could say I've been a good little Indian.

All my expiry dates have passed for parole. I'm out in nine months, four days from today, that's my statutory release date. You still have to report every two weeks, you have to report to a police station every month, let them know that you're still in the city, that you're still kicking around. Until '97, that's my warrant expiry, my time's up. That's when I'm a free man, do what I want.

If I got out tonight, I'd like to go see the dolphins in West Edmonton Mall. Sounds stupid, but that's one of the things I'd like to do.

I'd see my mom and my little brother. Those are the only two I really feel mean anything to me on the street right now. There's one brother I haven't seen for 10 years. My family wasn't the kind to really talk openly, to express feelings. The word "love" wasn't really mentioned in my family. It was taken for granted that it was there, didn't need to be said, because if you didn't know, well, you should have.

My little brother's 18 years old. He's a gang banger, a gang in Winnipeg and they got their rival gang. They've just been busted for all their guns, machetes, knives, so I'm really concerned about him. My other brothers say, "He's trying to follow in your footsteps."

I'd try, not tell him, to convince him that the life he's leading is going to wreck when he grows older. Look how long it took me to realize what kind of shit I was putting myself through. I had to spend 10 years in prison just to realize there's a better way of life on the outside, better ways of dealing with your problems. Doing everyday things, trying to build a name for yourself on the street before being the tough guy, or hanging out with the wrong crowd. There's more ways of having fun than drinking and getting high and stuff like that.

Suicide is a big part of prison. At one time in every criminal's life, suicide has probably come across their minds. It's just dealing with it in a way where you don't take that last step.

There was a number of times that I wanted to. You don't want to deal with it anymore, don't want to finish your time. I just wanted everything to be over. I gave up on myself because society gave up on me, and I didn't really think there'd be anything out there for a con. No jobs, no law, just harassment from police. That's basically how you're looked at on the street when you get out – once a con, always a con. It's like you'll never be good again, like you're a bad seed. There'll always be doubts, there'll always be suspicions, there'll always be something negative in the eyes of some family members, some cousins, some respectable people that know that you're out. Suspicion will still be there, no matter how hard you try to change.

I used to think that the only way out was just to kill myself, and I learned that that's not so. You don't really have to care if someone is thinking that you're never going to be straight. You got nothing to prove to nobody, but to yourself. You're not trying to do good for anybody else, you're trying to do good for yourself, to try and stay out of prison, to try to have your freedom back, and keep it.

That's just some of the things that I've learned doing time. I don't care what people think of me. I don't have to build an image for myself. I'm looking after myself before I look after anybody else. I'm trying to get out and stay out. I think everybody should learn not to be afraid to ask for help if they need it, 'cause that's the real killer. It's not you strung up, it's that moment of weakness when you still have that little last ray of hope to reach out and ask for help, but some people just have too much pride to do that. When you grow up with the lifestyle that most of us do grow up with, trouble, you don't like to ask for anything from anybody, and sometimes it's necessary.

I lost a lot of friends in the 10 years I've been in. Hangings, setting themselves up to get killed, like bad drug deals or something like that. I'm really glad I made it.

A Place for Rapers

Andy Morrissette

"This raper, who raped his own kids, got up and bumped my tray with his shoulder, knocked my milk into my food. I knocked him out. Broke his nose and jaw. They threw me in the hole . . . they didn't know what to do with me because no guards saw it."

ndrew Lawrence Morrissette, 28, was taught by his uncle to hate the police, never rat on anyone. From his early upbringing, schooled in crime by adults, he never had a hope of avoiding trouble.

In The City, performed by the Eagles, could have been his theme song. A mirror reflection of his life, found in the words: "I was born here in the city, with my back against the wall. Nothin' grows and life ain't very pretty, no one's there to catch you when you fall."

Since those early years, there have been violent times and federal times. Included in all of that: being forced to live with sex offenders, deviants, scum of the earth, the most despised people to darken the gates of any prison at any time.

was throwing a football around with a couple of friends, out in the prison yard, and me and a friend rammed into each other, and he ruptured my spleen with his knee. I went to the hospital and the guards took me back to the institution that night. They must have thought I was trying to escape, or I was on something, because I was in serious pain. They threw me in the hole, where the medical unit was. The next morning, they phoned for the ambulance to come and take me back to the outside hospital. I had to undergo major surgery, get my spleen removed. I could have died from it.

Andy Morrissette – "*My mom was pretty well run-ning from my dad, an excessive alcohol drinker, and then we got split-up, two kids would stay with my mom and two would stay with my dad. The youngest would stay with my mom, and the three of us would always bounce back and forth from my mom and dad, from Calgary to Winnipeg, until I was 10 years old.*"

I was born in Winnipeg on March 29, 1968. I have three sisters, and we were all living together until I was five. My mom was pretty well running from my dad, an excessive alcohol drinker, and then we got split up, two kids would stay with my mom and two would stay with my dad. The youngest would stay with my mom, and the three of us would always bounce back and forth from my mom and dad, from Calgary to Winnipeg, until I was 10 years old.

My mom was on welfare raising four kids. I was the only boy of the family, so I had less than my sisters, because they always got the hand-me-downs. There seemed to be a lot more for the girls, a lot more attention to them than myself.

We were pretty poor. We lived on macaroni, big quantity food that you could buy, like big bags of puffed wheat, porridge, canned soups and boxes of food, where you could keep it in the fridge and reheat it. I usually had to get my clothes from friends because we were so poor. My mom only could afford to take one of us out with her when she got the welfare cheque. Most of the time, we'd go out and shop with her, and then she'd treat us to a restaurant, you know, a Big Mac, or a hamburger, fries. Other than that we didn't get nothing. Just food and clothes.

At Christmas, we got a lot of vouchers from the Salvation Army. Me and my sisters, we used to go over to the Salvation Army, in front of the Safeway. They'd have those boxes where people would drive up and throw their bags of clothes in. We used to climb in there and take them out because we couldn't afford clothes. Our presents we got from Salvation Army, and food hampers. We were lucky if any of our relatives, our family, could afford anything. If they did, they bought it from second hand stores, nothing ever new.

I felt out of place at school. I got kicked out of kindergarten because I smashed a truck into this kid's face. We were playing in the sandbox, I remember, and he tried to grab the truck from me. I guess because I never had much I wanted to keep it. I hit him with the truck and made his nose bleed.

I felt poor. A lot of times I was late for school, we had to walk. We never really had nothing for books and stuff. At the end of years at school, we'd take pictures and my mom would have to pay for them. She never paid for any pictures of us because she couldn't afford it. The school would send her a bill and she'd say, "I can't afford pictures. What? Do you want the pictures back?" And they'd say no, and that would be it.

I never had birthday parties. The odd birthday I'd get money, "Oh, it's your birthday today, here's five bucks, here's 10 bucks." I can't ever remember having a birthday party at home or with my family with cake and presents.

I played a little bit of soccer, throwing a football around, but other than that, I spent a lot of my time roaming the streets. I had a lot of desire to play hockey, football, those two I think were the two most I wanted to play. And baseball, I liked that. I had a pair of skates once, one Christmas. That was from my dad when we were living in Calgary. I was nine or 10, and I used them a couple of times. I put them in the closet, where it had a gas heater, and the skates leaned against it and got on fire. Ever since then I never had skates. That was about it. I never got a chance to play anything.

I went to church when I was young. I didn't understand it, it scared me. The reason why it scared me was because it was people I never knew. It was totally different from my family, my structure. My family always drank, and they always fought. A lot of them told me to watch out for myself, take care of number one, be tough. In order to do all these things, I had to keep everything inside and when somebody tried to show something to me, I thought they were trying to hurt me in some way. Find my weaknesses and hurt me, so I always kept everything locked up inside.

I had a lot of difficulty in school because of my family. I got a lot of verbal abuse from my mother and no father around. I had a lot of anger because my family wasn't as normal as my other friends. So, I never really could concentrate on schoolwork.

Up until Grade 4, my teacher asked me, "Could you read this?" I just sat there, making jokes and laughing. I couldn't read. They kept passing me to the next grade to get me out of their class. I would be so bad that they didn't want to deal with me. Hopefully they thought the next teacher would try to deal with me. I had to go to a special school, learn how to read, and I did. I took Grade 4 twice and I went to a special school, a special classroom at a high school to learn how to read from elementary school.

When I got physical abuse it was only when I did something wrong, skipping school, minor stuff, until my two older sisters started stealing. They were stealing off my mother and they started blaming it on me. Mom started giving me lickings for stuff I didn't do. And, when she gave me lickings, she gave me lickings. She used spoons, cooking cords, threw me all over the house, grabbed me and whipped me across the room. It wasn't just bend over and smack me on the ass, it was all over the body.

I was always taught from my family, respect your elders and love them. No matter how much they abused us, I never swore at my mother, I never hit her, I didn't even think it. I was always pretty good at home, always good. It's when I left home I got to release it all, on the streets, and that's when I became bad.

I started smoking dope and drinking by the time I was nine, 10 years old. I was pretty well hanging around kids who had the same problems, so we could relate with each other.

I B&E'd a ceramic sales shop. It sold pottery of animals, pictures of Elvis Presley on wood plaques and clocks. They had a fire in the back, the door had a hole, and they just put some plywood on it. We broke the plywood and climbed through the burnt hole in the door. I stole a bunch of diamond rings.

I went and let my aunts try them on, and if they fit, I let them keep them. The rest I stashed on a roof. I was waiting to see if they were worth a lot of money, or worth any money at all, and then I was going to get the rest of them and sell them.

I lived right next door to the shop and I left my prints. They come next door, put two and two together, and I ended up in the youth centre. That was my first major charge. I had earlier been stealing bikes, candy out of stores, they grabbed me, brought me home, and that was it. It got worse.

I ended up going back to my family. The police drove me to them and said they wouldn't charge me or my family nothing. They stayed in the car. I was 10 years old, and I didn't want nobody in trouble. I went running into the house, went on the roof, gave them back everything. I didn't get charged for the rings because they got them all back. I did get charged with B&E because they didn't get some other things back. A fur coat, leather coat, some money and some plaques.

I ended up in the Manitoba Youth Centre. I didn't get any time, because I was young. I spent four months in a foster home. It was just to give me a taste of being away from home, more counselling than anything because of my age.

I was in a white, middle-class neighborhood, and I was the only kid there that looked Native. I got hit in the head with a hammer, because I couldn't find my runners. I thought another one of the guys in the home took my runners and went to school, so now I was going to be late. The youngest there said to the group home lady, "Grandma, why don't you hit him on the head with a hammer, knock some sense into him." Well, she grabbed a hammer out of the kitchen drawer, and the next thing you know I was falling down the stairs with a smash to my head. I went up to my room, jumped out the second-storey window onto their car, and ran. I was pretty dizzy, my head hurt a lot. I phoned home, and got on a bus. I told my mom what happened, and I got to stay home after that.

We had a a social worker. Mom explained to her what happened. To this day, I got a hammer groove in the back of my skull, where the hammer went. It didn't go flat, it went on the corner, and it caved in the back of my head where the hammer went in. I didn't get any medical treatment.

After that I just progressed. I started doing B&Es a lot more, pretty well any business on the street. It escalates from there. I always had someone coming to get me, up until I was 12 years old. All I was doing was break and enters, drinking, smoking dope, staying out all day, all night, running away, staying at friends and relatives. In order to stay there, I had to pay my way, so we'd go out and B&E cars, or garages, or get orders from the adults, what they wanted, tools, tires, car stereos, bikes, whatever we could carry. We'd take it all there and sell it.

I never got any normal loving or attention from my family. Never had anybody, really, to help me. Friends and relatives would always say: "Here, don't worry about it, have a drink. Forget it, be tough." They would try to make you laugh and then carry on. When I did crime, the attention I did get from my family, they didn't know how to do it properly. They were just doing it the best way they could.

When I was a little kid, I'd say, "I'm telling on you uncle," and he'd give me a whack in the head. Punch me in the head or a slap.

He'd sit me down and he'd ask me: "Do you know what a rat is?"

And I'd say, "Yeah."

And he says, "That's what you call people who tell on people. A rat. And you don't rat on people, don't tell on no one. The police are out to get you, you don't tell the police nothing, they're your enemies." I did a lot of crime with my dad's brother.

I never had a proper structure of life, family lifestyle. When I got in trouble when I went home, I'd get grounded for a couple of weeks and I'd get lectured. And anybody that would come over, family or friends, they'd lecture. They'd say, you shouldn't be doing B&Es, you shouldn't be doing this, you shouldn't be doing that, you got to behave for your mom, you got to behave for yourself, and they'd tell you all this. I would do good for three months without getting lectured.

"Look mom, I got 80 percent on a spelling bee!"

"Oh, that's nice," and then just throw it aside. There was no, carry on, you know, keep doing good, behave. I never got no attention, no real love or care. It was like they'd just do a count: one, two, three, four, OK all the kids are here, OK go to sleep. There was no talk or nothing, it was only when you did bad. That was the only time you got showed care and love, other than that there was nobody really to help me, to set me straight.

My mom would leave us. My older sister would babysit, and my mom would go and get drunk at the bar. She would come home maybe with her boyfriend, or just a few friends, and they would drink. When we didn't see her, she'd be at the bar or at her friend's, and she'd just phone home and ask us how we're doing.

I spent a year in one group home, and ran from there a lot. I ended up getting kicked out of a school, didn't even finish six months there. I had to spend about four or five months in the group home, in the kitchen doing school work, until they could find me a school I could go to. No school would accept me, except a girls' school run by nuns, strict teachers. It was a lock-down called Marymound. I got driven there, and they had to open the door with a key. Then I was locked in, and they wouldn't let me go until they saw the group home staff at the door. At the end of that year, I ended up getting a lot of B&E charges, a couple of assaults for fighting, and thrown in Agassiz Youth Centre in Portage la Prairie. I ran from there 10 months into my year, got caught, and was put into a wilderness camp near Beausejour.

A few guys I knew there were making another offender do something, making him bark like a dog. When I got up to them, this guy took the opportunity to run towards the cabin. I didn't want him using me as a scapegoat to get away from these guys, so I chased him and punched him in the head. I knocked him out, he fell down, and I booted him in the head. I put him in a coma, so the wildnerness camp staff gave me an ultimatum. All I had to do was do about six months and I would have been able to go home to my mother, or I was being charged for assault and the RCMP were going to take me to the youth centre. I chose the youth centre. Me and another guy were getting blamed for this, and as they got us back into Winnipeg, first red light, we jumped out, and we ran, went on the run. I was on the run for about a month doing break and enters, partying, roaming the streets.

I started hanging around on Main street when I was 13 years old, that's where I did a lot of drinking. Everybody I knew from youth centres, from the streets, cousins, relatives, all my friends, all their friends, their uncles, cousins, were all there. It was the only people that I knew away from home. That was like a home away from home. If they weren't friends they were my cousins, if they weren't cousins they were my aunts and uncles, we were related some way or another, we all knew each others' family, so I felt right at home. I got stuff I never had. I got to buy my own clothes. I got to buy anything I wanted. I'd just wear something, throw it away, buy something new. I got a lot of women. I wanted to act older so I didn't have to show my true feelings. I wanted to try and forget it because it was a lot of hurt, a lot of stuff I didn't understand, you know, I didn't understand myself. I didn't understand why my family lifestyle was like this.

I got picked up again, spent almost half a year in the youth centre, then got another year in the Portage home for boys again. I did about 10 months and ran, jumped a train and made it to Winnipeg. I was on the run for about a week, my mom convinced me to go back, turn myself in, and I could come home and live with her. The staff come and picked me up, drove me back, and I spent the rest of my year there.

I got out, went home to live with my aunt, and ended up getting picked up for assault, breach probation, B&Es. I ended up in the Manitoba Youth Centre. They used one of the cottages as a group home, and it was called open custody. While I was there, I was going to the Alcoholics Foundation of Manitoba for drug and alcohol meetings. I went AWOL, got picked up, went back to the youth centre, and ran again. They open up the door and let you go. I ran a second time, and ended up getting sentenced into Knowles, a lock-down centre. From medium to maximum, before I was 16 years old.

I ran from there three times and got thrown in the youth centre. This lady was coming to AA, a sponsor from the street doing the meetings in the youth centre. She got a group home licence, took me into her home, got me a job. I was going to AA meetings with her, two meetings a night.

I was at hotels, setting up rooms for functions. I worked there for a couple of months, and ended up leaving it all and going back down to the drag. Alcohol affected me. I didn't understand alcohol. I wasn't mature enough to drink the stuff. There was no course on how to drink alcohol. My understanding, with my friend, was to drink as much as you can and see who could stay up the longest and not pass out, function properly without looking stupid. I didn't know how to treat alcohol and I didn't know how to respect it.

Nine out of 10 times my crime was under the influence of drugs or alcohol. I was running low on money or something, I'd get the courage to go and kick-in a house, go in a car, or fight. Those were the times I got caught, because I was under the influence. I didn't care. I figured, I'm on the run already, they already want me for a B&E or assault, I might as well just carry on. I'd get away with the ones that I was straight, but got caught when I was drunk. I'd leave my prints. I wasn't thinking straight.

I spent a lot of time, three, four days in a row on Main street, with no sleep. I was selling T&Rs, Talwin and Ritalin, to people that I knew. I had a girlfriend that was 16 years old, she wanted to be a hooker. My buddies' girlfriends worked the streets, I knew all the other hookers, so this girl worked on the street, got a girlfriend that wanted to work, and she got another girlfriend. I had three girls working under my name, and they gave me $100 each. That's all I asked. But they ended up giving me everything, and we'd all end up spending the money on each other anyway at the end of the night. I didn't consider myself a pimp or nothing like that. I considered myself a protective friend, just hanging around with them. They were more like family, you know, people that were down there, those were my people, so I learned to respect them as people, not as anybody lower than myself.

That was a risky business. They were going with people they didn't know, they were helping people with sexual gratification, they were helping men out. It was like Russian roulette, because you never knew what kind of car you were getting into, it could be a cop's or a sicko's, if you were going to get a disease, if you were going to make it out of that car alive or if you were going to get charged. When you do a B&E, you go in there when nobody's around, it's empty, there's hardly any chance of anything going wrong. You're dealing face to face with somebody by hooking, and you never know how they're going to treat you. I was more a big brother to the girls.

I was doing T&Rs, just come out of a hotel. I was standing there with a 24 of beer, and this girl I knew that worked the street, Carla, come running up to me from this car she pulled up with this guy. "Hey, brother, what's going on?" She hugged me, and whispered in my ear, "Listen, you're my brother, you're coming with me." She heard that this guy ripped off a couple of working girls on the street, so she wanted me to protect her just in case he tried to rip her off. I ended up going with them, to this guy's house, and she did her thing in the bedroom while I sat in the living room and drank vodka. I had a big hunting knife on me. Carla came out of the bedroom after they were done what they were doing and we got high, we fixed a couple of T&Rs together. It was getting late. She wanted to go back down to Main, continue working the street. I was pretty hammered. When they dropped me off in front of my place, I was staying at a friend's, I thought of what she said about this guy, so I offered to sell her the knife for protection, against him and whoever else. She looked at it, said no, and gave it back to me. As I was getting out the back seat, the knife fell. I grabbed it, took it out of the case. This guy thought I was going to rob him. I was so drunk that I never got a chance. He ended up running, phoned the police and I left.

Some days later, I was hanging out on Portage Avenue at a restaurant called Family Hamburger House. That's where a lot of the homeless, the head bangers, the kids that are into rock and roll, smoking dope and drinking, hung out. A bunch of our buddies got into a fight with these guys and they knew what school they went to. We went to this school, started fighting, just grabbed anybody and everybody. There was a bunch of us, 50, 60 kids fighting. The cops came, I started walking away, the cop pulled up to me. I figured I had no charge, I wasn't wanted for nothing, so I gave him my real name and he ran me through and said, "You're under arrest for armed robbery." I went into the Manitoba Youth Centre and they raised me to adult. I spent two and a half months at the public safety building, the guy come to court that I supposedly robbed, and said I didn't rob him. They turned around and charged him. I got released.

I went to Calgary because my dad was having open heart surgery. While I was living with him, I was doing B&Es, selling dope, basically to support my dad, help him with the bills. When he made it out of the hospital, got home and feeling up to going back to work, I continued doing my crime and getting picked up. I stole a car, ended up smashing this car up, almost killed myself. I was on mushrooms and acid and I was drinking shooters, rye and cokes, draft beer, and blacked out. I almost died on the Centre Street bridge. I got 16 months.

While I was in that young offender centre, I took some courses, worked out, played floor hockey. I got into a fight with this guy, he called me some names. I ended up almost killing him. I wrapped a towel around his mouth from behind as he was sitting in a chair. I slammed his head off the wall, and the concrete floor, a couple times. I kind of had him, like a rock and a leather lasso, and I was swinging him around. I held him in the chair, with the towel wrapped tight in a knot, and kept hitting him in the head. A friend of mine, who he called a goof too, sort of wanted to get in on the action.

Goof means lowest form of life. That's like calling me a raper or a rat, a sicko. That word means the lowest of anything, you know, you can call me anything but that. I ended up giving this guy multiple concussions and fractures, and he ratted me out. So when they were taking me to the hole, he was sitting out by the hall and I ended up punching him in the head. His head bounced off the wall, I knocked him out, and he hit the floor. I said, "You can throw me in the hole now for something."

When I turned 18 they didn't want me in the young offender centre. I finished the rest of my sentence in Spy Hill. About six months later, I got out.

I wanted to straighten my life out, and took a course at an adult vocational centre, a basic job readiness training program, to prepare you to find a job. I wanted to get a grant, student loan, whatever, and go to university or something like that, take upgrading, you know, try to get my Grade 12. I didn't have it at the time, I only had Grade

10. I was either going to try to get into mechanics, woodworking, roofing, plumbing, or something, a paying job. But, I barely finished the course, just passed with 50 percent, and I got a certificate. After that, I was collecting welfare at my dad's. When I got my cheque, I ended up going back to Winnipeg.

Right after Christmas, I picked up a possession charge. A whole bunch of us were drinking together before going to a party in a station wagon, and we got pulled over because there was too many people in the car. All they wanted was two people to get out and walk, because it was too many in there. The window was rolled down about two inches and one of my friends said, "Oh, I think I'm wanted for warrants."

The cop was standing right there and he said, "Everybody out!" There was a couple of guns under the seat, syringes, narcotics, alcohol. They took us down to the station, I gave them a bogus name, they gave me a pink slip to report for fingerprinting and I didn't do that.

Later, they charged me with B&E, possession of stolen property, failing to appear and giving them the wrong name. While I was out on bail I went to my mother's place. I was sick, sick from fixing sets, T&Rs. I was up for three days straight. While I was there, my mom told me she was going out, and she told me to clean up the place. I was washing the dishes, my sister was sitting on the couch watching soaps. As I finished washing them I told her to dry them. She didn't, and I told her to get off her fat ass. Then she got up, and said, "Clean the couch up!" So I was fooling around, grabbed the pillow, and hit her in the head. She was on the little carpet in front of the kitchen sink, slipped, hit the floor, started freaking out, trying to fight me. I grabbed her arms and swung her around in a circle, like a swirl to the floor.

She was mad because I was laughing at her. She got up and hit me a couple times, I punched her in the arm, and my other sister came downstairs to see what all the noise and yelling was about. My sister told me, sort of pushing me out the door, to go for a walk to calm down. While I was standing at the door, getting ready to go, I saw my sister on the phone. She was going to phone the cops on me for assault. So I went back in the suite and I grabbed the phone. I said, "You want to charge me for assault, I'll give you something to charge me for," and I punched her in the head a couple times. I threw the phone at her and left. I broke her nose, I think, because she had two black eyes. I got charged for an assault and I had the other charges.

I got two years probation for that. I went back to Calgary, continued to do crime, B&Es, selling goods and stuff. I picked up 14 months in

Spy Hill provincial, then went on the run from the minimum security section. I got another year added on for being unlawfully at large and some more B&Es. I got out again after serving some time and was supposed to go to a halfway house. I didn't. I went on the run for six weeks, and got into cocaine. I done robberies, robbing people, knocking them out.

A couple of guys we knew from Spy Hill wanted to do this armed robbery. So I said, "OK, we'll be right over." This guy and me went over there, and were going to do the armed robbery. I was just going to be his backup. By the time the robbery was getting ready to be done, he got scared and didn't want to do it, so I took over his part.

It was the office of an apartment block, where you pay your rent. I had a knife. I had $54 000 in my hand, cash and cheques, $10 000 in cash, and I handed it to the guy I was with. He got caught on the spot. There was three guys working out of the boiler room and they were just leaving work. I ended up running down an alley, being chased, and I turned around, started chasing back with the knife, and escaped.

The guy I was with ratted out on me, so they were looking for me for an armed robbery now, while I was already on the run from Spy Hill for six weeks.

A month later, I was back in the remand centre. It was three to five years on the armed robbery. I got three years. I got a year for one B&E, three months consecutive for the possession of stolen property, all consecutive. I got two years concurrent, one each for the other B&Es. In actuality, I only got four years three months, but I got six years three months on paper.

I was sent to Bowden, a federal prison. When I got into the institution it was not bad, the way it was built, but when I found out it was a place for 80 percent of rapers, you know, people who rape women and children, I couldn't handle it.

There was some suspicion of threatening to kill a few of them, wiping food on them in the cafeteria as I was walking by, mustard, ketchup and relish.

I went to a book sale, where they were selling magazines, birthday cards, and there was a raper as a door man. He talked to me, trying to stop me from going in with my friends. He said there was enough guys in there and I told him, "Get out of my face. You're a f——ing skinner, you're a no good piece of shit. If you ever talk to me again like that, I'll f—— you up," and he got scared and left.

He put in a kite against me, wrote it down on paper, sent it to the warden. They had a bunch of kites on me. Guys would say, "That guy's a raper," and all that, and I'd just look at him and say, "You f—ing goof, piece of shit. You're no good, you sick, sick puke."

I'd let him know that he was no good. When I went to the cafeteria, when I got the one-sixth point of my sentence and applied for day parole, after I read I wasn't going to get out, this raper, who raped his own kids, got up and bumped my tray with his shoulder, knocked my milk into my food. I knocked him out. Broke his nose and jaw. They threw me in the hole for two months. The first month they didn't know what to do with me, because no guards saw it, they just had kites against me, people writing in what they saw. The second month I put in a voluntary transfer to go to Drumheller.

It was basically the same but there wasn't so many rapers roaming around, a lot of them stayed locked up. I just stuck to my own anyways. I did my workouts, my programs and I got my general education diploma in there.

I got a one-third parole to Seven Steps halfway house in Calgary. I didn't go, went on the run the first day. I figured, I did the crime, it's my time, I'm going to do it the way I want to do it. I earned the parole so I went out on the run for 10 days.

And then I got arrested, accused of robbing a bank. They said I had a gun. I was just charged because I looked similar to the guy that robbed it. But the guy was 30, 40 years old, and someone said he looked East Indian, 5'10", with a beard and a moustache. I'm 5'8", part Native. I don't even shave once a month.

I got sentenced for six years and then I beat it on my appeal. I didn't do it, but was sent back to Drumheller. I lost all my good time, got out in '92 on mandatory, which is two-thirds of your time. I have a common-law, old lady, and while I was out I was trying to find work. I got on welfare, trying to get them to help me, and I was going to try and make some money on the side by selling cocaine. I started getting into it, doing, you know, using it. Then I began doing scores. While I was fixing cocaine, I was away from home. I almost lost my old lady for good, she went home, moved downstairs in her parents' house.

I went there and told her that I owed money to some guys from the street, and I wanted to get our stereo, cuff it to a dealer, and get some blow. Then I'd sell the blow and pay back what I owed these guys, and pay back the stereo. Well, she didn't want to do that. But I insisted, started to unhook the stereo, and she came toward me while I was bent down. I gave her a backhand, fracturing her nose, hairline fracture. They say it was broke, but it wasn't broke from the outside, it was an inside break. She just sat down and I left. She phoned her cousin to come over and comfort her, tell him what happened, and he phoned the cops on me.

She wanted to drop the charge, but the police can charge you without getting personal consent, so I got charged. It was more like a common dispute, you know. But I got two years for that robbery, just a robbery.

I also got charged for an armed robbery, robbing a dwelling. A guy ripped me off, I went there to take back what he took, and he wasn't there. It turned out to be his mother, which I didn't know at the time. When I sat her down on the floor I told her: "We're not here to rape you or hurt you in any way, just sit down and be quiet." When I sat her down, she hurt her knee. She later said she broke her leg, but she waited for 27 days to go to the hospital. Nobody breaks their leg and waits 27 days. She was in court with a cane, walking casually, in a few months' time. My partner got eight years. I mean sure, I tried not to hurt her and that, but because there was a lot of houses being done similar, I ended up getting nine years for it.

I had breached my mandatory release, never finished my first federal bit, and so that was added on to my sentence which was combined to total 15 years, five months and 24 days.

At the Edmonton Max, I think of how my life has gone every day. I never really stopped to think of it, and it's a shame that I have to realize this with age. In my case, it's never been a positive lifestyle, so I had to learn from the negatives. People who live positive lives, a negative comes along, well they know how to deal with it because they lived the positive way all their life. My way has been always negative and I never bothered to think about the consequences. When you live this way all your life, you tend to think that your morals and your honor, your standards and your values, are more important than your freedom. Your freedom comes second. It's you who comes first. You're doing life whether you're inside of jail or you're outside of jail. When your time's up, your time's up.

It's a learning school in jail. I've taken the best out of it, been my own teacher. I never had a childhood. I tried to live fast and hard, tried to get as much of life as I could, because I never had it when I was with the family. I never had a family, I never had nobody to help me or teach me, so I was my own teacher.

I learned to take care of number one. You have your ups and downs. And you have more downs living this way than you do living a normal lifestyle. I'm a tough individual, and if I can handle it this way, I can make it another way. I've had my fun this way and now it's time to think really what the hell I'm doing with my life. It ain't a game no more. I'm a man now, the childhood's gone. No sense trying to relive all that.

I don't think you can get a job on the street with what they have here to offer. I do have a little bit of plumbing skills. Roofing, painting, other than that, job wise, I don't think the institution has anything to offer that I can prepare myself when I get out. I've got a building service workshop certificate for 36 hours as a janitor, maintenance person. Maybe I can be a caretaker or something. If I look for an apartment, I could maintain the apartment block.

It's a small world, you're always going to be bumping into somebody you know and the situation's always going to be there. The prison has helped with programs. I've taken a lot of substance abuse courses, AA, I've got my 12 steps certificate. I've taken them all, life-skills programs, psychology for success, substance abuse courses. I'm going to continue on and still take some, twice, three times, just to learn. You're always learning something new.

The system could be more helpful. For people who are doing time, there should be a lot more for them, such as programs, counselling. What they have to offer is only a fraction of what you can learn to prepare yourself when you get out. It's a tough road out there, and it's like society, it's like they don't really want you to rehabilitate yourself, because if you get rehabilitated, there's no jobs, there ain't going to be no jobs, like they want you to come back. If they had more concern for you as a human being than as a number, then maybe you would have more respect for yourself and others. You're paying for it already with your heart and soul, in suspended time, paying for it every day.

It's reality in jail. There's nowhere to go, you have to face it everywhere you look. You can't run from it, you can't hide. Whether you go in the hole or in your cell, it's always there. You see animals in a zoo, going back and forth to the cage. Every turn he's got, he's facing it. It's the same with us. But we're people too, we got feelings. You may not believe it.

What I learned from the system is, go ahead, rape our women and children, we'll give you a lot less time. You steal our money and that, we're going to give you a lot of major time. Believe it or not, people that do property offences tend to make sure there's nobody around, so they don't have to hurt no one. We tend to think there's going to be insurance, so they will get reimbursed. We're not out to hurt anybody, we're just out to do a certain job, take the money and run.

We're human beings, we don't understand our feelings half the time, but you got to be tough, and sometimes you're over-tough, because if you get weak, if you face your feelings, you don't know how to feel them, and you end up committing suicide, or losing it, going into a mental institution.

I think the future holds for me, a steady job, a roof over my head, and a financially secure family. Other than that, my freedom.

When I first get out, I'd like to see my relatives. It's been a long time. I'd like to be with my common-law wife, hopefully she'll be with me.

I have a son who's 12 years old. His mother left me when I was in Winnipeg and she went to B.C. I don't know where they are now. All I know is my son's name is Brian, that's it.

My Family's Reaction

Hugh Peters

"A couple of my aunts were crying and my mom and dad were pretty shaken up. But for me, I wasn't stunned with the verdict. It wasn't a shock. It's just hearing the words: 'Life without eligibility for parole for 25 years.' At that point it is final."

In early January 1995, a former army corporal who went on a murderous rampage was released on parole to a halfway house in Hull, Quebec. Seventeen months later, in June 1996, he was granted full parole, the most freedom he can win for the rest of his life.

Denis Lortie was dressed in battle fatigues when he burst into Quebec's National Assembly in May 1984 and sprayed it with submachine-gun bullets. He killed three people and wounded 13 others. Defence psychiatrists testified the military supply clerk suffered from a form of psychosis. For his killing spree, he was sentenced to life in prison with no eligibility for parole for 10 years. A judge was later quoted as saying the crime wasn't particularly heinous.

On January 26, 1995, Roger Warren, 51, who was found guilty of murder in connection with the bombing deaths of nine miners in Yellowknife, Northwest Territories, was sentenced. The judge said his crime was "stupid and despicable . . . nothing less than an act of terrorism." He was given a life term without parole eligibility for 20 years. Asked if he had a statement, he said: "No, I have nothing to say."

This is not the tale of Denis Lortie or Roger Warren. Nor is it by any means meant to be construed as an in-depth account of glaring disparities in court sentences, inconsistencies invariably dismissed by the argument: "Circumstances were different." That said, a comparison of the Lortie and Warren sentences, together with the one that follows, provides stark evidence that the number of people murdered or maimed in Canada does not always make a difference when punishment is meted out.

This is the saga of a 21-year-old man who, seven months prior to the Lortie and Warren cases, was the object of a Supreme Court of Canada decision that confirmed his double life sentence. He must spend at least 25 years in custody before he will be considered for release.

Hugh Peters (his name has been changed along with that of one of his victims, who cannot be identified by court order) was a teenager living in a small, stable farming community when the unthinkable happened. In November 1990, he watched a television movie with two schoolmates, tied them up, slit their throats, doused them with gasoline, and then tried to burn down the murder house. One of the victims barely escaped with his life. The other's charred body was found at the scene, the index finger of his left hand raised as if placed in a "rude" gesture, according to police.

The case was moved to adult court where a plea of not guilty by reason of insanity was entered. Included among those who testified:

- A police officer, who said he found numerous books in the home of the accused dealing with guns and the law.
- The survivor, 14 years old at the time of madness, 15 at trial, who told the court that his assailant said he "shouldn't be mad at you guys," but rather at his hockey coach, who had just cut him from the team. The witness also stated that when the accused left the room during that terror-filled night and returned about 20 minutes later, he said he had shut up the other boy and added: "Now you have to die." Court was told that later, with blood flowing everywhere, the attacker asked: "Why won't you die?"
- A doctor who treated the blood-soaked boy gave evidence that the injury victim couldn't speak and twice handed him notes saying "I don't want to die."
- A pathologist, who said the 15-year-old victim died from a 12-centimetre-long wound. His windpipe was severed along with the carotid artery and jugular vein.
- A defence psychiatrist, who described the accused as a paranoid psychotic with an antisocial personality. He further gave evidence that the accused believed everyone in the community was out to punish him, and that the accused thought he "would become part of the community" by joining mourners at the

funeral of the two boys. The doctor further revealed: "He felt his life in danger, that his mental health was in danger."

- A defence psychiatrist who declared: "He felt the entire community was together in a plot to end his life. He was more or less at war. It was either them or himself. He believed townfolk either intended to goad him into committing suicide or that someone would run him over with a car." Additionally, the doctor said under oath, the accused believed the local paper was printing messages intended solely for him. The messages never named him, but told him his life was in danger. The final straw, according to the expert witness, was when the accused was cut from his hockey team, and at a party hours before the burst of violence, believed people were talking about him. In a psychotic bid for redemption, court was told, it was the last in a series of events to cause the mind of Hugh Peters to snap.

- A prosecution psychiatrist, who disagreed that the accused was psychotic. The doctor claimed the accused enjoyed slitting the throats of his prey. "It was a pleasurable experience for him," said the witness. "He seemed to take pleasure in the idea that he might be evil, that it gave him a perverted sense of power." Court was told that the accused was a bully who enjoyed hurting others, but was capable of understanding his crimes were both legally and morally wrong. He would often smile or grin as he detailed what he had done to his quarry, court was told. He "had the fantasy of killing someone for a long time," the all-woman jury heard.

- A forensic psychologist, who also talked with the accused, said he had an "antisocial sadistic personality disorder" but was not psychotic. "For some time, he always felt like he'd kill someone," said the witness. "He said he always knew he would."

- A Crown attorney, who described the accused as a clever, cruel human being who delighted in hurting others.

- An acquaintance, who said the accused told him two weeks before the killing that he disliked the youth who died. And that he called him a "goof" and added he "wouldn't mind beating the snot out of him."

Hugh Peters, upon being found guilty, told the judge that he had been "stepped on" by society.

Afterwards, the mother of the teenager who will carry the scars of the attack forever, claimed the parents should have known about their son's dangerous tendencies.

When I walked into the penitentiary, all I knew was that Hugh Peters was there for murder and attempted murder. I was aware the victims were teenagers, that their throats had been slashed, and the house they were in had been torched. That was all the advance information I had.

I was ushered into a small, thick-glassed cubicle, in full view of a manned control room. A secured doorway leading to the cells opened, and the muscular prisoner, 6', 205 pounds, entered. We shook hands, and we talked, a getting to know each other period, but primarily about him telling his story *In the Words of the Offender*. Quite simply, I would ask questions, he would answer. Then the tapes would be transcribed, and his story would unfold. He was the one who asked numerous questions, listened attentively, expressed reservations, wanted to think about it, wanted to phone his parents, check with them. It was a fairly quick meeting. We went our separate ways. I walked out into the sunshine, fresh air, free to go anywhere. He retreated into his inner sanctum: bars; cells; fellow criminals; guards; rules; and no legal way to leave until possibly 2015.

Not too much time passed before I received a message. I could return to his iron-bellied domicile. He was willing to share his story, agreed that it might do some good.

One of the first things this articulate, well-read inmate told me was this: "If things had gone differently, I could be in university." Doubtless that is true. What I also believed to be true, having since become familiar with the printed record of his case, still holds. Hugh Peters, under the circumstances, provided a chillingly, candid account of what he felt could be talked about. He had the right to remain silent, but he thought by taking part in this chronicle, it might help people understand how things went so horribly wrong, and what life is like for someone who kills.

f anybody recognized that maybe help was needed, if they did, they never said anything. Many people came to my trial and afterwards they were saying: well this, and this, and this could have been done, and that should have been done; and my thinking is, why didn't you say anything? If you knew about all of my problems back then, why didn't you say something back then? Hindsight is 20-20 vision.

There's been quite a few times when you sit back and you go, geez if this wouldn't have happened or that wouldn't have happened or if I could change this, but you get to a point where if you spend the rest of your life looking back you're going to go insane. That's what would happen. You can't change it so deal with what you have now and go forward.

It is important that my real name not be used simply for the fact that my family right now has finally gotten over all the media attention. My family doesn't want to be in the media spotlight. I have no problem with my name being used. It's my family I'm concerned about.

For about two weeks, I was in the paper every day. One paper, the Winnipeg Sun, I was front page news for maybe five, six days out of the two weeks I was on trial.

They made a CBC television documentary about the town itself. I think it was called '*How a Town Heals Itself.*' There was a lot of media coverage.

We're a pretty private family, conservative I guess, and to have your life put in the newspaper or on television continuously, basically everything that you have done is scrutinized, and it is not a pleasant experience. I don't think my parents did anything wrong, but to have their life scrutinized like that, I don't think anybody would enjoy that.

They live in the same house, and my dad has the same job. He's a supervisor for a large corporation in a town near ours, about six miles away. My mom lost her job as a result of my arrest. She was a librarian at the high school, where I and the two victims attended. Because of my arrest, she resigned, but if she had not resigned she would have been fired. She had worked there about 11 years.

I was born in Regina, and when I was about two or three moved to central southern Manitoba, not far from the United States border. It's a small conservative Mennonite town. I think there's about seven churches in town, so it's very religious.

It was sociable to go to certain churches and not sociable to go to others. My parents and I and my brother, who was two years older, went to the United Church, and I guess it wasn't as sociable a church as some of the others. It did affect me, but I don't know to what extent. When I was younger, we went every Sunday. When I was about 10, I stopped going to church.

I guess the biggest special occasion was Christmas. That was a pretty close time for our family. Birthdays and stuff like that were also special, but Christmas was the biggest occasion for us. We also went on several vacations, which were also very special times.

I played hockey. I played baseball until I was 14. I was a fair athlete, about average. I wasn't a standout in any of the sports.

In school I was actually pretty good. I was a pretty good student, usually B or better. Some years the Cs popped in, but for the most part I was a B student.

When I was in Grade 3, I saw a psychiatrist, because I was having problems with the teacher in school. I think that was only once. The psychiatrist said I didn't have any problems, nothing that he could see.

When I was in Grade 6, they put me in a special group for smarter kids. It was called Apollo, and I started getting bugged about it by my friends. After that year I dropped out of it.

I was doing pretty good. I was really good at math and most of my other subjects. Most of my teachers liked me. I was a pretty good student then.

I had some problems dealing with some kids during my two years in junior high, Grade 7 and 8. Most of the teachers liked me, there were a few who did not, and my marks were still pretty good. I guess I had trouble dealing with some of the kids, not all, but there were a few. Everybody had a different thing I guess. "Your haircut is like this" or "Your mom works here." It was all kinds of different things depending on the person.

The teasing just wouldn't go for a short duration and stop, it was continuous, and then I would get aggressive. I had confrontations with several students in school. I was a bit bigger than average for my age. I was not the biggest, but I was one of the bigger kids in school. I could take care of myself.

When I was in Grade 7, I also saw a psychiatrist. I was having, well, not problems with a teacher this time, it was with the kids. I think I saw him three times and I stopped seeing him. I don't know why, but it was either his choice or my parents' choice. That's been the only therapy, other than when I was in Grade 3, that I've had.

When I was about 15, I started breaking into places. Nothing that I consider major. It wasn't car theft or arson or murder or assault or anything really violent. It was breaking into places and things like that, mostly by myself. It was more for monetary gain than anything else. At the time I smoked and I needed cigarettes. The best place to go was this gas station where there were lots of cigarettes. I broke in there three times.

There was a period of time where I got into some more trouble. They called me down to the police station. I went and they said: "We're charging you with these crimes." I didn't have any priors, I was a good student, I lived in a small town, I had good family. It wasn't serious enough charges, where I was concerned about being sent to a youth centre.

Finally I was convicted. I had two convictions. One was break, enter and theft, and one was mischief, damaging public property. They were different incidents. I had maybe $2500 restitution and fine, plus two years probation.

It wasn't the punishment itself, the fine or the restitution or the probation that really made a difference. I said to myself, "I'm getting tired of this, it's not worth it," simply because of the aggravation it causes me and my family.

I guess my parents viewed it as simply going through a rebellion stage as a teenager. There was disappointment at home, and more or less, "Try and change your ways." There was also a lot of support. It was, "Whatever we can do to help you change, let us know and we'll do it."

I paid my restitution on time and I also attended my probation consistently, once a month. I kept going to high school and played sports. Hockey basically, and team sports over the lunch hour. I maybe had some sports heroes, but I can't really recall any hero that stood out in my mind. What I had hoped to do was attend university, hopefully in the field of law or perhaps accounting, and hoped to get a degree and job in one of those careers. Perhaps medicine.

We earned our money helping my dad. Both me and my brother spent the summer and most days after school and in the evenings helping my dad with his beekeeping operation. This occupied most of my spare time. I was also busy taking high school correspondence courses to better my education. I spent a lot of time reading.

I was 17 when I was arrested November 17, two or three months into Grade 12. I'd been having a tough time. Not with school itself, but basically every aspect of my life, I was having trouble. I couldn't deal with people. Sports wasn't going good for me. I wasn't relating to my teachers well. I wasn't relating to my classmates well.

I went to a dance, November 16, a Friday, and there were two guys that I knew from hockey. One guy had just recently moved from town, the other lived in town all his life. I got there about 9 o'clock, actually arrived late, and there were some comments, basically teasing, made toward me by both the individuals. I went home angry, about 10 o'clock, and decided that I was going to kill them. About 11 o'clock we were watching TV at home, me and my brother, and my mom and dad. About 11:30 my parents went to bed, and I went upstairs. My brother was watching television.

I went into my room and I got a gym bag, and I threw a bunch of stuff in there that I figured I would need to kill them. I had two handguns, which I had broken into a house and stolen about a month earlier. I put one of them into the bag. About 12 o'clock I snuck out of the house through my window. My parents were asleep. Nobody knew I was gone.

I went over to (the name has been changed) Trevor's house, which was just maybe a block and a half away. His mom was away, so Trevor and Curtis were at Trevor's house alone. I went to the door and knocked. They came to the door and started talking with me, and it was cold outside, so they invited me in.

We sat down and watched a movie, *The Hunt For Red October*. I guess it was about 2:30, the movie was over, and I pulled out the gun. It was a .357 magnum and I pointed at them and told them to get on the floor and I tied them up.

I got Curtis into Trevor's mom's room and strangled him and then I cut his throat. Then I went back into Trevor's room and tried to cut his throat and he went down and I thought he was dead so I left the room. I heard a creak, the door opened and he was in the bedroom doorway. So I went after him again for a second time, this time with a fireplace shovel and hit him with it, and again he went down and I thought he was dead.

I went back into my bag, I had brought gasoline along, and started pouring gasoline all over the house and started setting fires in different areas. He got up again, and I went after him. But the house was on fire and because of the amount of smoke in there I couldn't really do anything so I had to let him go. At that point, I was just thinking of saving myself because the entire house was full of thick, black smoke, so I went to the back door.

I was outside and I remembered that I forgot all the stuff I brought inside so I went back in the house. The smoke was too thick so I went back out and I was standing there. Trevor had gone around to a neighbor's house and started ringing the doorbell and he was looking at me while he was ringing the doorbell. I was about to go after him when the porch light turned on and a person came out and yelled something at me and I took off and went home.

One died, he was strangled and then his throat was cut. He had tape over his eyes, he had his hands taped behind his back. He kicked his feet a bit when he was being strangled, but he was unconscious in about a minute. I was strangling him with a cord and the cord snapped. Then I went into the kitchen and got a knife and I cut his throat. About a minute later, most of the blood had stopped coming out. It was a trickle at that point and I knew he was dead.

The other one lived. I missed the carotid artery by about an eighth of an inch. He came very close to dying. He had been burned. I thought he was dead and I put a blanket on top of him and poured gasoline on it and set that on fire so he had his throat cut and he also had burns on most of his body.

Feeling powerful are not the right words. You feel like you're playing God. But at the time, it didn't seem like a big thing. It was not: "Wow! What am I doing?" It didn't really even register at the time.

As far as what was said at the dance to trigger what happened, I can't even recall if I ever did tell anybody. I can't really say for sure. The whole school year, from the middle of summer on, I was becoming almost like a hermit. I couldn't deal with people. I didn't feel comfortable around people. I didn't want to be around people. At that point, I hated people. I'd just as soon be in my room studying and doing stuff alone. I was golfing alone, I was shooting alone. The only time I would socialize would be at parties, Friday night or Saturday night, go and have a few beers. This was the first problem I ever had with them.

It was gradual. Looking back I can't really say where it started. It happened over a period of time. Little things would bother me just a little bit, then little things would bother me a lot. Things became unbearable and I couldn't deal with it. I didn't know how to deal with it. I never asked anybody for help.

I went back in through my bedroom window, went downstairs and had a shower and cleaned myself up, and then I went to bed. This is about 4:30 in the morning. I was so exhausted my mind shut down. I think that's what it was. Everything was going through my mind and I was trying to think about it and rationalize it and understand what had happened. I was exhausted, physically and mentally, and I guess that's what happened. I just went home and went to sleep. I'd been up since 7 that morning. Physically that's a lot, and mentally it was quite a strain, the whole day itself. I think I basically shut down.

I left the one handgun at Trevor's house, but when I went home that night, I had another one under my pillow. I fully expected the police were going to come over. I didn't know what I would do if they had, but I had the handgun under my pillow just in case.

I woke up the next day at 9 o'clock. My mom went shopping and my dad was gone. My brother wasn't home. I went to where Trevor's house was to see what was left. The house was still standing, but the inside had been burned out. I didn't care at that point. The whole day I was indifferent. I was resigned to the fact that I had screwed up and it was just a matter of time before the police came to pick me up.

I went back home and went to sleep. I got up about noon, had breakfast, drove my parents' truck downtown, went and cashed a cheque, went into the town mall for a little while, and went to go see a friend at his house. About 2:30 I went home and got a few rifles and I told my parents I was going out to the farm to do some shooting. At 4:30 I was arrested.

There were three RCMP officers. One I knew and the other two were from the city. I watched them drive along the country road leading to our farm and they'd actually passed our farm and gone to another one. Then they stopped and came down the road to ours, and I was standing there with my .22 rifle in my hand and they pulled up. All three of the officers got out of the car, they pulled their guns and said: "Drop the rifle!" And I put it down. They said: "Get on the ground!" And I did. They came and handcuffed me and took me to the RCMP station.

I was numb at that point. I knew what was going on, but I didn't care. They didn't say anything in the police car. When I was at the RCMP station, I told them I didn't want to talk to them until I had spoken to a lawyer. Then a police officer came in and he said my dad had called and said that a lawyer was on the way and not to say anything until I speak to a lawyer.

I was charged when I was still in the RCMP station. Still, at that point, things weren't registering. Everything happened so fast. My mind was trying to grasp what had happened, and at that point it hadn't. I guess the only thing I would say about it is that it was uncomfortable for me, the physical aspect. I got very little sleep. The lights were on, the doors were always banging back and forth, they had a radio that kept going.

Every time somebody came to see me I was strip searched. They had no blankets there, the cells had nothing. A form of cruel and unusual punishment, I guess.

They sent me to the Manitoba Youth Centre. I appeared in court every week there. I originally was charged with three charges and they brought another eight charges in. When I went to trial there were only the two charges. The others were dropped.

I pleaded not guilty by reason of insanity to first-degree murder and attempted murder. I was found guilty on both counts. First-degree was life without parole for 25 years, and for the attempt it was also a life sentence.

I was pretty sure that's the decision they would come back with, based on what had happened at the trial and everything else. I guess I was sort of resigned to the fact about what was happening. My family's reaction is what upset me. A couple of my aunts were crying and my mom and dad were pretty shaken up. But for me, I wasn't stunned with the verdict. It wasn't a shock. It's just hearing the words: "Life without eligibility for parole for 25 years." At that point it is final.

I was unable to hug my mom or say anything to my dad before I left the courtroom. My parents came at about 10 o'clock to the public safety building in Winnipeg and visited me for about an hour. They made a special arrangement, because the decision had come down that day, that my parents could come in and see me because visiting was not allowed at that time of night.

About a week and a half later, Pen placement came to see me and I was told that, because of the amount of time I was doing, I would be considered a maximum security inmate and that I would be shipped to Saskatchewan Penitentiary.

I was in the remand centre until just after Christmas. Then they sent me to Stony Mountain Institution. Stony Mountain is way up on a hill, it's all wires, bars and brick, and driving up to it you're handcuffed and shackled. Not scary, but I guess creepy is the word I would use. It's an older building, it's dark, it's grim and it's almost like going into a haunted house. I was nervous because I didn't know what to expect. I'd been told about the prisons by guys in the remand centre who had been there before.

They processed me and put me in the hole. I just kept thinking, "What am I going to do? What's going to happen?" I was trying to go through everything in my mind. At that point, I didn't have any contact with any other inmates, so I didn't know what to expect.

The hole was six feet by eight feet, a brick bed with a mattress on it, a toilet and a sink and that's it. You get your meals brought to you three times a day. For a phone call, they bring a telephone and put it in an opening on your door and you can make a phone call which lasts about 15 minutes.

I'd been told when I went into the institution that the next load leaving by bus was within a week, so I knew I wouldn't be there long.

There must have been about 20, 25 of us on the bus. Everyone's in a separate cubicle. The bus had a centre aisle and each seat had a cage around it and a door. They would put each person in one of the units, handcuffed and shackled. There was a guard up front who was armed and there were two guards in the back who were armed. Most of the guys were pretty quiet. I didn't know anybody there so I didn't really associate with anybody.

You're near a window, the windows were tinted. I just looked out the window and tried to catch the scenery because I knew it would be a while before I would see it again. It was about a nine-hour trip. For me, I just wanted to see everything. I didn't know when the next time this was going to happen, if I would be able to see it again. Some guys were sleeping, some guys were talking, but I was looking out the window. I just wanted to see. I hadn't seen trees in a long time. I hadn't seen cars. I hadn't seen a lot of that in a while so I wanted to see it that one last time.

They dropped off some guys in the back, at the Special Handling Unit, and then they came to the front, and they unloaded us there. We came in the middle of the night and all I could see was wall. That was my first impression, a huge wall with lights, and two trucks going around it.

It took about an hour to get processed. Some of the guys they let into reception, which is an orientation range. I didn't know at that time, but they didn't have my file. Because they didn't have any information about me, they put me into segregation. They brought me some food on a little tray, but I wasn't too hungry so it just kind of sat there on a shelf. I watched a bit of television that night and was trying to think about the next day. What's the next day going to be like? What's going to happen then?

I was locked up. I didn't know the routine but they came around with breakfast. Then you had to clean up your cell, then they had time for showers, lunch, and then you could go for exercise in the afternoon. We came back in, were locked up, had supper, and were locked up until the next morning.

I met some people in segregation, they were telling me the ropes, who to talk to, who to stay away from, the set up of the institution. I was there for a week, so in that week they kept me informed of what was going on in the prison.

The penitentiary can give you the basics of, you eat at this time, you do this, your cell is supposed to be like this, but the stuff like who you talk to, who you should associate with, what you can say, what you're not supposed to say, you can only pick up through the inmates. Some people aren't lucky. When they come in they don't click on to anybody that knows what's going on in the institution. They get in the wrong crowd.

Some guys go through the provincial system before they come here, so they come in and they know guys from the provincial system, for example. I'm from a small town, middle of nowhere, first time being in. I think I was 18 at the time when I was shipped here and it's a real eye-opener. You have to learn quick.

I wasn't worried about going into population, because I knew that murder was an acceptable crime in prison, plus the amount of time I was doing. With a double life sentence there was not too much worse that could happen to me, so my attitude at that point was: "I really don't care." In prison, once the people found out how much time you're doing, your crime kind of puts you on a scale. It's a hierarchy system. Murder is considered a "good crime," child molesting is probably the worst. Informants are also on the bottom, rapists are on the bottom and armed robbery is closer to the top. There's a hierarchy system, plus the amount of time you're doing also has something to do with it. The common saying is: "If you're doing life, what have you got to lose?" I mean what are they going to do, give you another life sentence? So in that aspect, when people find out you're doing a lot of time, they tend to leave you alone.

Not all of them knew the details of my case. Most of them weren't from Manitoba. But there were a few guys who came in and passed the word around, "this guy's doing double life," and so some guys knew me in here and word got around. Most of it wasn't firsthand to the rest of them. It was only a few who knew and they passed the word around.

The severity of what took place has sunk in. It happened a few months ago when they turned down my appeal. There was always some hope that the appeal might change things, might overturn my conviction, order a new trial, maybe reduce my sentence, something of that sort, but when the Supreme Court threw out my case, I knew that I would be doing a lot of time. It sunk in and there were a few days there I was kind of depressed, but after that you say, "This is not going to change anything." And you move on.

Thinking of suicide, that's been pretty constant throughout. From the time I've been arrested until now, actually. It pops in every now and then. Things get really stressful and are tough to deal with and you get to the point where you're saying: "Why am I bothering with this? What's the point of this? I'm going to be in prison for a long time and this is not where I want to be. I don't want to be around people like this. I have no future." You almost get into a tailspin at that point. You start thinking about all of the negative things. It's pretty tough to stop. It's a landslide. What I do is tell myself: "Wait until tomorrow, and if tomorrow you feel the same way, well then maybe consider it." When I'm having a bad day, I sit there and say: "Well you're probably not thinking rational right now, so sleep on it and maybe things will be better in the morning."

I didn't actually see them myself, but there have been two people who comitted suicide in here since I've been here.

Almost a year and a half ago I started lifting weights. Typical prison thing to do. I didn't lift weights when I first came in, but working in the recreation department is a good place.

I get up, do a bit of reading, go for breakfast, then I go to work, clean up the weight pit, usually do a workout in the morning until about 11 o'clock, from 11 to 11:30 we're locked up, 11:30 to noon we're fed. From 12 to 1 we're locked up, from 1 to 4 we go to work. I usually go back to the gym and do another workout and either go to my cell to sleep or go to the library and read. Come back at 4, 4 to 5 is count, and I usually listen to music, and read. Five to 6 supper, then 6 to 10 is exercise. I usually go out for two to four hours in an evening. At 10 o'clock we're locked up until morning.

I usually call home once every two weeks. I get about maybe five or six visits a year. I have started having trailer visits here. I write to six people back home. Some of the people I write to are people I have met since I have been incarcerated. Basically, my communication is with my immediate family and a few other people. I don't have any contact with any of my high school friends. There were a few girls I associated with, but no girlfriend, nothing formal. Most people I ever associated with on the street, I don't have any contact with.

The odd time I think of the crime, but for the most part I've stopped. I guess what's happened is I think more about what's going on in here today and tomorrow, than what put me here. I analyzed that for a whole year while I was in the remand centre and basically I've stopped thinking about it. That's a different part of my life right now. Right now I'm in here and I deal with what's in here, the people in here, and try and keep my days as full as possible, as busy as possible, reading, and watching TV, so that I don't fall into a rut and start thinking: "What happened? Why did this happen?"

It was a stupid thing. Most people couldn't believe something was said, and that I would kill them for it. But it was the proverbial straw that broke the camel's back. It was not that incident, it was everything that had led up to it. I was anti-social. I could not deal with people. My dealing with people was too minimal, in school, outside the school, sports, everything. I had a few friends I was comfortable talking to, but for most people, I simply did not want to be around them, and I did not want them to be around me. Everything just built up. My marks weren't as good as I would have liked them to be in school, and that week I'd been cut from the hockey team, which I made the previous year. I was losing friends at a pretty rapid rate. I snapped. Everything got to me. One thing piled on another and finally I broke.

As far as what stands out as something significant that I've learned, I don't know. Philosophically, one thing with me, all the people that I had on the street that were my so-called friends, even some of my family, as soon as this happened, they scattered. Everybody has trouble understanding. I have trouble understanding; my parents too. My one aunt and uncle come up and see me and they have trouble understanding. But does that mean that you bail out right away? Maybe go and try and understand it yourself. Go ask. Nobody came and asked me anything.

They didn't want to associate with me, they didn't want to have any contact with me, that bothers me. I don't let it bother me as much now, but it used to really upset me that people can like you one day, but you do something, and all of a sudden you're not significant in their life or important enough to talk to. That bothered me.

Another thing that bothers me is this life 25 sentence with no eligibility for parole for 25 years. To me it does not make sense because you did something wrong, and obviously it's very bad, but it's one thing. For everyone to judge me on one thing that I've done in my life, I don't think is fair. If you take a whole puzzle, you got 500 pieces, you take one piece. It doesn't tell you what the puzzle looks like, it doesn't tell you anything about the puzzle. It tells you about one piece, a fraction of the puzzle.

I don't see any future at this point. I came in at 17, if I'm lucky I'll leave at 42, and it strikes me as being unfair and too much time. To me, what's always been more idealistic, is maybe a life sentence with no parole eligibility for 10 years. Then the parole board could review your case every year. If you're ready to be released, let's say after 12 years, they can let you out. If you're ready after 18 years they can let you out. You might be ready after 30 years, and maybe you will never be ready to be released, and never are released.

This minimum of 25, they raised me to adult court, like I said, 17 when I came in, 42 when I leave. I'll have no life out there. I'm resigned to the fact that I'll go out there probably with no job skills, because they don't want to pay for an education while I'm in the penitentiary. I've asked for university courses, they say I have to pay for them myself at $400 a course. I make $1200 a year. They don't teach you any skills here, they have no courses to take, and I'll go out there with next to no skills because of the limited resources in here, and that will severely limit my opportunities. I'll have no practical skills and on my resume I can say what? "I've cleaned the weight room for 20 years?" Sure, punish me, but at what point does it stop being punishment and start being revenge?

The death penalty has always struck me as being stupid simply because there is no room for error. Despite all the appeal processes that you have available to you, the system is human by nature, and mistakes are made. David Milgaard is a perfect example. Twenty-one, 22 years later they go: "Well geez, I think we might have made a mistake." If you made a mistake with capital punishment, are you going to say postmortem: "Oh, we're sorry. You're not guilty now." Well if he's in the ground already, it doesn't really change anything, does it? That's my thinking. I would sooner have maybe life without eligibility for parole like they have in some states. I think there's two or three where life means you'll spend the rest of your life in prison. At least what you're doing with that, if you find out 20 years down the line you made a mistake, at that point you can try to correct it with compensation or whatever. If you've already executed the person, what do you do at that point?

Insofar as counselling or treatment since being in prison, I've been told I'm not a priority, because of the amount of time I'm doing. Sloughed off to the side. I guess they figure I am doing such a large amount of time they'll worry about me more down the line.

I don't like it, but they have limited resources available for them to use and they have people going out on parole or want to get parole soon so they have to use those resources for them. Hopefully, some day when I come up for parole they'll be willing to set aside some of those resources for me. It bothers me that if I wanted treatment, that it's: "We can't help you right now. You're not a priority on our list." And it bothers me with the university education too.

I want to better myself so when I go out there I won't re-offend and come back in here. Give me at least a little bit to work with, and they won't. They won't assist me in any way and what am I supposed to do?

I see a lot of prison time and I haven't really even thought about what life could be like out there. I can't. I haven't even lived. I'm 21 now. I'll spend 25 years inside a prison by the time I'm released. I've got another 21 years to go, and that's when I go for parole, so my mind can't even comprehend it. That's my entire life that I've lived so far twice over, and I can't see life out there right now, because I don't have anything. If I had an education I could say "I got this education. When I get out there maybe I could go do this or do that or seek employment here." But I have nothing. I completed my Grade 12 education when I came in here, but Grade 12 in 2015 isn't going to get you too much. Even now, people with university degrees are being laid off.

I do a lot of reading, try to keep my mind occupied, always have something to think about. I find if you don't, if you have a lot of dead time, time where you're thinking about the past or what you did or this or that, it gets you down, it gets you depressed. It doesn't really change anything. I think the key to survival in here is keeping your mind busy. You should always try and think of something, whether it's reading a book, a magazine, an editorial, and thinking about a different point of view. Maybe it's playing sports in here, always involved in team activities and stuff of that sort. As long as you're keeping yourself busy. It's the people who sit in their cell all day and do nothing, for them I would think time would be tougher to do, but maybe for them it's easier that way.

For any kid who thinks stealing cars is a rush, I think they're only kidding themselves. It's no rush being in here. It's not the physical constraints that get to you, it's the mental ones. It's watching your back all the time. It's worrying about fights. It's the loss of privileges. You have no choices. I can't get up at 2 in the morning and decide I want to have a piece of cake. I eat what they give me and that's it. I do what they tell me. I go where they tell me I can go. If they decide I can't go out in the yard today, I don't go out in the yard. If I do something wrong, I get thrown in the hole. It looks good on television, how prison is so glamorous, but television glamorizes a lot of things that aren't. It's very bleak.

My brother has his own apartment, works for a security firm, and is doing pretty well. How ironic we both ended up in two extremes. He's working for a security company and I'm inside a prison.

This is What's Gonna Happen

Darcy Watmough

"My lawyer presented his case and what he was hoping for. When the judge finally made his ruling, in a way it was almost relief. In another way it was: 'Holy shit! How am I gonna survive this? What have I done to my family? What have I done to my friends? What have I done to people who shouldn't have been involved to start with?'"

On March 31, 1988, the body of 23-year-old Bernard Tallman Jr., a young Blood Tribe member, was found face down in a ditch southeast of Lethbridge. He had been shot in the back of the head, executed gangland style.

Less than a month later, Chief Roy Fox sent a letter to Alberta Premier Don Getty. It said in part that the Blood Tribe: "... is greatly concerned about the increasing incidents of deaths and murders of our members under peculiar and mysterious circumstances" and the "apparent unwillingness/inability of the authorities to solve these tragedies."

It was then announced that the RCMP reopened investigations into five deaths that sparked the outcry, even though they had never closed the file on Bernard Tallman Jr. On April 29, 1988, Darcy Lee Watmough, 20, and Albert David Morin, 25, were arrested and charged with his murder.

A week later, as the prisoners were being moved for a remand appearance, a disturbance broke out at the Lethbridge courthouse, spreading like wildfire onto the street. There were allegations of a white gang systematically hunting down and murdering Natives.

Eventually, the Government of Alberta ordered a public inquiry. In a twist of irony, it did not specifically consider the case of Bernard Tallman Jr. It remained before the courts and was, therefore, deemed outside the probe's terms of reference.

On Chief Fox's expressed concerns about policing, the report of the public inquiry, which entailed 86 hearing days, 232 witnesses, and thousands of pages of evidence, found: ". . . no evidence of bias or racism . . ."

The mood surrounding the separate murder trials that followed the shooting death of Bernard Tallman Jr. was tense. Security was tight. Observers were required to walk through a metal detector. The courtroom was packed. More than 40 people, many from the victim's reserve at Standoff, couldn't get in and helplessly congregated outside. Local aboriginals testified they stole a gymnasium bag full of drugs from a parked truck. Court was told that when the drugs, valued at $3000, went missing, the accused went looking, trying to get them back. Witnesses made it very clear that the murder victim had nothing to do with the rip-off, basically he was in the wrong place at the wrong time.

A prosecutor declared: "They both intended at that time to kill this captive man lying at the side of the road with his legs curled up, begging not to be hit."

A charge of first-degree murder against Al Morin was reduced to second-degree and later to manslaughter. He ended up with an eight-year term.

Darcy Watmough, who pulled the trigger and pleaded guilty, was sentenced to life imprisonment with no chance for parole for 15 years. Locked behind prison gates, this is his story.

ell, I killed a man. It was one of those things that you don't think is going to happen until it happens. It's hard, it's a long story to get into.

I appealed the sentence and the judge's exact words were: "You were lucky to get what you got." I really can't argue with him, because for the crime that I committed, even though I was out of it on drugs and that, it's not something that anybody should do.

I've been in seven years. I was a year in remand and then once I was done court I was sent here. I've been here ever since. I have a feeling I'll probably be here another two or three years, and then I'll transfer into Alberta where I'm closer to my family, so when I get out on parole, if I get out on parole, I'll be closer to where I finally want to call my home.

I was born in Fort Macleod. It's kind of a laid back town. It seems like everybody knows everybody. The population is probably around 5000 to 6000. It seems like everybody knows each other's business. It's one of those gossip towns.

My family is very strait-laced. There's been no charges, trouble with the law or anything. I seem to be the bad apple out of the bunch. I was the third boy in a line of four. Two of them are married, one is married twice, and my youngest brother's got kind of a live-in family. His girlfriend or common-law had kids when he moved in with her. As I said, I'm the bad apple.

I can't say that any punishment I got from my parents I didn't deserve, because I did. I had my own ideas and if I didn't get my own way I was going to do it one way or another. There was a few times I got lickings from mom and dad that I can't blame them for, because they told me "No." And I did it anyway. My parents were fairly strict in their guidelines and rules. They told me what I could and couldn't

Darcy Watmough –
"I guess justice wasn't done because the victim's family probably would have liked to see me dead. I can't remember if there were tears coming down or I was just hanging my head in real sorrow, because I realized this is it. I'm going to jail. How am I going to handle this?"

do. My brothers more or less followed their discipline and they've never had any problem with the law.

The way I was raised is probably like any average family. The only difference being that I wanted to be independent. I didn't like to do the other things like the other kids did. I always wanted to have my own special way. I guess you could almost say I was kind of a loner type. I didn't need anybody around. If I wanted to get away from everybody, I'd go out and play in the backyard and no one would see me for hours. I had a lot of acquaintances, but there was very few real close friends.

In the early years, I was always an A student. The closer I got into the age of 12, 13, where you start thinking about girls, sports, vehicles and that, my grades seemed to falter. By the time I hit Grade 9, I noticed a big slip. I was struggling. Grade 10 I failed a couple of courses and had to take either summer school or come back and redo Grade 10.

Mom and dad kind of talked to me into going to summer school and I stayed with my grandmother and grandpa in Lethbridge and went to summer school at the Lethbridge Community College. Those courses just flew by. I had good marks in them. I came back the following year to take Grade 11 and my marks picked up again. I never had any problems after that. I graduated with a general diploma.

I played softball with my family as I was growing up. Any chance we had where the family got together, or softball tournaments, or something like that, I always played. I got into baseball in my Grade 12 year. I also played volleyball and basketball. I was into track and field a little bit. In my graduation year I ended up going to zones in Red Deer. I got beat out by a couple hundredths of a second for second spot, so I didn't go on, but I was pretty sports active.

The thing that gave me probably the most joy in life was always fighting for top spot on the teams that I did play on. And the second one, which my heart's still in today, is woodworking and cabinetry. At that time I was thinking of maybe a career in construction or cabinetry. Building houses and putting in cabinets and doing furniture. Since I've come to prison, I've learned how to carve and now I've put it together with my cabinetry and do hand carved furniture.

We do a lot of wall plaques, carvings out of wood. Basswood is the main source of wood we use. We're slowly working into mahogany and trying to work our way into carved furniture. Nobody seems to see any of that around these parts. There seems to be a lot of interest in it. We work in the mornings, afternoons, evenings. We've been kind of lucky, they allow us out there seven days a week, an average of nine hours a day. What we make is what we earn. We have to pay rent on the shop. We sell it through the Saskatchewan Penitentiary arts and crafts department and through family and friends. We can send stuff out to friends and family and they can resell it out there and send the money back. Or we can send it out C.O.D.

I would have been 18, 19, probably around '86, '87, when I first started getting my fingerprints in the books. I got a simple possession charge for drugs first and then an impaired driving. I didn't serve any time up until this charge here, convicted on second-degree murder. I was 20 years old.

I probably have to back up a few years, back to when I was 14, 15. I started drinking and partying with friends whenever I could get out of the house, away from mom and dad. Go stay at a friend's house or something. They'd have a small party if they were living in town. If they weren't, there'd be maybe four or five of us just drinking. About a year of that and I was introduced to marijuana. I started smoking marijuana and I enjoyed it. I could forget about everything. No troubles on my shoulders, nobody existed. It just slowly graduated up the ladder until I started taking acid and coke and heroin.

Next thing you know I'm getting into trouble. When I got that simple possession and impaired driving, I was kind of in the middle of selling drugs and it was hectic. I wasn't so much drunk, the alcohol itself was kind of a secondary drug, something to ease the dry throat of the other marijuana and smokeables, because you always get a dry throat when you're smoking that stuff.

As I graduated up the ladder into the heavier drugs, I started getting more and more aggressive. For a small guy like me, it's amazing I lived as long as I did, because I'd never learned to fight when I was a kid. I was a loner. I didn't want anybody around me. I didn't want any complications or anything like that. So the more aggressive I got, the more people started noticing me and started confronting me. So, I either had to put up or shut up.

There was an instance when I was engaged, we had broken up, me and my ex-fiancee, and I'd gone out with some other people to the bar. A couple of days later she showed up at the same bar and we started getting along again.

We went back to her place, just me and her, and we started getting friendly again and she tells me she slept with a couple of my best friends. So I went the next day and hunted them down and give one of them a punch and was looking for the other one. He was nowhere around. One of his friends, the guy I give a shot to, kind of started defending him, telling me a different story than what my ex was telling me. So I said: "OK, let's all meet at her place and let's straighten this out."

Well, the guy who was the friend of the guy that I give the shot to, kept giving me different stories. I knew what the true story was just by looking at my ex, 'cause I'd lived with her long enough and I knew when she was bullshittin' and when she wasn't.

I was getting into my truck to leave. I was sick and tired of it and didn't want any more to do with it. I knew that me and her were never going to get back together again. The guy reached in the truck and give me a shot. That was it, my fuse was burnt.

I went back home and changed. I was in dress clothes at the time, went back home, changed into a rough T-shirt and some sweats, came back and more or less beefed it out with him. I think he sprained his ankle and had a broken nose or something like that. It was a kind of run to the hospital repair job.

When I started winning these fights, this isn't so bad. People are going to give me some respect. Now that I've quit drugs and alcohol, that wasn't me. I don't know who that was. At the time, my head was clear. I knew what I had to do and nothing was going to stop me from doing it. Now that I look at it from a distance: why did I do that? Was it worth it?

I had taken baseball bats and a club and a knife to fights, but they were never used. That comes later.

I was living with the ex and I moved out to mom and dad's after we'd broken up. In-between the time I met her in the bar and got into that scrap with that one guy, I moved back into town to a kind of a dive. It was an old house. It had about five suites in it. It was only about $250 a month.

I started working at this plywood plant and I was making plywood, all different sizes and kinds. I got to know some of the guys working there and they were all drug users too, so we started hanging around together, me and this one guy, and we partied it up. That kind of went sour after a while, and I quit and went to work as an apprentice mechanic.

That didn't last too long. The drugs had kind of overtaken my life and I wasn't givin' my employer a fair shake at it. He was kind of a friend of the family's and I respected him enough to tell him: "Hey, I've got a problem. I can't seem to fight this lazy streak," is how I put it. I told him about the drugs and how they were taking over my life, that it was just useless for me to work there because I wasn't gettin' as much accomplished as what he shoulda had done. So he said, "OK, I'll give you your severance pay and we'll call it quits and go that way."

I'd gotten into dealing again. The money was great. I didn't have to work. I always had a pocketful of money. I could go out and party whenever I wanted to. I didn't have to be anywhere at any specific time. It kinda became the fast lane I guess they call it. And things just kept gettin' deeper and deeper. The stresses kept building up and building up, so I started taking more and more drugs just to get myself away from the problems and kinda put 'em on the back shelf, out of my mind. Out of sight, out of mind, you know. So you don't see the problems, they don't exist.

In order to do that, I kept taking more and more, my tolerance kept building up, but what I wasn't noticing at the same time was the people I was hangin' around with, their actions were rubbing off on me. The whole thing could have been a big dynamite can.

I'd been out partying a few nights. We went to a party in a different town. I got wasted. I didn't know what it was or what I was doing. I was drinking straight out of a 40 percent bottle, 26 ounce, takin' acid, I was in la la land. I didn't even know anybody that was there other than the guy I went with. He said I passed out.

I had my wallet stolen and shit like that and on the way back from the party the next morning, me and the driver of the other vehicle were kinda racing. I'm still out of it, cause' acid, the effects, last for quite a while.

Well, we're racing and we're coming up to this one corner that I normally wouldn't take at 80 miles an hour. Anything more than that and you're in trouble. I come into this corner at 120. Next thing I know, the truck's slidin' sideways and I'm bouncin' off the guardrail. Lucky for me it was a new guardrail.

I went back and looked later and there was about 10 posts broken off. I stopped at the bottom of the corner, looked for damage, and there was just one scrape along the side of the truck from where the posts from the guardrail were hittin' it. I just shook my head. I had four people with me in the truck. It just straightened me right out. I put these people's lives in danger just out of stupidity. That problem was chewin' at me too.

I'd started going out with a new girlfriend and things were going great. She took my mind off of everything. I'm still in contact with her today. She still seems to care for me and if she stays until I can get out, that's the woman I'll be with.

Like I say, things were great. Then one night my roommate, he was kinda dealing for me at the time, 'cause I was preoccupied with this woman, so he was doing most of the business. He was going to another party. He took most of my drugs and left me just with my personals.

He comes back the next morning, right out of it. "All the drugs got stolen," he says. Now I'm pissed off. There was probably about $3000 worth of drugs there. So I said, "OK, I'll make a few phone calls and see if anybody knows anybody that's bragging about stealing some dope, out selling it or having a good time with it and we'll try to find them."

I get a phone call the next afternoon saying "The guy has weed on him." Well my roommate's down at the bar playing pool with a few of his buddies gettin' all loaded on acid and that. Where he got the acid from I don't know, 'cause he said all the drugs were stolen. I never even give it a thought. I go back, pick him up at the bar and he's arguing with me then that we'll never find it. I says, "Well never mind, you're the one who stole it."

This guy says he's got a lead on it. We're going to go check it out. I pack him up from the bar, take him back home, get ready to go, pick up the weapons that are needed, which included a gun. He got pissed off at me just before we were ready to leave. Instead of hitting me, 'cause I knew he wanted to fight me, he turned around and hit our front door window.

He cut his wrist and it was a good cut. He was spurtin' blood all over. I went into the bathroom, just calmly, like nothin' ever happened, wet down a towel, came back, wrapped it around his wrist, and hightailed it to the hospital to get it looked at. I wasn't sure how serious it was. We get him into the emergency room and he calls me over to him. The nurses are trying to fight with him to get him to lay down, and he leans over to me and says, "Here, take my wallet."

And I says, "Why, all your identification is in there?"

He says, "Take my wallet." Right then I thought there was acid in there. I knew the cops were going to show up, 'cause any emergency like that they're always called in, so I grabbed his wallet and hightailed it out of there.

I take this acid with me. I think there was about 100 hits or something like that. I'm pissed off. I'm not feeling the effects of the drugs or anything anymore. I figure, "OK, I've gotta calm down," so I'm takin' about 20 hits of acid from this white blotter. You put it in your mouth and swallow it or you can hold it between your fingers and just the sweat off your fingers will absorb into the skin. There's a number of different ways of doing it. It seemed to calm me down. I could still think clearly and everything, I thought at the time. But when I look at it now, I wasn't thinking clearly at all.

I left for Lethbridge to meet up with this guy who said he had a lead on it. He takes me down to the local bar. I keep following him. He seems to know what he's doing, so I'm just playing along seeing where this is gonna lead. It's gettin' late in the night and he hasn't found out anything yet. I'm gettin' choked and more choked as the night goes on. I can see that he's not gettin' anywhere. I finally get flustered.

There were a couple of guys who said they could get some oil at the time. That was part of the parcel that was lost. It's more or less like a fermented pot, it's mixed with a few different chemicals, melted down and cooked.

So we take this guy and he's going to take us to his cousin's place. He goes in, and for some reason, things aren't strikin' right, so I turn my head and talk to the guy I was with and says: "He's not comin' back out. We're gettin' burnt here." He reaches under the seat and grabs the gun and I pull out the knife. I'm still behind the wheel of the truck, and he goes up and knocks on the door. This guy comes out and says, "OK, let's go try a different place. These guys don't have any more." What the story was inside I don't know, 'cause neither one of us went in.

For some reason, as we pulled out of the parking lot, or the driveway, I got this mean urge in me. I don't know if I knew I was being storied, or whether I was just frustrated from not finding anything out that night or what. I put the knife to the guy's side and says, "Hey look, let's quit f——in' around here." The guy I was with, he pulls out the gun and more or less holds the guy where he's at and starts askin' him questions while I'm drivin' off down this back road. We pull over and the guy I was with pulls him out, smacks him around a couple of times and keeps askin' him, but this guy isn't answering. Whether he didn't know anything or what, I don't know.

We seemed satisfied with the answer at the time. He seemed to think he might know where somebody else is that has some oil that we could check out, to see if it was ours. You get differences between batches, so you get to know what's yours and what isn't.

So we go to the bar. It's closing time. We go in, and on the way in, 'cause we had beaten this guy up and was askin' him questions, and maybe he felt his life was in danger at that point, we told him, "Hey, we're going in to pick up some off-sales, you alert anybody to what's happening here, we're gonna dump you." It was just a threat at the time, to keep him shut, so he's not warning somebody else that we're on our way to look for these drugs. He goes in, buys the off-sales, comes back out. There was no problems.

I can't remember where we were headed, it was in the north part of Lethbridge, and just out of the blue I got pissed off again. Whether I thought this guy was giving me a bum steer or what, I don't know, but we took off into the country again. He says, "Well, where you goin'?"

I says, "Oh, let's go drink some beer first and we'll talk about how we're gonna approach this next." We're sittin' in the truck. We have to get out of the truck to get the beer, 'cause it's in the back. I wasn't gonna allow beer in the front of my truck anymore after that impaired. We all get out and grab a beer. The guy I was with grabs one for me, grabs one for himself and he's gonna go hand the other guy a beer and I says: "No! He doesn't get one."

The guy I was with says, "Well, why?"

I says, "He hasn't answered what we want to know yet."

From there, knocked him around a bit more and got him laying down in the ditch from where we were parked. We're beatin' him around, kickin' him, hittin' him in the head and pokin' him, just more or less rough-housing him, trying to get some answers out of him. It seemed useless. We weren't goin' anywhere. Whether he didn't know, I don't know. We'll never know, I guess, cause' he's not around anymore.

He just wasn't givin' the answers that we wanted and the guy I was with says, "Well, what should we do with him?" I started thinking right away, what's gonna happen when this guy goes back after the shit-kickin' he's taken tonight and brings the rest of his people into it? We don't have enough firepower to hold off a whole gang of people. I was wondering. I dealt with myself and a few other people that I had for suppliers. If one person didn't have some I'd go to another one and buy theirs, so I'm thinkin' to myself, "Hey, we have to resolve this. How we gonna do this?"

I asked him, "If we let you go what's gonna happen?"

He says, "Nothin', nothin'."

Well, just the quiver in his voice or whatever, I guess the guy I was with picked up on it and says, "He's gonna go back and tell his friends and they're gonna come back and look for us."

I says, "Well, what do we do?"

"We could always shoot him."

As soon as he said that, I don't know if he was joking or whether it was just something to scare this guy or what, but as soon as he said we could always kill him, just, right there, in front of my eyes, I didn't think of anything else. Nothin' else existed. Like, the guy I was with, he was no longer there. I had one thing set in my mind. I've gotta save myself, give a warning out to other people that, hey, you don't f——with me.

I went back to the truck, pulled out the gun, loaded it and came back. The guy said something to me, the guy on the ground says: "No, don't. No, don't." And I just put the gun to the back of his head and pulled the trigger.

It didn't blow off. With the gun being so close or whatever, or me being so out of it, it was almost like an airgun sound and that was it. I can't remember if they were solid tip or hollow tip, but the bullet went in and just shattered. It was a .22 rifle.

We pulled him down into the ditch, put the gun underneath the seat of the truck, got in and drove away.

I never opened a beer until we got back to the guy I was with's place. I really can't remember if we talked. I don't think so. I remember it seemed like a long drive.

We just left him where he was at. Once we got back to his place, we sat down and had a beer. He started talking to me and says, "You know, we killed somebody."

And I says, "Yeah."

He says, "Well what are we gonna do now?"

I says, "What do you mean what are we gonna do now?"

He says, "Well we can't just leave him there. What are we gonna do with the gun?"

I says, "Well we can go bury him and bury the gun. Sooner or later somebody's going to find out."

We drove back out there about a couple of hours later to try and find him, but whether I was so wasted, we couldn't find him. We're startin' to think here, what are we gonna do with the gun now? So we think, OK, we'll bury the gun and see what happens from there. We'll just leave everything else the way it is, hear how things go.

I dropped him off at his place after we buried the gun and I drove home. Got home, took the shovel out of the back of my truck and put it into the guy's truck who was staying with us at the time, went in to bed, laid down and went to sleep.

I slept like nothin' had ever happened. There's some times when I think about it now that I have trouble sleeping.

At the time, I don't think I had been sober for two or three months. I was on a constant binge. I'd wake up in the morning. I'd usually either have some joints rolled up in my cigarette package, or if I didn't, I'd roll one up right away and have it before I even crawled out of bed. So what I was thinkin' about when I first woke up was never there any longer than five minutes. I completely forgot about the killing for about a week.

It didn't exist. Then what sparked my interest again was when they found the body. Up until they found the body it was a fantasy. It was one of my dreams.

I didn't talk with the other guy until after they'd found the body. It was about a week later. It was in the news and in the papers and on the radio that an investigation was underway. I knew the guy I was with that night was gonna be in town. I drove over to a place where I knew he was gonna be and approached him, "Hey, what's gonna happen here?"

He says, "I don't know. I don't think they found out anything yet."

I says, "Well they found the body. There's been no report of them finding the gun or anything. What if they match up the tire prints from the scene with the tires I got on my truck right now?"

He starts thinkin' about it. "I don't know. Did we leave any tire marks?" I can't remember. He says, "Maybe we better change the tires."

I reached in my pocket, I didn't have enough money at the time, and says "I need some money. I gotta go to Calgary and see someone there and I'll change the tires in Calgary so there's nowhere around town in the area that are gonna see this receipt."

I went down there. It seemed like nobody was the wiser, but I was on edge. I knew I f——ed up.

About a week after they found the body, I tried to clean myself up. Go cold turkey on the drugs, try to be a respectable citizen again, to try to draw off any heat that might be coming my way. Well, there was enough people that night that had seen us that we were automatically under investigation.

They couldn't prove that we were there, but they'd seen us with that guy earlier that night. They knew we were looking for drugs and so whether the police had put two and two together, and were just looking for the proof, I started noticing that people were following me. I always felt watched and it was just driving the hell out of me.

Finally, about a month almost to the day, I broke down. I dug into an old stash I had, got loaded, went out to my parents' place, and I was planning on just up and moving, taking off, just get away from everybody. I got to their place and they noticed the condition I was in. I guess I was shaking and everything and things were built up to the point where I was about to explode again. They started asking me questions. For the condition I was in, whether I didn't think about who I was talking to or whatever, I felt secure with them. I started telling them that I know about this murder. I didn't tell them that I did it, but I told them that I knew about this murder.

Mom and Dad were looking at me and they could see I'm shaking, so they started feeding me alcohol to try and calm me down. I think it was rye or something and rye doesn't agree with me to start with, so I started getting on the fight, and my Dad phones the police and asks them to come in.

At the time, I never thought about my Dad calling the police. I wasn't thinkin' clearly. I had just taken, I can't even remember how many hits of acid, and then Mom and Dad start feeding me some rye. I was out to lunch.

The police come and pull me up and Dad tells them what I've told him and they pull me into their police station, put me in an interview room and start questioning me. This was in Fort Macleod.

I guess I was scared or whatever, I don't know. I started giving them bullshit stories about how I'd seen this, but wasn't the responsible party. Like I'm right out of it. I don't know whether they know I'm bullshitting or whether they just don't believe me because I'm so loaded. They leave the room for a bit. I think I was talking to my Dad or something for a few minutes and he said that I had a lawyer coming.

They came back and arrested me for first-degree murder, and locked me up. They put an undercover cop in with me. He tried to find out what I was there for and that, but I didn't know this guy from Adam and I wasn't talkin' to him. I guess they did the same thing with the guy I was involved with and from what I understand and from what I've seen, he told them. I'm trying to remember his exact words. "We snuffed him," I think is what it was. Right there was all the evidence they needed. I guess he'd even drawn out a map where the gun was buried. He didn't know that he was talking to an undercover. I don't know whether he was scared or on drugs himself and didn't know what he was doin', but right there I knew we weren't gettin' out.

They arraigned me about a week later. I sat on remand while my lawyer built his case. You know, I even lied to him. I was just so scared of the results, how long I was going to be behind bars from what other people had been talking about, that I didn't even tell him the truth.

I got life 15, second-degree murder. It was a combination of different feelings. My lawyer prepared me a couple of weeks before I'd gone up for it, that, "Hey, this is what's gonna happen." I'd been thinking about it for a while. When I walked into the courtroom, the day that I was sentenced, sat down on the bench, prosecutor gave his statement and what he recommended for time, my lawyer presented his case and what he was hoping for. When the judge finally made his ruling, in a way it was almost relief. In another way it was: "Holy shit! How am I gonna survive this? What have I done to my family? What have I done to my friends? What have I done to people who shouldn't have been involved to start with?"

I never screamed. It was kind of, as I said, a relief in one way, because I knew it was finally over, and justice was done. I guess justice wasn't done because the victim's family probably would have liked to see me dead. I can't remember if there were tears coming down or I was just hanging my head in real sorrow, because I realized this is it. I'm going to jail. How am I going to handle this?

I can remember walking out of the courtroom, and whether it was one of the victim's family, or a friend, I'm not sure, yelled over the box, and said something to the effect: "You don't deserve to live."

And I looked at him and said, "I'm sorry." That's when I left the courtroom. I think I was through the door at that time. I went back to the holding cell and I just sat there. I can remember wantin' to break down, needing to break down, but I couldn't. Whether it was pride or shock or what, I don't know. And that stayed with me for a couple of weeks while they were tryin' to get ready to transfer me.

It got to the point where the doctors and nurses knew there was something wrong, and psychologists I guess, but they didn't know what it was. They figured maybe I was suicidal or whatever. They put me on some medication that just knocked me on my ass. It was almost like going back to the drug days. I had been straight for just about a year, waitin' to go to court and trial and all that, then they give me these drugs and, Holy Christ! It was probably then that I noticed that,

"Hey, I can't take these anymore." I was already startin' to feel aggressive. I quit takin' them. Then they transferred me up here.

I'd kinda heard stories goin' through remand. Waitin' to be Pen placed. I heard stories about people who are gay and they muscle you for sex and they beat you up for your money and more or less it's a violent jail. What people wanted they took. I'm having thoughts about this as here I am, 160, 165 pounds, walking into a prison that probably has 200, 250 people. I was scared. I really was.

When I first got here they put me down in segregation for a couple of weeks. I'm not really sure why. Whether it was just to observe me or find out who I was or why I was here or what. I'm not sure. Maybe they sensed a fear or just wanted to get me by myself for a while, let me adjust slowly. You're locked in your cell basically 23 hours a day. You get fed through the doors. They got a little opening in the doors that they bring meals to. At 7 o'clock every morning you get up and have your breakfast. Right after breakfast, they bring a mop and a broom around. You get a mop and sweep your house.

You've gotta scream more or less to the guy next to you. In order to do that, you know everybody else is gonna hear you, so a lot of the times, you just throw your headphones on and listen to the radio and just write your letters and ignore everybody else.

The first night I was here I was wondering about how my family was going to take this. I was eight hours away from where they lived. They're not going to be able to visit me once a month, three or four times a year, 'cause that's a long drive for someone gettin' up in their years to drive just to see somebody. I was wondering if my friends were going to leave me and what they thought of me. Basically, just what everybody thought of me. How it was going to affect them, and whether they were still gonna remain in contact with me or whether I was there by myself. No one to fight for me but myself.

Finally I got ornery down in segregation and told them, "Hey, why am I here? Put me out in population, so if there are any people here who want to deal with me, here I am." It was kinda what they call the fish range. It's kinda like orientation, where you get to know what's in the institution, where things are, what's expected of you. It's more or less one step away from main population. It's just to familiarize you with how things are operated.

I didn't mind that. It was a chance. You got out of your cell probably about four hours a day and you could move around and associate with different people. Get to know a few people and go out for exercise. It wasn't too bad. Then about a week into that, they took us around to the various shops you can work at and gave us a list of programs available in this institution.

When they were doin' their tour of the shops, when I came across the carpentry shop which is my love and joy, that was enough for me. I didn't need to know about anything else. They came back, we filled out employment forms for the work board and I says, "Hey, this is where I want to work."

They says, "Well you're going to have to wait to go through the work board." They open the doors at about 1 o'clock, to do your exercise, running around, see whoever you have to see. You come back and then lock up. I went straight out to the carpentry shop, did kind of an interview with the shop instructor. It wasn't really the way you go about it but I was determined to get in there. I was gonna go to him before he seen my name on a list and wondered who the hell is this guy. I was gonna go and see him and explain to him what I've done in the past, on the street, and through school. He says, "OK, you start Monday." This was about a Thursday, so I'd actually started working before I went before the work board. How much these guys appreciated that, I don't know.

When I first moved into population, what shocked me the most is how fictitious the stories that I'd heard were. I'm sure there are people who are gay and do their own thing. They don't bother anybody else, they don't harass anybody else. They don't try to pick up other people. They know who they are and they do their own thing.

As far as muscling and that, I've never seen anybody in here muscled unless they absolutely deserved it. Like a guy says, "OK, shark me this much money and I'll pay you this much back." Payday comes around. "Well, no, I can't pay you back. I never got paid. I'm waitin' for this guy to pay me." Sometimes the guy will just let it go and wait for another payday and just add the interest on. The next time the guy comes around, "Oh, no, I can't pay you this, I can't do that," then that's the only time I've ever seen anybody muscled. And the guy took his lickin' and that's it. It was over.

I can't say that I haven't seen drugs, 'cause you see a few people, you know the symptoms and that. But I can't say that I've ever seen anybody outright use it other than myself. I dibbled and dabbled when I first got here, because just the stress buildup from first arriving, not knowing anybody, not knowing who to trust. A guy offered a couple of joints and I took 'em and smoked them. It seemed to ease me into prison life, let me get a different outlook on the people who are here.

It's been about two years since I've even touched drugs. And two years ago, I maybe used it once and hadn't used it for a year before that. I finally come to the decision that if I ever want out, I can't do this anymore. They're gonna start doin' random urine samples and if I get caught with a bad sample, where's that gonna put me? I've got seven years in now and I'm just about over the halfway hump where parole eligibility is up. If I get caught now, where's that gonna put me? It's not worth it.

The worst times in here are probably around Christmas. Our family was close-knit. We always got together for Christmas, have our own little party, family reunion type thing for just the immediate family. Christmas morning we'd all open up gifts. I can't say I've ever felt closer to anybody than my family. Even though I was out of it half the time, I always looked forward to those times.

My family has been very supportive. I gotta give them credit. They've been there for me. Whenever I'm feeling down I give them a call. They help me sell my work, look for different opportunities for me and come out and visit me three or four times a year. It's way more than I ever expected. I owe them a lot. More than I could probably ever repay. They help me keep clear headed.

I know what I would like to do when I get out, but I don't know whether it will be available for me to do. I'd like to start my own cabinetry business where you do custom carved cabinets. You don't see that around very often. It's an area I really enjoy working at and I'd like to have my own business. I've got probably another eight years to go to try to build towards that goal. But are trees going to be around when I get out? Is lumber going to be accessible? With the environment out there today, who knows?

The only thing I could probably think of right now that would have made a big difference in my life and maybe others would have been alcohol and drug education – about the effects, what it does to people, how they react on it. Basically, educate me: either during, while I was using, or just before. They got a program in here called addictions education. It's not a real well-presented course, but the information in that course, if you want to sit down and look at it, is invaluable. Going through it now and seeing how similar the reactions are between what's in the information and your own life you can see it. You can put yourself in that spot exactly. You can recall maybe a dozen instances on the effect.

One effect they mention in this course is how you hurt your family and friends.

The Judge Said 60 Years

Rodney Munro

*"How I was figuring it was, I'm going to jail for the rest of my life.
I couldn't see doing 60 years without picking up more time somewhere
for something. With the type of mentality that's in the prison systems,
somebody gets into your face you've got to deal with it. Whether it's
right or wrong is not the point, 'cause this is a different society than
what's out on the street. Out there you can turn and walk away from
it. In here you can't. You have to deal with it, and some of the people in
here, there's only one way you can deal with them, and that's head on."*

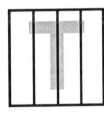he rate of imprisonment per 100 000 population is 130
in Canada, 368 in South Africa, 529 in the United
States and 558 in Russia. Spain, New Zealand, the
United Kingdom, Italy, France, Australia and Germany range from a high of 115 to 81. At the lower end
of the incarceration scale are the Netherlands (51),
Norway (60), Finland (62), Sweden (68) and Denmark
(71).

In Canada, substance abuse, as you have come to learn and will
ponder even further, has been directly linked to the majority of those
sent to jail.

In January 1995, relatives of two cousins senselessly murdered in
Montana released an impact statement asking for the death penalty
to be carried out on Ronald Smith, 37, of Red Deer. He had been
resigned to such a fate a dozen years earlier, when he confessed and
asked to die for the August 1982 kidnapping and killing of Harvey
Mad Man Jr., 24, and Thomas Running Rabbit, 20. His wish was
granted. Later, he changed his mind, forcing a continued legal battle,
with his life hanging in the balance.

Six foot, 200 pound Rodney James Munro, born October 24, 1956,
was there for the abduction and double killing. In telling his story, he
has admitted that it was him – not his partner, Ronald Smith – who
murdered one of the victims. With his eight tattoos, shoulder length

brown hair, and eyes of the same color, now very clear, he minds his business, does his time, and waits for the day he might be able to leave the confines of the Canadian penitentiary that has become home. His warrant expiry date: 2042.

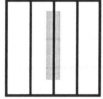knew sooner or later I would pick up some time somewhere. I didn't quite expect 60 years and I never thought I'd end up facing the death penalty. It just never occurred to me. I figured I might pick up, I don't know, maybe five years somewhere down the line, but for what I was doin' at the time, what's five years? Well, I'm doin' 60 now. It's a different outlook.

If I could change things I'd change them in a heartbeat, but I can't. It's just something I have to live with, but if there's just one kid out there who can take something from any of this, any part of this book, and just make them stop and think, then to me it's worth it, just keepin' any kid outta here. If just my saying something will help keep one kid out of jail, I think it's worth it. This is not the place to be.

I'm in my 13th year. Each prison is different. Some prisons are actually quite laid back, nothing happens. Other prisons you've got people stabbin' other people over silly things like gambling debts, if they borrow money and don't really want to pay it back. I've seen guys hang themselves just 'cause they're tired of doing time. So each joint, prison, is different.

If you get caught up in all the games that happen in here, you've got no choice but to play the games and that includes the violence part of it. When I first went down there was some of it.

If someone's just coming to prison they can expect some hard times. When you first come in you will have people pickin' on you, basically because you are young, you don't know the rules of the games. So you do get picked on. It's that simple with every place.

Your best bet is don't associate too closely with anybody, and if somebody does start to play the game, you put your foot down right away. You may have to take a beating for it, but if you do it and you do it fast, just don't take the crap from people, they just leave you alone after a while and then you're fine from that point on.

Another good bet is you just don't say nothing about anything. Once the other inmates realize that's the way you are, that solves half the problem right there.

Rodney Munro –
"I actually think
about the victims
quite a lot. I've
woken up with
lumps on my
knees from hitting
the wall. Other
than that, always
during the day is
when I'll think
about it. At least
once a day the
whole thing kinda
goes through my
head."

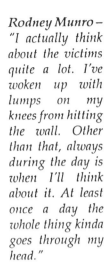

Prison life sucks. You can't do anything. I guess some people can take it differently. For some people, this is better than wherever they've ever been. For me, well, it probably was the best thing that happened, but it's not the life I want for myself.

When I first came in, every time I turned around it was charges. Somebody told me what to do and I basically said, "F—- you," you know. About the first five years, I was always in and out of the hole. For threatening officers and for what they call "causing riots," to pickin' on protective custody cases to just pickin' on people.

A lot of it is frustration. A lot of it is to get what you want. A lot of it is just bucking the system. When you first come down, especially doin' the type of time I am, you've got nothin' to lose. I mean, where're you goin'? This is it. I'm doin' 60 years.

I was involved in killing a couple of guys. A bunch of us were out partyin' and myself and my fall partner* took a 100-lot of acid, just spread it in half and did 50 hits apiece. Somewhere between when we did it, and hell broke loose, exactly what triggered it, to this day, I'm not really sure. I got the feeling somebody said something and then just being that high it just seemed to roll around in a guy's head until it happened.

We were just partying down through the States and all hell broke loose and a couple of guys ended up dead. Both of them had a bullet hole in the head and one was stabbed. I was the stabber. The one who was stabbed, in my opinion, was basically dead before he was shot. The shot was just to make sure.

I was 25 at the time.

I was born in Williams Lake, British Columbia, but the first place I remember would be Rocky Mountain House, Alberta. It was actually quite fun there. It was a small town and I was there for about seven years.

My sister and I never did seem to ever get along. As for my parents, we got along fairly well. I mean, I got the belt the odd time or two, but other than that I always thought it was normal.

I sorta got into trouble for climbing water towers. Just kids' antics, I guess, would be the best way of putting it. I didn't really play much sports. I was born with a hole in my heart so for the longest time I wasn't allowed sports, 'cause every time I did I ended up with nosebleeds and stuff like this. I used to just ride my bike a lot. I only had one or two friends. That would be about it.

When I first went to school I thought it was great. To me it was just a big kindergarten. By the time I hit Grade 3 they said: "No, no, no. It's no kindergarten. You have to work here." I didn't like that, so I ended up failing Grade 3 and then it was just mediocre grades from that point on.

From Rocky I went to Hinton for about a year. When I was there, I ended up getting the strap quite often in school. Just stupid stuff, not paying attention, stuff like that. From there I went to Grande Prairie for about seven years and that's basically where all hell started breaking loose.

---

*The term fall partner refers to Ronald Smith. It is prison slang which means a cohort in crime who becomes a scapegoat. He takes the blame that should fall on others.

I'd been doin' drugs, smokin' pot. I started that, oh man, I think I was still just a kid. I don't even think I was in my teens when I first started doin' chemicals. By the time I hit Grande Prairie, certain actions started coming out in me, ignoring what people were tellin' me, just doin' whatever I wanted when I wanted.

I used to run away when I was a kid, but I'd always leave for a while and come back home for a while. Split for a while and come back home. I always wanted to see what was around the next corner. Once I knew everything that was around me, I was more interested in what I didn't know in the horizon than where I was at.

I got busted for possession of drugs a couple of times, ended up on probation for failing to appear in court. I think legally I was kicked out of Grande Prairie for a couple of years. The authorities really didn't want me there, so I kinda started all over the place. I'd come back once in a while and see how everybody was doing.

I was selling drugs. It kept me high. I had enough money to party with, to live with, pay my rent with. That was with me right up until I got busted.

If I needed extra money I'd go find a job somewhere. I worked in sawmills. I drove truck, worked for a landscaper a little bit, labor jobs, just whatever.

I ended up getting married and we moved up to Fairview for a while, but for some reason or another things didn't quite work out. I was given a suspended sentence for theft under $200, and we ended up in Red Deer. I have two children, a boy and a girl.

Once in Red Deer it became one big party. Finally, the family just couldn't handle it anymore, so they went their way and I just kept doing my thing.

At that particular time, it's hard to describe your whole way of thinking. The constant partyin', drugs, alcohol, sort of starts to warp your way of thinking and the way you feel. You still know what the hell you're doin', but as for consequences of your actions, it just doesn't seem to matter that much.

When the family left, it just became even a bigger party. I could open my fridge and cupboards and there was nothin' in there but booze and drugs. The freezer was oil, acid. It was just everything.

Drugs paid whatever habit I was doin'. Between the drugs and the booze, I was spending a lot of money. It paid my rent, my groceries, utilities, phone bills. It paid everything.

I wanted to be somewhere around the kids and the ex a little bit, so I moved to a small town in B.C. for a while, but that didn't really go over too well. I got convicted of impaired driving. I went back to Red Deer and then she and the kids moved off and I just partied.

By '82, about a year after my family left me, I basically just didn't care. I didn't care whether I hurt somebody. I didn't care whether I got hurt. I didn't care whether I was here, there, lived, died. It just didn't matter. All that mattered was to get high and whatever happened, happened.

Myself and my fall partner decided to go down through the States: see the States; party, travel, see what it was like. My fall partner, that's what I call the guy that did the crime and is doin' time right along, basically, with me, only he's still down in Montana.

We were just hitchhiking along and they happened to pick us up. Like I said earlier, I'm not exactly sure what triggered what. We were goin' down the road and things just unfolded. The gun and the knife come out and it was like, "Pull over." And we took 'em off into the woods and bang, that was the end of it.

There wasn't any real feeling there. Every time it comes into my head I can see it, I can picture it, and I get the same feeling that I had then. It's kinda like nothing's there. I know that sounds hard to understand, to hear, but being that high you don't have the type of feelings that you would have if you were straight. It's real hard to explain.

It would have had to have been just a couple of days later when I was arrested on suspicion of an armed robbery in California. Everything kinda went from there. I got arrested, they dropped that, and then the FBI picked up the Dire Act, which is interstate transportation of a stolen vehicle. From there, they shipped me back to Montana and they dropped that and the state of Montana charged me with two counts of murder, two counts of aggravated kidnapping and they were trying for the death penalty at the time.

When you're sittin' in jail and these guys are tryin' to execute you, you kinda like, "Well, this sucks. I don't want this." So I escaped. I tied up the one jailer and my fall partner and I escaped and we got to about the edge of town before we got caught.

We were brought back to the jail. My fall partner went to court before I did, and he walked in and he said he shot both guys and to kill him. He asked for the death penalty and they dropped the murder charges against me. All I ended up on were the two original aggravated kidnappings, aggravated kidnapping for when I tied up the guard, escape, and the use of a dangerous weapon, which was the knife used in the crime.

When I was sentenced, I felt relief. At one point, you're lookin' at four, five counts of the death penalty, then they turn around and drop some of that, but the state is still asking for 100 and some years. The judge said 60 years. Thank you judge.

How I was figuring it was, I'm going to jail for the rest of my life. I couldn't see doing 60 years without picking up more time somewhere for something. With the type of mentality that's in the prison systems, somebody gets into your face you've got to deal with it. Whether it's right or wrong is not the point, 'cause this is a different society than what's out on the street. Out there you can turn and walk away from it. In here you can't. You have to deal with it, and some of the people in here, there's only one way you can deal with them, and that's head on.

I was in the state prison at Deer Lodge, Montana. Their max is total lock up, 23 hours a day you're in your house. They feed you in your cell, you get an hour yard. They run it about 7 o'clock in the morning, so in the wintertime you don't feel like going out and freezing or nothing, so basically you're in your house constantly. That's the setting you're in.

I was in that lock-up situation for pretty close to six years. Then they moved me out to what they called their medium, which is you get yard in the afternoon and again at night. It's a bigger yard, you're around more people.

It took me seven years before I was finally able to transfer back to Canada. I had to apply for it. It took a while to get it through the State Legislature. It had to go through their State Government, their Federal Government and then the government up here.

I got the word in '89. I think I had my stuff packed in a matter of no time. It was putting my stuff in a wheelbarrow and out we go.

When I come across the border it was back east in Ontario. I spent two weeks in the hole at Kent and then from there I went to the SHU here in Prince Albert.

I kinda had to laugh, 'cause on the plane out here the guards are all saying, "You're goin' to the SHU. It's the worst place you can be in Canada." When I got there I had more freedom than I had down in the States. The cells were a lot bigger, you got to go to the gym, the yard, and after you're in the SHU for a while you even get to eat your meals with other inmates. I mean, great.

You tend to meet a lot of interesting people no matter where you are in here. Some of them are a little off the wall, but some of them are OK. You can deal with most people.

I spent a year there and was told I either stay in the SHU or I get to come to Sask Pen. So I said, "Okay, I'll come here."

When I first went down it was just day by day. Once I finally got back to Canada and I knew that somewhere down the line I might have a chance at a parole, then it kind of stretched into not just day by day, but what might be. What I might be able to do. Now with my kids startin' to write to me and my ex writing to me and being polite, I'm a little more hopeful that I just might be able to straighten my whole life out, which would be nice, 'cause I'm tired of it. I'm tired of the games. I'm tired of time. I'm tired of the drugs, the booze, the whole thing. And that's what keeps me going.

If the individual changes and wants to change, he will change. If they don't, they never will. That works in any system. It's a matter of time. Time will change you. I know I've changed. Whether it's for the better or for the worse, in most respects I have to say for the better, but for the overall view, I won't know until I actually get out.

I've been eligible for parole since about '90. I figure I'm still looking at another five to 10 before they seriously start thinkin' about it. It's gonna be hard, because the longer you're in, the harder it is to get back into society, because so much passes you by. It's a sudden culture shock.

If I look out through the fence and cars go by, I can't even tell what cars are what anymore. My kids have grown up to the point where I really don't know who they are. I'm just starting to communicate with them. They're 15, 16. We're just starting to get to know each other.

I haven't even seen the kids since I've come down. The last time I had a visitor was pretty close to a year ago, I guess. It was a woman who was writing to me from Edmonton, but she got a boyfriend and her boyfriend didn't like it, so that ended that.

I get to write to my fall partner. The warden said it was all right. We write back and forth. This way we can both try to help each other out because we both know what we went through and I just want to keep in contact with him, see how he's doin', makin' out. Other than that about the only other people I write to is his sister, his mom, and now my ex and my kids and that's it.

I don't think my fall partner wants the death penalty. I think he did that so that I might at least have a chance of getting out some time rather than both of us being in, period. At least that's my way of thinking about it.

Given the choice, I'd go for the 60 years. At least I've got a chance to try to make some type of a life for myself even if it is just a small, bit of a life. I never would have known I could carve if I would have gotten the death penalty and I find the greatest satisfaction in just sitting down and carving something.

I was seriously out of control. There's no doubt in my mind, between the drugs, the alcohol, the way I was thinking, the way I was feeling, it was just way out of control. I'm surprised I'm even alive, 'cause if I hadn't been arrested, either I'd be dead from an OD somewhere, or the cops probably would have ended up shooting me.

The worst thing about being in prison is watching the waste. There's a lot of talented people in here, if they would ever stop and use their talents, but they don't. Some people will use it when they're in here, but as soon as they hit the street it's gone. They start drinkin' again and this and that, and what I find real hard is that a lot of people just don't learn from being in prison. Sometimes it's just like a vacation to them, in and out, in and out. They just don't learn.

The first thing I want to do when I get out is hug my kids, if that's ever possible. Only time will tell. Other than that, I want to get on with my life. I want to find a job somewhere, because I want to set up my own little workshop in my backyard, so I can continue with my carving and make carved furniture. You don't see it anymore today, anywhere out on the street. I think it will help keep me out of trouble, 'cause it takes a lot of work and a lot of time to do it.

Crooks have been romanticized too much, I'm afraid. Kids will find this life vastly different from what they think it is, and a lot of them won't like it. Some kids may think they're tough enough, but I've seen some of the toughest people end up doin' themselves in, 'cause they just couldn't handle it. I think they ought to just stop and really do some hard thinking. The drugs and the partying becomes a lifestyle. Once it becomes that, it's hard to quit, so they best be careful.

I'm president of the lifers' group right now. We're just trying to get it organized. There's a couple of things behind it. One is to try to make the lifers, guys who are doing life, ease into the system to where they understand this is it for them, or at least for a lot of them. This is home. It's to get them to adjust mentally, to get themselves into a routine where they're not havin' to play the games. Once you start on those games, it's a rough road to hoe.

To try to help out in any way we can, we have a goal, or at least I think we do. I have to bring it up at the next meeting, but I would like to try to find a way of helping some of the kids on the street. They do have a children's aid downtown here. If we can find some way of maybe helping to support them or some charity like that, because kids are the most precious thing we've got, and if we can do anything to help keep them from getting into places like this, I'm all for it.

I actually think about the victims quite a lot. I've woken up with lumps on my knees from hitting the wall. Other than that, always during the day is when I'll think about it. At least once a day the whole thing kinda goes through my head. Sometimes it's just a quick flash. Other times something will be shown on TV or something and the whole thing just plays like a film. I'd have to say pretty close to about once a day. It would be just like the whole thing was put on film, just going through my head.

There was no really crying out. Actually, quite simply, the silence of it all. There wasn't any real crying out or pleading or anything, just a lot of silence.

I've Seen Guys Die Here

Ed McLean

"I watched them drag a guy, a kid by the name of Robertson, all because he wouldn't bring a can of thinners into the guys to sniff. They waited until he got showered and then they stabbed him in the heart, the chest and threw him out. I saw them pull him out on a carpet and the kid that was standing beside me, in fact Eddy was his name too. I said: 'That kid's dead. He won't live. He's finished.'"

It has been said, with much certainty, that the only sure things in life are death and taxes. Let the record show there are at least two more absolutes: child maltreatment is an enormous problem; and there is never enough time, unless you're serving it.

Ed McLean, 45, knows much about all of the above. He was beaten as a child, as an adult, he slit a man's throat, and in total has been locked up longer than he has known freedom.

Ed McLean blames no one but himself for his actions, even though some might say he easily could. From childhood, his life of crime was destined, his days of freedom doomed.

This is a man with a criminal record that may be longer than both your arms, lengthier than that of any other offender in this book. He has served time in BC Pen, Dorchester, Kent, Renous, and a lot of other lock-ups along the way. From the Saskatchewan Penitentiary, this is his story.

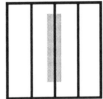was transferred from Renous Penitentiary here. First I was transferred from Renous to RPC (Regional Psychiatric Centre) on the condition that if I went to RPC they would send me to a medium, because I'd been in a maximum for almost 13 years. They sent me to RPC in Saskatoon. Then after they done what they wanted me to do, they were going to send me back to Renous, so I was sent here to be held to be sent back. Held on A1 block here in this prison. It was up to this prison whether they sent me back to Renous or not. I gave warden Jim O'Sullivan a letter. I said: "I'd like to stay here in this Prairie, because I was born in Saskatoon and if I go up to Renous I have no way of getting out of prison. I have no family. I have no friends. Everybody's against me up there." He allowed me to stay.

Renous is the end of the world penitentiary. It was originally built to double maximum security for all lifers, and me, doing 25 years and double life. It's way up by New Brunswick, way out in the end of the bush there. It's a very secluded penitentiary. It's a forgotten warehouse. Once you enter it, you're there for 25, 30 years, before you go up for parole. Most guys anyways, because they're all lifers. They send a lot of the guys from the SHUs there, to get rid of them, hide them, so nobody knows who they are.

I was born in Saskatoon on June 9, 1950. My mother and myself and one sister and two brothers moved to Fox Valley, Saskatchewan. I was very small, so I'm not sure what went on.

I was about five years old when I walked into a house that my brother had broken into and I stole some stuff. That's when my career in stealing started, pretty well then. Some ties and clothes and whatnot. I remember getting beat up, punished. I was punished for it, but not my brother.

Then my brothers left home and there was just my sister and my mother. We lived in a very old house. I remember us putting pots on the floor to catch the rain as it was coming through the roof. We were very poor people.

Then we moved back to Saskatoon. I was about six. I don't remember much of my childhood, because there was a lot of beatin's and I couldn't remember too much of that.

I think some of 'em was my mother, but I had a vision that somebody else beat me and it was a man. I had my arms up protecting my face, so there was a man there that was beatin' me and I don't know who he is.

I didn't have a dad in the household. My mom would meet the odd man and they'd have an affair and he might stay with her for a while. She picked and choosed who she lived with. By the time I was seven years old, I was livin' at 511 Albert Avenue in Saskatoon. I was stealing out of stores, pretty well doing my own thing. My mom was a maid. She had room-and-boarders in the house. I was left alone most of the time.

I'd steal a little beer. I think one time when I was caught stealing beer out of a CNR train, my cousin and I, he was around six years old, we went to some criminal court for that in the YMCA in Saskatoon. An army court, I think it was, because all I remember is brown uniforms. Then I was sent home. I got a dirty beatin' for that one.

I was introduced to drugs by a psychiatrist. They found me in a basement. I was foolin' around. They thought I was trying to hang myself, so they sent me to the University of Saskatoon Hospital to take tests. They give me Valium, so Valium started me in my thing.

Ed McLean –
"I seek no pity. I know I deserve what I got and if it means dyin' in prison, fine, I'll die in prison, because then it's worthy. That's what I got. I did it. I'm guilty you see. That's the way I see things now."

By the time I was eight years old, my mother was very sick with cancer, so they moved her to a hospital. That's when they put me into an orphanage, my sister and I. It was from there that everything started escalating up.

I went to the orphanage. My sister went to my aunt's. Then they sent me to one of my mother's aunts to stay there for a while. But I couldn't handle it. They hated me, sent me back to the orphanage.

From there I learned about drugs, crime, pretty well everything, because that's all kids talked about. You know, you got all runaway kids there. You got female prostitutes 13, 14 years old. I was learning everything, including whatever came along the line sex wise. It was all there: the girls would sneak in drugs; sneak in homebrew; sneak in whiskey and beer; and give it to the boys. We'd party at the institution. I was eight, nine years old, doing these things.

My mother was still alive, so I would sneak and hide down by riverbanks. I would go up and visit my mother at nights and in the evenings some times. During the day, I'd steal out of stores and gardens, live along the streets, in cars, lumber yards. I slept on the riverbanks or on top of bridges.

I'd crawl underneath and sleep on the dikes on the bridges, but I wouldn't leave Saskatoon until my mother died, because she was very important to me. She was all I had left. All my family. I have a number of brothers and sisters, they never seemed to care for me. They all just left me. They didn't want nothin' to do with me, so I was always on my own. When my mom was put in the hospital, she never got out. She died a few years later and I just kept getting worse and worse. I would go from car thefts, to break and enterings, to stealing. I was adopted out to two or three different foster parents and homes.

One used the horsewhip on me one day, so I thought it was time to leave. It was one of those small quirts I think they're called, leather stripping. Split all the back of my legs and skin off my leg. I run away from him and I say: "I ain't coming back to this fellow's place to live no more." I didn't like it there.

By the time I was 12 years old, I was sent to Regina Boys School. I started to learn the ropes. You know, like how to be tough, how to stand up for yourself, because I got punched out a lot there. I got beat up a lot by other boys, so I had to fight on my own.

I'd escape and run away. They'd catch me. I was always stealing, breaking into places. Stealing cars, joyriding, stuff like that.

Finally, I was sent from boys school to a foster home. These people treated me good, but I was so ruined and messed up I couldn't live with them, so I ran away from them. I went to Winnipeg with another fellow and I was caught by the police. But I had a brother who lived there and he didn't know what happened to me, so he offered to take me in. Then he turned me in to the police for running away, escaping, car theft and whatnot. They sent me back to boys school on the condition that I'd only be there for six months. Then I could come back and live with my brother. He did help me by doing that.

From the age of 15, I lived a pretty normal life, I guess, for two or three months at my brother's place. Then I got into a group of fellows and we started stealin' cars and joyridin' and that. That turned into us gettin' caught.

I got locked up on Vaughan Street. Went to trial. I don't know exactly what happened, but they put me back in my brother's custody again. My brother drove me to Saskatoon and when we hit Saskatchewan I said to him: "Well, goodbye. I'm an adult now, at the age of 16 here, so I don't need you no more." And I went my own way. From then on I turned bad. I mean really bad. I started stealing, breaking into places.

Me and a couple guys went to North Battleford and stole out of all the stores there. Took a whole mannequin out of one store, the clothes and that, stealing off 'em.

We actually went up to North Battleford to help this guy get his girlfriend back. What we did was, we picked her up, threw her in the car and drove her outside of town. Then I said: "No. We're bringin' her back. We can't take this. This is wrong." But now, she didn't want to get outta the car. She says, "I'm goin' with you. You got me this far, you gotta take me now." So I went to Saskatoon with them. They got pinched later on in Edmonton. I went back to North Battleford to get another two fellows and I got pinched there.

On that pinch, I was 16, there was a wild car chase. The police shot out the back window of the car and shot our trunk up. I guess the bullet must have hit the gas tank, because the whole car was full of smoke. You couldn't see nothin' but smoke and I'm tryin' to drive. It was about an 18-mile car chase. I was tryin' to run 'em off the road. There was no gas, so I had to come to a stop. That's when I got my first six months. I also got another two months breach, to give me eight months in Regina jail.

When I got out, I come to Saskatoon. I pulled a few capers right away. I made some money and I got out, because I found out there was a camera in one of the places and the police were looking for me. I drove out to B.C. with a buddy.

In B.C., the only way we could make money was by breaking into houses, garages, buildings and stealing stuff. I met a guy there that was a fence. He owned a bookstore and I'd sell him hot goods and he'd give me the cash. This is how we made our money.

Then me and a fellow got caught on another wild car chase. At about 100 miles an hour the car spun outta control. They caught me, but the other fellow got away. I started doin' my time then. Time started getting serious. I got two years in Haney Correctional Institute. I spent most of my time in the hole. It's as big as a small table, nine steps round. You can touch each wall and touch the roof. It's so dark in there you can put your hand on your face and you can't see your hand.

During the day they would let the bakery smell come down in there while you're on bread and water. You're on a concrete or marble floor that goes to a dip. They got a hole in the bottom of that which they can spray water up about three feet if they want to do so on you. You can't lay down straight, because you've gotta lay at an angle on the floor. It's very cold in there. I used to get numb. After the third day your whole body's so numb you can't even realize you're there.

I couldn't feel nothin'. It was complete numbness. Then it didn't matter how long they kept me there. They would feed me three slices of bread, and water, one of those little bowls of water each day. On the third day they'd give me a regular meal. Then I'd go back to bread and water again for another three days. On the third day again they'd give me another regular meal, then back to bread and water.

After 15 days you don't even know any more. I spent many days in that little hole. They've got about eight cells like that and I was in all of 'em. I was considered a rebel.

You think about everything evil. I would think about murder. I would think about how I was going to get out. Get the guards and the people that worked in the institution. How I'd kill 'em. Torture 'em. Things like this. These are the thoughts I had when I was in that hole. Thoughts of being really bad and evil. I hate to say that, but that is the truth.

This built into me something I don't know, because I became very violent after this institution. It was considered the worst hole in Canada in all prisons. In fact, this hole was labelled as that at one time. There's no other prison in Canada that had a hole that was considered as cold, as hard as this one.

Anyways, me and another fellow escaped from Haney. We were caught, out in the bush. They took us and sent us to Oakalla Prison farm. One day the power went off and they had me down what was called Westgate B. It's a bunch of cells with no roofs, just little cages inside a building. There's a big feeding trough up at the front where they put the food. Like a pig trough, where the hot water runs down. They put buckets of food in there to keep it warm, so that's what you eat if you pick your tray up and go along to the tables.

The power went out and some guys tried to rape a fellow. The fellow was a friend of mine, so I stood up for him. I walked into the cell. I had a knife in the back of my pocket. Everybody's got knives. I said, "Let the guy go." They said, "Is he your kid?" He wasn't my kid, but so they would stop I said, "Yeah." I was scared.

About a week later, seven or eight of them attacked me for this. They tried to pull my eye out. They broke my nose, or they bent it a bit. I wouldn't say completely broke it. Then they got another guy and they tore his eyes out. I was charged with that. I told the guards I did it, so I got 15 days. Number one diet and the hole.

The hole there was under the cow barn. They'd lock you in a cell. There's a set of bars. Three feet in front of the bars is a solid wood door and with a one way window they can look in and you can't look out. There's a light bulb on. It burns on you. It never shuts off. That's on you 24 hours a day. The cow manure and the cows' pee runs down the side of the walls into the cells in some of the blocks. Some of the hole cells, not all of them. So you've got a pretty good idea of what you're up against. You got a foam rubber mattress. A pair of coveralls. A black, little bucket they use for your toiletry. That's it.

I spent many times in there. I spent 33 months in the institution, counting Haney and my escape there, and most of the time I was charged for doin' things that weren't, you know, they were phoney charges. Like one day, we were pulling stumps and I couldn't work any more. I was sick. I had something like a temperature of 100.3. The guard told me to keep working. Finally I just took my axe and I started walking up to the guard. I said, "I'm not gonna work no more." I walked him and the shotgun all the way back to the road, so they phoned the truck and took me to the hospital. Things like this. I'd get charged and I'd get locked up and I was very sick.

There was gangs in the prisons, and if you were a loner, a lot of them would try and jump you. They jumped me twice. This time I was waitin' for it. I sat down beside one guy. I was 17 years old. He was about 300 pounds. I knew he was going to beat me up. I had been tired of these guys instigatin' and that, so I put a knife in my pants, stuck it in through the material, weaved it in. The guy was sittin' there.

I sat down beside him, the guard left the range, and I took the knife out. He come around, he smashed my nose. He broke my nose. I went underneath him and I gutted him. I stabbed him. Once through the stomach, one in the groin, one under the left lung, and one through the back. Four times I got him. Someone screamed: "Take the knife!" The knife was taken, shot through a window to another part of the building, and disappeared. I was charged for stabbin' this guy, but I wouldn't say nothing. They took me to the hospital. My nose was flat right against my face. I saw him laying on the ground. He was close to 300 pounds this man, and he's laying on the ground. I remember cursin' him, sayin' it looked good on him. I would never say that today, but I said it then.

After that happened, guys started respectin' me a bit. They said: "Oh, oh. He's not like the rest. He uses knives." That night made me all of a sudden something different in the eyes of all the convicts. Now, even though I was still a loner, I had respect. They didn't push nothin' on me no more. They backed off.

I wasn't taken to street court. I was taken up to isolation block in Oakalla Prison. They told me the guy is gonna live. He's not pressin' charges. And they don't want to press charges because they said: "We believe this guy deserved what he got. It was coming a long time, so we're just going to leave it go, but we're going to have to charge you inside." I was charged inside and locked in the hole for 60, 70 days. Then they put me in the maximum security part of the prison itself.

I began to use drugs, heroin from the addicts out there. The guys cut me in on heroin.

I did get into homosexuality. There were guys out there who thought they were women. There was the odd time I would get one guy down and let him give me oral sex or I'd sodomize him, but in these cases here I was always the man. I wouldn't let them be doin' it to me. I don't do that no more. I can't even stand that, you know, but I'm tellin' you the truth. You want the truth, you're gettin' the truth.

What happened was we'd go down to the end of the range and have a couple of guys at the other end of the range to keep point. If the guards come, somebody would whistle down the range. Then you could stop whatever you were doin' and play chess till they go by and then go back to whatever you were doing. Sex was wide open there. Half of the guys in that place were gay and a good percentage of them even thought they were women. They would dress up like women. The guards allowed all this. They didn't stop it. Even some of the guards were gay. It wasn't nothin' new in there.

You didn't have to be gay at all. You could take it or leave it. It was never forced on you. There was instances I seen guys raped. It was forced on some guys, but I don't believe in that.

I did one time try to intimidate a guy with a hard look, but I would never force him to do it. In the end I would say: "Go on. Get away from me." Most of the times I didn't have to, because there were so many around that you just give 'em a chocolate bar, or just look at 'em, and they'll call you in a cell and say, "You want to get ironed out." Because that's their trip. They like doin' it.

I could go down and a guy would give me, I'll use the term, blow job. You could get one: morning; breakfast; noon; and night. You could be standing in line and they'd be willing to do it. Sex was somethin' that was really heavy and thick in there at that time. It has slowed down a lot in the prisons out here now. You don't see it as much, but it is happening. Guys are still doin' it and you can't stop that, but it's not forcefully done. Guys are doin' it, because of the fact that they want to do it. They found themselves a partner. You know, two guys will be partners together and that's the way it is. It's allowed in a way, as long as it's undercover.

A guy coming into prison today, this day and age, don't have to worry about nothin'. All's he has to do is mind his own business and nobody'll bother him. There's no more groups and cliques like they used to. Oh, they have groups and cliques, but they're watered today. The men I grew up with, they were as hard as nails. They were like fire and when they came at you, you knew you were in trouble. This group of prisoners they have today, they're wishy-washy. They're nothin' like the prisoners of 20 years ago.

I see guys here, if they ever dared to open their mouths to say the things they say now, 20 years ago they would have been killed. I saw a guy stabbed. I've seen guys die here 20 years ago. I watched them drag a guy, a kid by the name of Robertson, all because he wouldn't bring a can of thinners into the guys to sniff. They waited until he got showered and then they stabbed him in the heart, the chest, and threw him out. I saw them pull him out on a carpet and the kid that was standing beside me, in fact Eddy was his name too, I said: "That kid's dead. He won't live. He's finished."

I saw guys hanged. I saw a guy who talked to me one night. He asked me, he said, "Is there a God?"

I said, "Yeah there's a God. I believe there's a God." About three weeks later, I saw him hanging in his cell and watched the guards cut him down.

It don't affect me. I just say: "That's his way. That's his lot. That's his life. That's the way he was supposed to go, or he wouldn't of went that way." I have no pity for nobody. I don't seek pity and I give no pity. I believe every man in this prison, institutions, and everything we do, we got nobody to blame but ourselves. So why give pity to other people when they got themselves into that mess? Just as me. I'm in this mess here. I seek no pity. I know I deserve what I got and if it means dyin' in prison, fine, I'll die in prison, because then it's worthy. That's what I got. I did it. I'm guilty you see. That's the way I see things now.

It was a doghouse where I lived in. It was all dogs. Everybody was dogs. They'd rip you off for everything they could get and what they couldn't get, they'd still steal from you. They'd stick a knife into your back and ask you with a big smile, "How you doin'?" You always had to watch your back then, and I was learning too.

I finally finished my time. I had done 33 months. I got out. I was out for about a month and a half and I got charged with a B&E. They give me four years. Two years definite. Two years indefinite. I said, "I can't do another 40 months in Oakalla."

The morning I escaped, I run into some people. They took me to a big party that night. They bought me a plane ticket. I flew to Calgary and, just by chance, met my sister and my brother, who I hadn't seen for years. I was with them for a few days. Then I went my way. I got charged for breakin' into a garage and stealing a car. I got another two years added on to the four years. They sent me here in 1970, then moved me to New Brunswick.

I've thought of suicide. These were playing around, but still I thought of it. My arms show it. Where I've taken a razor, cut this open, pulled the line out, snapped 'er off. I almost died on that one. They dragged me to the hospital. They had to cut my leg open to find a vein to pump blood back into me. They thought I was going to die. The only reason I didn't, the guards that dragged me out put me over the sewer, they weren't gonna help, but the radio man, Billy McFarlane, opened the door and saw through the bars what they were doing. He threw a rope and said: "Tie that man off." Then they got scared, because I was almost dead. They tied me off and whipped me to the hospital really fast.

This was in Dorchester Penitentiary, back in '73. When I was there, I got charged with stabbing two prisoners in the gym in a fight. I was locked in the hole. From the hole, after about six months, they shipped me to BC Pen. I think eight, nine months, I spent in the BC penthouse.

That's a different hole. It's like the old SHUs. Then BC Pen shipped me back to PA again and said: "Now we're starting over." I spent about two years in the hole.

When I came here again, Tom Ellis was the warden. He left the institution to go to region (CSC's regional headquarters). Mr. O'Sullivan became the acting warden.

I started a big bingo. Went to all the shops and told everybody: "No work. We all go in the gym." Fired the committee. I said: "We're all startin' over here. This is where we're going to have it."

Only prisoners there at first. I stood up on the stage and I said "OK," because mostly were partly Native and part white, and I told everybody on the stage, I had an iron bar in my hand, I said: "I started this. If it turns into a riot I'm gonna get 10 years, so that means anybody that has any violence during this whole thing, or starts a fight, they can use that and read the Riot Act on us, and that's gonna give me 10 more years in this penitentiary. The first man that has a fight against anybody in here, I'm gonna cave his skull in with this bar, and that's the way it's gonna be. You guys got that right? We're here for a legal protest, nothing else."

They followed through. They did what I said. We started havin' meetings. They brought the press in and that. Mr. O'Sullivan was allowed to come into the gym and say he would change things. We had some written. Five o'clock in the morning we had everything arranged, so we could call off the protest.

Everybody could go back to their cells. We could work out the deals. We had a new committee. Everything would be changed around by Mr. O'Sullivan's orders. In fact, he even had the kitchen bring us down some ice cream before we went. We all had some ice cream that night.

Then Mr. O'Sullivan called me up and he said, "You know, when I heard you were running this outfit down here, I thought that was it. You kept it pretty good." I policed the whole thing. I got certain guys to watch other guys, so there'd be no fights and no violence and whatnot. Mr. O'Sullivan became the warden after that. He handled that situation properly.

That was around '74. I got out not too long afterwards. But when that bingo was over, about three months later, we had another bingo in the gym. Three guys died in here. They were Native guys. The Natives said, "We backed you white guys up. Now you back us up." I said, "If you have a bingo now, with all the stuff you've been given, you're gonna lose it all, regardless of those three suicides." They wouldn't listen, so I said, "OK, I'll stay in the gym with you, but I won't be involved with anything." This time I wasn't running nothin'. I said, "You guys blew it. You ruined everything." I was getting out on mandatory in about seven days' time.

During the protest, there was a tunnel dug up against the wall. They found out about it. They closed it down and said: "Now we can read the Riot Act. You can either surrender, or we're coming in with tear gas, the guns, the beatin's and everything." Everybody surrendered. I was locked up in PC. The penthouse.

I got out as soon as my mandatory started. I was a very bitter man. The feeling I had was: "Now what are you gonna do?" But if I walked through the prison today, I'd turn around. I'd look at the prison and say: "Thank you. You helped me find out who I am." There's a different man sitting here today. The man that was in this prison those years was a cold-blooded killer. He had no respect for nobody. No conditioning. Nothing. I was cold. As hard as rock. Today I can't stand violence. Anybody even doing it around me, I get him away from me, or I get away from him. I'm very thankful I do hate it.

I went to Calgary, but the police wouldn't leave me alone. They picked me up. They beat me up. They picked me up. Finally, I went to my classification officer and I said: "Hey, the next time a cop picks me up in this town I'm gonna blow him away. No more. I'm not takin' no more." He says: "You can't stay here. You gotta go. They're not gonna leave you alone. Go to B.C."

I went to B.C. But it was just as bad there, because of the drugs. I got whupped up into drugs. I started into robberies and stealing, anything to afford the dope. Then I started selling drugs.

I went to Edmonton and got a job. I tried to work. I really did try to go honest. I got a job in industrial block, making wire rope. I was getting paid four something an hour. I worked as hard as I could. The guy that got me the job, the foreman went up to him and said: "I don't know where you got this guy, but get more like him." They loved me there, but none of them knew I had a record. None of them knew I was in jail. I wanted to keep it that way.

One night I got drunk. I left the house. I was gonna go and visit my girlfriend in Calgary. I drove. The stupidest thing I'd done. I got in a big police chase out toward Ponoka. We were going about 105 miles an hour when I hit an exit. I left it like a 707. They found the car 40 feet, totalled, on the other side of the highway, and me, somewhere out in the bush, unconscious. I think the heels were almost ripped right off my shoes. All my clothes were tattered. They took me to the hospital in Ponoka. When they weren't looking, I got out of my bed with this white smock and booted it outta there.

I phoned a certain fellow up in Edmonton and said, "Pick me up. I'm on the outskirts of town. I'll throw a blanket up, or you'll see me." He picked me up. Drove me to Calgary. I went and stayed with two hookers.

They told me: "The police are going around. They've got your picture on their hat. They're asking us if we can find you. They say we've gotta help him. He's a sick man." The whores were telling me: "They're gonna blow you away. They're not tryin' to help you." The prostitutes were hidin' me. I was always fortunate in that case. The women liked me, because I was always treatin' 'em good, you know. As far as good as I knew what good could be. I would never really smash 'em around, or hurt 'em, or beat 'em, but I would stick up for 'em. If I saw the guys hurtin' a prostitute, I'd go up to them and I'd grab them. "That's a woman. You don't do those things to her." The girls all liked me. Many of the prostitutes helped me out many times. When I needed a place to stay, they'd hide me.

I hid for a while. Then I went back to Vancouver. I had a gun. I took it up to this guy's apartment. There was a warrant for his arrest. I left the gun in a bag. I said, "I'm gonna go and get some dope. When I come back, we can decide to go down to the States. See what we can do." I left my girlfriend, the gun, and him, in the apartment, because he told me: "Don't carry it with you no more. Put it here." He was scared I would use it. Probably would have too. Anyways, I go and get some pills and dope. I come back and the police busted in. I got not bad ID, phoney under the name of Gary Angus I was using, so they were going to let me go. But they said: "We know you. You're Kenny. Here's a warrant for your arrest. You've got to go back to Drumheller." Walking out, I grabbed the bag with the gun in it. They jumped on top of me. They got the gun away from me. "Now," they said, "We've got all three of you charged with possession of a restricted firearm." Eventually, I took the beef on that. I said: "I stole it. It's my gun. They had nothin' to do with it. Didn't know nothin' about it." The charges were dismissed against them. I got 18 months for the gun, another 18 months for drugs.

They let me out after that. I got downtown again, started sellin' dope. The narcs jumped me. Throttled me. I had two bundles of drugs in my mouth. They got one, but couldn't get the other. They didn't know I had two, so they were satisfied when they got one. I took the other one in with me. I got two years for possession of heroin, two counts.

I finished that bit, got out on the street. I was a complete wild man. I started smashin' people in bars. I started fightin'. I don't know what went wrong with me. I just went crazy. Crazy. Everybody was very scared of me down there.

Then I got hired to pick up money for drugs. I'd go along to these people and if they wouldn't pay, I let 'em know that certain things would happen to 'em. One of them was for $20 000. Another was for $50 000. Another for about $150 000 owed. It was big money. It was big people I was working for. I can't say who they are, but one of the guys that was with me ended up getting murdered. He was killed in a parking lot. I'm the one charged with that murder. They called it a drug-related murder and my whole life has been around drugs.

He worked with me. He was with me. I was informed certain things about the fellow that I didn't know about. I was high all the time on percodines, heroin, drinkin', so I could use that for an excuse, but it had to do with drugs anyways. I took him outta the car. I executed him right there. Just cut his throat.

It was a very sick feeling. I felt blah, but I couldn't show what I felt, because the other guy that was the driver of the car, I couldn't let him show that I did feel sick about what happened. I pretended it was just like lightin' up a cigarette. I went our way and said: "Don't worry about it. It's over." I'd never killed a man before. It really bothered me. Still does to this day. I never did get over it. There's times I think about it.

What I did, after I killed him, I went up and got my girlfriend and drank some more. Took her to another hotel. Had sex. To keep from thinking about what was going on, we spent the night together. I tried to act real normal. Nothing. Don't worry about it. Yet parts of it was eatin' at me. And it has. It's never stopped. Even up to this day, I still have thoughts of that man. The sounds that went down that night.

About a week later, they picked me up in a hotel. Charged me with first-degree murder. They said: "If you plead guilty to it, we'll drop it to second-degree. Give you 10 minimum." So I said: "Well, 10's better than 25. OK, I'll take it." I pleaded guilty, got 10 years with a minimum. Now I've got 16 years in and they're gonna make me do 25 anyway.

This was in 1979. I was in BC Penitentiary. While I was there, I sawed the bars off the gym. They caught me out in the yard trying to escape over a wall. I had a grabbing hook with a rope attached to it, and a nine-inch blade with me. They circled me with guns. Me and another fellow. There was one guy that did make it about a week before, but I missed out. I was the last guy to try and escape from the BC Pen.

From there, I was locked up in the BC penthouse. It's a very ratty place. I remember mice crawling up the walls, the bars, across my table, bedding at night. I'd catch and throw 'em off, or shake 'em off my blankets. It was a very dirty penitentiary. With the riots and all that, it was a really filthy, slimy bucket. Everything was bad there. It's closed now.

After that, they sent me to Kent Institution. I was there for about three, four months. I ended up charged for attempted murder. Stabbing an inmate.

One day they found me in a shower. Somebody laid the boots to me. I was completely bruised over. I was right unconscious. The guards told me they thought I was dead, because they couldn't even find a pulse on me.

There was a war goin' on in there. Drugs and who was gettin' drugs. I happened to be on one side, against the other side. There was a power struggle going on and a lot of them guys wanted it to go their way. I didn't want it to go that way, because it was the wrong way. It was hurting a lot of people. I wasn't really trying to have a power struggle with anybody, but this one guy really was a rotten, instigatin', slimy person.

I said: "I gotta straighten this guy out. One way or the other." He got me while I was drunk. I got a dirty beatin'. They took me right out to the street hospital on that one. I woke up there with a brain concussion. They brought me back and locked me in the hole and I told the warden: "Listen, I just fell. I was drunk and fell off the sinks into the shower. I won't hurt nobody. Just let me out." He let me out and I waited for about 30 days, because my balance was very bad from the brain concussion. When I could focus straight, see straight, I went huntin'. And I got my man. If that's the way you want to look at it.

He almost died, because I drove it right through his stomach, into his spleen. They locked me in the solitary block. Kept me in the hole for a year on that one. Finally, the charge was dropped to assault with intent to maim.

I was transferred to Millhaven. I got there and they had a big war going on. The East and the West. A power struggle. It didn't seem to matter. I get there and Mclean's the name, he's the big man all of a sudden. Guys were lookin' at me saying, "What should we do?" I said:

"Do nothin'. Just do your time. That's all, man. Just do your time. That's all I want to do. I've got life to go."

But they wouldn't leave me alone. They pushed me, prodded me, got me into a situation where it looked like I'm the head honcho of the guys from the West. I didn't want that situation, but it became a part of it.

A guy got stabbed there. I was blamed. They locked me in SHU. The cells up there are completely solid iron. Your bed's iron. Your floor's iron. Your walls are iron. Your tables are iron. Your windows are iron. You've got a big steel slate over your window, and in the wintertime they give us plastic to cover that, so wind won't blow through. It gets very cold in there. In the summer, it's like an oven.

I was charged and taken to street court with some other guys for attempted murder. I pleaded not guilty. One guy pleaded guilty. The charge was dismissed on two other guys. Finally, the charge was dismissed on me, by technicality. But I did not stab that man. What I will say is this: I am guilty, because I knew it was there. I won't lie about it. I did set it up for that man to get hurt, so I'm as guilty as the guy that did stab him. They were right in locking me up in a SHU for two years. They shipped me from there to Dorchester. I was there one night and I got in a fight. There was a big hullabaloo with drugs. I was there maybe two, three weeks, there was a big fight in the gym. Nobody could get in. Guys were running around smashing one another out. I knuckled one guy. Another guy knuckled me. I had my eye cut. It was crazy. Finally they said, if we turn ourselves in, the guy they want us to turn in, they won't charge nobody. The fellow they wanted, his name was Mike. I won't use his last name. He was my partner at one time. If he reads this book he'll know who I'm talkin' about. Mike was there and I talked him out of his weapons. They took him to the hospital. Locked him up. Then they let us all go back to our cells. I thought it was around 11 o'clock at night. I found out it was 3 o'clock in the morning, so you have an idea where I was.

Because of my past when I was there before, like the fight I had in gym when I stabbed two men and it cost me that six months in the hole, people were always leery of me. They said: "He always uses a knife." Guys were always scared, because of the number of men I stabbed. I found with a knife, I'll use a phrase, I felt like I was a god. That was my only protection. I would use it no matter what. Today I curse a knife. I hate knives. I hate people that use 'em. I won't have nothin' to do with people that use 'em.

When I was sent to Dorchester in 1983, my life changed. I decided I'm gonna do somethin' with my life. I'm at the bottom. I'm lookin' up. I said, "I got nowhere to go." I turned and I said: "If there's a God in this world, then give me help." About two days after that: I stopped smoking; I stopped doing drugs; I stopped all violence; I separated myself from all the prisoners in the penitentiary including the guards, including the hospital staff. There was only one prisoner I allowed to be in my company, off and on. I went like that from that day till this day.

I no longer believe in misusin' people or abusing them. It's completely true. Everything I say, think and do has got to be honest or I won't have nothin' to do with it.

I believe I had a spiritual encounter. It was God tellin' me: "I'm real if you want me. But you gotta do what you gotta do to get me."

I was preaching, teaching in the chapel. I found out that wasn't it. I says: "There's somethin' wrong here. If I was a Christian like you people say we are, how come I can't stop smokin'? How come I can't stop doin' drugs." I says: "I got a lady that's visiting me and I can't get my hands out of her panties. I'm mauling her day and night." I said: "That's not a Christian to me. How come all of the disciples could stop all of a sudden?"

I asked the nun about this. I asked the preachers about this. None of them could give me a direct answer. They said: "Oh, no. You're a Christian. You're learning." I said: "Hogwash. This is all lies. This is phoney, this chapel. So is all chapels and churches."

I went to myself in here. I found out how to change myself. To find out who I am, I had to go inside myself. I had to relive my whole entire life over again. All those painful things that I've done and that were done to me. Grieve 'em. Seek the truth. Find out who I am, so I could be upright in heart, destroy all the negative influences in my life.

I don't go to manmade churches. I believe the Bible is in my heart. I got everything I need inside me. The only thing I need man to teach me how to do, if I ever get out of jail, is to show me how to pay bills. I don't know any more. I haven't got a clue.

I don't expect to get out of prison. I believe they're going to keep me in prison as long as they can. They can't justify holding me any more. I haven't had any fights or any violence for over 11 years. I've got a trade. I've got an education, but I got nobody to help me. They've thrown me away, so I say: "I'm lost."

While I was in Dorchester, I asked to go to Renous. The guards hated me so bad in Dorchester they were doin' everything they could to make me blow up, cause me to do somethin' violent, so they could say, "See." Finally I said, "Get me outta here."

From Renous, a year later I came here, which was two years ago. I have a very clean record. They can see that I am exactly what I am, just being myself. I don't fight. I don't join groups. I don't smoke. I don't drink. I have nothin' to do with drugs. I stay by myself, mind my own business. That's my full duty to do that. I don't have no problems other than a spiritual problem that I'm workin' on. I consider myself spiritual, but I work on that. That's a private, personal thing. It has nothin' to do with anybody and I don't share that with nobody. That's for me alone.

I had no youth. I had no parents. My mother could never be with me. She worked all the time. I never saw my father. I never knew my father. I was always left alone to find my own way. A lot of times we didn't even have food in the house. I'd have to go out and steal food out of gardens. A lot of times we didn't have clothes. I'd take clothes off clotheslines, socks and that, for myself. You see, we never had nothin'. We just had the poor neighborhood where we lived. That was it. I remember finding rats under a baby's crib in our next door neighbor's house. If they were there, I'm sure there were some in our house too. It was a bad neighborhood.

I've spent over 30 years of my life in institutions. I hate crime with a passion, but it doesn't help me. These people won't let me out. I don't know what to do. I've been eligible since 1989 for parole. I don't hurt nobody in prison. I ask for help they say: "Well, do our programs." What for? I'm not an alcoholic. Why do an alcoholic program? I'm not a drug addict. Why do a drug addict program? It don't make sense to me. I said I would go sit through some of them. They said: "How about the anger control?" I don't have an anger problem, but I said, "I will sit through some of your programs and listen to them. If there is somethin' there that is helpful I'll take and use it." But I've cleaned up my entire life. There's nothing negative inside me. I won't sit with people who are negative.

They keep me in prison, because they say: "We don't know how to judge you any more. We don't know how to categorize you any more. You're different. You don't say nothin'. You don't do nothin'. You just work, mind your own business." Well, what's wrong with that? You know, what's wrong with that? There's nothin' in the Criminal Code says there's anything wrong with that. There's nothin' in the Criminal Code saying I have to talk to people. I don't like talking to people. I got nothin' to say. Everything that comes out of the mouths of these people is lies, deceit and guile. I'm tired of all that. I'm tired of hearing it. I'm tired of people telling me excuses.

I've never had a parole in my life. I've only been out on mandatory supervisions. That's the only paroles I ever had. I never once considered them supervision, because they were phoney. That was my good time. But as a national parole, a full parole, I've never had one in my life.

I can't even get a day pass. They won't let me out. The only way I can get out is if somebody on the street will help me, and I don't know anybody out on the street any more. I've been in prison this time almost 16 solid years. I have a trade. I haven't had any violence since '82.

I don't have no mandatory. I'm doin' life. They could keep me here for the rest of my days. The only way I can get out is if someone is willin' to stand up for me and say: "Hey, I know this guy wouldn't break the law when he gets out." I wouldn't even spit on the sidewalk, because I follow a different moth. I have a simple religion now. I believe totally in the truth. My religion is this: as long as I'm not hurtin' anybody mentally, emotionally or physically, then I can't be doing anything wrong. And that's the way I live.

I have no future. I don't see any future. I don't make any plans ahead of time. I just live for one moment at a time. If tomorrow I'm alive and I'm here, then that's meant for me. I have nobody that will open a door for me.

I know I would never do a crime again, but who's gonna help me? Who's gonna stand up for me? They're ain't nobody out here.

I have a brother in Saskatoon. He says he'd give me a place to stay, because he lives on a farm. I could live at his farm with him and his wife. They would never turn me out, they said.

I'd have to work from there. He wants to raise buffalo. It costs a lot of money. I haven't told him this yet, but I've been thinkin' I could paint enough pictures to make enough money to help him buy those buffaloes. Maybe go into partnership with him. That's what I've been thinkin' off and on, if I ever do get a chance to get out of prison, but I got nobody in prison who will get me out, give me the chance to prove it.

I wanted to add in that if there is somebody out there that knows a man when he's upright and hard, give me a hand. Help me get out. I don't think I should stay in prison for the rest of my life. I've paid dearly for my crimes.

I don't act. That's the difference between me and these other guys. I tell it like it is. If you can't handle the black and white of the truth then I'm sorry. I won't change that. My classification officer can't stand me, because I tell her she's a liar. I say: "You make these commitments. You broke 'em all. That makes you a liar." What else can I say? Use a little discretion? How do you discrete that? I've used all the discretion I can. You're a liar, so let's stop bein' a liar. Let's do somethin' about it.

I mean, here's a woman that worked in a hamburger joint on the street. All of a sudden she's in charge of men's lives as a classification officer. What can you get done with somethin' like that? She has no understanding of men. She has no understanding of life. None of 'em do. So how can a person get a fair shake here?

A Thing of Hope

Jimmy Eldridge

"I once read a quote from a warden of the most high-security Texas prison: 'I never tell my lifers that they'll never get out, that they'll never see the street. You can't take away a man's hope and freedom and expect him to remain sane.' And this man is one of the most well-respected wardens in U.S. prisons, amongst the wardens. It's not just somebody who decided to throw his opinion in."

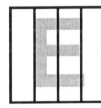very year in Canada's federal prisons, there are about 100 "major security incidents." Included are: murder of staff; murder of offenders; hostage-takings; suicides; major assaults on staff; major assaults on offenders; major fights between offenders; major disturbances; and escapes.

Jimmy Eldridge, 36, four years older than the average federal inmate, has survived it all. At 125 pounds, half an inch taller than five-foot-three, he has been directly involved in a penitentiary hostage-taking as well as the stabbing death of a fellow inmate.

His criminal record began nine days after his 18th birthday, when he was convicted of possession of a narcotic. Next was a one year term for escaping lawful custody.

Not too much time passed before it was murder and then, almost freakishly, outlasting years of prison mayhem, volatile times, that claimed the lives of many men who thought they were too smart, too big, too tough, for the system to devour.

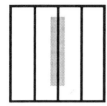had to go through 18 months of RPC (Regional Psychiatric Centre) to piece more of it together. I don't know how easily understood a mild form of mental illness is for most people. How serious depression is understood by most people and how serious social maladjustment is seen by most people. All I really know is how it feels and how it ends up making one think. How it changes his thinking. Talking to one of the psych nurses in RPC, about the most vivid description I could give, was that just prior to killing that man, everything I looked at in life, for my future, I told him it was: "Like looking up the ass of a dead horse." It's a crude saying. It's rude. But life was black and it stank. To me, I was worth nothing. I had no future. Nothing but self-pity.

I had been in the prison system 15 years before I was sent to RPC. I'll be 37 in December. I've got 19 years in prison now on this sentence. I'm serving life 20. The earliest I could get out on life parole is 1997. If my parole is not granted, I could stay behind bars for the rest of my life.

I don't really think about it. I came to terms with my life sentence about eight years ago. At that point I began living for what things made me feel good for the day. What things kept me happy, occupied for the day. I started planning my days a week at a time. It later turned into a month at a time. Now I can plan for a few months down the road. But life within prison, this is my life.

I was born on an American Air Force base in Germany. When I was two, we went to the States. When I turned five my mother brought me up to Canada, separated from my father. He was too abusive, an alcoholic, a homosexual. She just couldn't handle it any more. She took us, the kids and me, across the border. She's Canadian, so she took us back home to northern Alberta.

My father was an American stationed in northern Canada, near Grande Prairie. I'm not sure exactly how he was stationed there or what the agreement was between the States and Canada at that time. This was in the '50s. He was stationed there and that's where my mother met him. She was going to school in Grande Prairie and that's where they got married. All my grandparents on my mother's side, they're Irish Canadian. There was no aboriginal blood, not till closer to my immediate family. They began marrying into native people.

From what I'm told, all the children were subject to my father, especially my mother. From before the age of six, I don't remember a thing.

We started off living back at my grandfather's farm, busing to school. Our farm was isolated. There wasn't anybody my age. School was an experience that I can't say was good. It wasn't bad. It was just sort of forgettable. I just had one friend then. At the age of six, seven, the things I was happy doing were the things I was doing alone, in the bush, walking in the bush, exploring.

The next thing that happened, we moved to the small town of Guy, Alberta. We had our own house at that point. It was a small place near a store. My mother worked at the store. That's where I started interacting with other children more. At that point, this friend that I had early on, became even closer with me, and I became friends with a couple of other people. We were together just about all the time doing pretty much normal things, building tree houses, swimming.

There was no trouble with the law. At home, there was no abuse. My mother, though, was under a lot of stress financially. There were four of us children. She was trying her best to support all of us. She was on some sort of pension. Something to do with an agreement with the government, because my father was not permitted back in Canada. With that, plus her part-time work, she was just barely making ends meet.

I remember she used to get a bit uptight and strange. She explained to us later that she had a nervous breakdown. We were too young to understand what was happening. All we knew was that her moods would be very inconsistent. This was for about a year. She had all of us scared, but she gained her strength back and today she's quite well. She's a very strong, good woman.

Our school only went up to elementary. I had to start busing to junior high. Later we moved the house back to my grandfather's farm. I don't know exactly why my mother did that, but I was already busing, so it didn't really make that much difference. I went into my high school years busing to school from the farm.

When I started going to high school things became more difficult for me. I was doing quite well in the elementary grades. I was quite often at the top of my class for math and science, but when I started going to high school, things changed quite a bit.

I felt different than the other students. I was pretty much alone except for a couple of other people who were socially maladjusted, I guess you would call it. It was at that point that I started to associate myself with other students who were not part of the mainstream, so to speak.

That's where I started skipping classes. My grades fell dramatically. I was drinking a little. Not enough to really get into trouble, just more in keeping with the lifestyle of the people I was associating with.

My first brush with the law was being stopped in a car with some other kids. We were smoking grass. They were all older than I was. It didn't end up with me charged with anything. One of the fellows in the car took charges, but that was the first time I really encountered the law. There was no real consequences. The other kids didn't let me get into any trouble. They kinda covered me. One fellow told the police that I knew nothing of what was going on. That sort of thing. So I kind of respected them for that. I looked up to them for that. To me, they were more my friends for it.

The first time I was ever locked up in jail was in Calgary. That was for stealing a motorcycle. I was on remand for a few weeks and released. My lawyer had the charges dismissed. I was guilty of the crime, but I never even met this lawyer. It was over the telephone. I spoke with him. He appeared in court. That was it. It was over.

I job hopped throughout my teen years. I couldn't hold a job. I worked Canada Manpower for a while. I worked in the bush for a while. Whenever I needed money real bad I would end up finding a job. My motivation was zero for keeping it. My motivation for finding it was almost zero. It took a lot for me to get one. It was after a series of short jobs that I had actually tried to keep, but couldn't keep for various reasons, that I ended up deciding to pick up a gun for the first time.

I hitched a ride to Edmonton. It was on the way that I pulled the gun out and told a man, he was about 22, to pull over. He didn't. He looked at me. He said something to the effect: "You wouldn't really use that?" At that point, I pulled the trigger.

I grabbed the wheel and pulled it over. I stopped. I sat there for two minutes, just sort of not thinking. Then traffic passing by kinda made me realize that I'd better get the car off the highway, which I did. Then the fear started setting in.

He was dead. I had shot him in the head. With a .22. I wanted him to pull the car over, get out, give me his money. I was going to take the car and use it for armed robberies.

I was hoping he would pull the car over, hand me the keys and his money. That's what I was expecting him to do. I visualized everything happening just that way.

I pulled him out and put him in the bush. I drove away, and I got to Vancouver. I had an accident on the way. When the police came to the accident scene they escorted us to the nearest town. I had to sign for the tow truck, and I signed my own name. To this day I don't know why. I wasn't thinking of getting away.

That's what caught me. Signing my own name for that. They just followed me right into Vancouver and picked me up. They originally charged me with first-degree murder.

I went for a pretrial psych assessment. I never testified on the stand, but I gave pretty much everything to the psychiatrist and then my lawyer. I had already confessed everything to the police, the moment they picked me up. I pleaded guilty. At first, they had me charged with first-degree, then for some reason they dropped it. I didn't even have my plea entered or anything at that point, so I don't know why they did that. But I just pleaded guilty. I wanted it over with.

Life 20 was the sentence. I was numb even before I shot that guy. It's really hard to explain. Nothing mattered. Nothing in life mattered.

There's a thing in the law that gave me a chance to appeal within 30 days and they kept me in provincial for another 30 days before taking me to Saskatchewan Penitentiary.

I came through the gates October 1977. It was just like everything else. Like the whole thing was beyond me. Just another proof that my life was out of control.

I went onto the range with my bedding. I remember looking up. I do remember thinking that I wouldn't survive it. I do remember thinking, sort of like the end of the road type of thing.

It was exactly in keeping with what you see in the movies. You walk in and there's four tiers, bottom and three higher landings. It's in a circular type of thing where people can stand on the edge and look over. When I walked in, back in those days you didn't have radios and televisions and there was a very regimented type of system, so the smallest change in routine was of major interest to all of the prisoners. When people came in you had a lot of inmates standing along the higher landings looking over and making comments.

A few whistles. Some calling out, "Fresh meat." To most of them it's just a game. They've been in jail a while. They're just having fun, but it's no fun for the person walking in.

I didn't know what I'd do if someone had grabbed me or tried anything. I didn't think that far. I'd already been in a couple of fights. I learned that someone my size, the best you can do is get in close, try to pin the fellow down. Try to hold the arms down to keep him from beating you up too bad.

I'd never seen a knife used. I'd never thought of a knife being used, but within my first couple of weeks here I was approached by a couple of homosexuals. I was first kinda just felt out. And still naive to think that they'd go away and not come back. They did come back and told me in no uncertain terms that I would have no choice in the matter.

That was the first time I went looking for a knife and found a pair of shears, big cloth shears in the sewing shop where I worked. I took the shears. I broke off one handle. I waited for them to try and force me into anything. I had learned just enough by then, my first three weeks here, to know that word gets around quickly, so I let some people know that I was carrying this knife. I let them know I was doing a life 20 sentence and I didn't really care too much about anything.

I don't know if that's part of the reason why these people didn't come back, but it was all in keeping with my observation when I first came in. People who care the least about their own lives and the lives of others were most respected, most feared. It's in that way that I started sort of coming back to life. I started building a life in jail in that direction.

I wasn't here two years before I'd gotten involved with some associates in a hostage-taking. Myself and these other inmates, we took two staff hostage. One of my associates kind of pummelled and kicked one of the staff while he was tied up. It was a personal thing about the way the staff member treated him while this inmate was in segregation. He was venting his memories on this officer. From what I understand now, they thought they were going to die. They really believed they were going to die. The officer I was watching over for a while was just a normal man. He wasn't a bad person. He didn't mistreat inmates or anything. He just didn't want to die. At that time, I was making myself be callous.

We ended up being transferred to the Millhaven Special Handling Unit. It made Sask Pen look like a kindergarten. People died a lot in that place. A lot of stabbings. And I became a part of that.

The Special Handling Unit is a place where they send people who are too dangerous to be kept in any inmate population in Canada. When you have a group of inmates like that together, you have a little community developing that forms its own rules, forms its own laws, and its own sentences for breaking those laws.

The first thing I started doing was taking all the survival instincts I'd learned in Sask Pen for those first two years and applying them fully. By that time I'd done a lot of exercising, running, weightlifting. I could hold my own in either a fist fight or knife fight. When I hit the

Millhaven SHU it was like every bit of ability I had for violence had to be used to survive.

There was more than one incident. One time for example, a guy flipped out over a card game, just started swinging. We went down fighting. He tried to take my eyes out. I managed to get myself away from him enough to start using my fists.

It just so happened by that time that we had both gained enough respect amongst the other inmates, so that other people intervened. We both walked out to the yard with the knives and were prepared to get into it, but my partner stepped in and everybody kinda said: "Enough's enough. Neither of you are what's called no good. Neither of you are rats. You shouldn't be fighting like this." They kinda stopped it.

I spent seven years at Millhaven. There's two things that I remember vividly that are going to be with me for the rest of my life. One of them is a man getting stabbed 32 times because he was labelled for nothing. His name was Sean. He was just a kid. Two inmates jumped him, and over a period, it seemed like half an hour but it was only about 10 minutes, he kept fighting his way clear of each of them and they kept stabbing him. The staff didn't intervene. Nobody intervened. They were watching from the tower. It was right in front of the tower. It was just sheer luck he was still alive. I don't know how he lived. It started as a person thing and a couple of guys wanted to make a name for themselves. They decided he was the target and that was it.

The other thing I remember is my involvement in the death of another man there. My partner claimed that when he put the hammer on him, fingered him. Even to this day, even some of the people who were there, none of us knew that this man was going to die.

My partner was a big fellow, black man, who was feared by most inmates. When he called us out to the yard we didn't question it, we went out. I didn't question him because it was just another routine type of: "OK, let's go out to the yard, man, and have a discussion."

My partner called a meeting in the yard. We're on lock-up. He called down to the range: "We're having a meeting out in the yard. We all gotta go out there." So we all went out. I knew for a fact some guys didn't want to go out, but they were scared. I went out because he was my partner. He told the guys out there, he said: "In about 10 minutes we're going to get together and talk."

He told Stuey to sit down next to him and said: "Let's me and you talk first." Nobody knew what was happening. Next thing I know, I thought he was wrestling with him at first, he's holding him down, and I see the knife, stabbing Stuey. Then he throws the knife down. I didn't know why he did that, but he threw the knife down, and he started garrotting him with a shoelace that he had pulled outta Stuey's parka. Stuey was being throttled to death, but he was still conscious enough to grab the knife out of the snow. I seen this, stepped in, grabbed the knife, pulled it out of his hand, threw it. And then James killed Stuey.

He told us after, that Stuey had ratted out on him. It wasn't until a year later that I found out that that wasn't true, that it was partially true. Stuey did ask the guards to take him to the hole, but he asked the guards to take him to the hole because he was being muscled for sex. I don't know whether or not he actually told the guards that it was my ex-partner James that was doing this to him. At this point in my life, it doesn't matter.

Back then everybody had somebody to watch their back. Everybody had somebody who'd be there on call. My partner would be there on call for me. I'd be there on call for him. No questions asked. It's part of a way of surviving. Part of a way of not getting a knife put into you.

Sex doesn't have to be a part of it and normally isn't. It's first of all a trust, common understanding. A faith that your partner's not going to turn on you. It's no different than any street gangs. No different than any large city street gang anyway. You have your partners. You have your associates.

Everybody out in the yard was charged that time. It turned into a large court case with seven inmates and lawyers. They give us a voir dire to separate. Because of the amount of money involved by that time, it was turning into millions of dollars, they had a SWAT team like you've never seen no SWAT team before, covering us from point A to Z. The amount of publicity generated by the media was such that we didn't stand a chance. There were guys out in that yard who just weren't guilty. They knew nothing about what was going to happen. They knew nothing about what was even happening until it was over. There were only two inmates actually guilty and that was my partner and myself. I was guilty for taking the knife away from that inmate's hand. I was guilty of aiding and abetting. My partner was guilty of the crime. Nobody else should have been convicted of anything, but by this time there had been enough violence and the Crown was under enough pressure that they decided to set an example in this case.

They just charged everybody in the yard and they pulled witnesses. One of the three witnesses told the truth 100 percent. The second witness told part of the truth and recanted. He was scared of repercussions. He became a useless witness. The third witness lied heavily.

The first witness told the truth insofar as there were two of us involved and that as far as he could see from his window, nobody else knew what was going on pretty much until it was over, and that even if they did know what was going on halfways through, there was nothing they could do about it. The third witness, the one who lied, said everybody in the yard surrounded the murder scene with their jackets open as a barricade. So the Crown was basing their case on this third witness with the first one sort of semi-circling in.

The outcome was a massive plea bargaining. Our lawyers, there being nine of them, were prepared to keep the case going for another month or so, with the full jury and everything. That was their only way of countering the humungus amount of publicity being generated.

I can't explain as nearly as well as I'd like to how the Crown managed to orchestrate a scenario. They had, for example when we were going for our preliminary in Kingston, a bulldozer driving in front of the inmates. In front of the escort cars. They were stopping traffic. They had traffic stopped all along the route between the junction where Millhaven highway meets the Kingston highway. They stopped traffic right into the city and they drove us with a bulldozer in front and some really big garbage trucks in the back.

It was like that every week. Once a week we'd go into the city for our setover by the judge and the publicity was ongoing for a month straight. Anyway, when we finally got our voir dire to Sudbury, they cordoned off a three-block circumference around the courthouse. They stopped all traffic, had SWAT people posted throughout that perimeter, and the Crown told the media it was because there were inmates who had mob connections. That we had access to millions of dollars and were going to escape. You can imagine what the media did with this.

Our only way of countering that was promising the Crown a really drawn out, extended court case. Finally we got a plea bargain. The plea bargain was such that each of us got a sentence in accordance with our current sentence, to run concurrent with our current sentence, so that warrant expiry of the current sentence was also warrant expiry of the new sentence. The Crown wanted convictions and got them.

Each fellow got a different amount of time. One guy got two years. Another guy got five years. Werner, my partner, got 15 years. I got 10 years. And that was 10 years ago.

Millhaven was just closing down. They were closing the Millhaven SHU because of this inability to control violence and they opened up the Sask Pen SHU. It was 1985 when I started serving my sentence in the Sask Pen SHU. That's also where things started to change in my life.

The difference between the Millhaven SHU and the Sask Pen SHU is like night and day. The Millhaven SHU had been open a decade with violence nonstop, from beginning to end. Even when the staff tried to control the violence by locking the place up as tight as possible, giving the inmates recreation for 30 minutes, one inmate at a time, inmates would still come out, manage to get their handcuffs off and still stab a guard.

A perfect analogy is an escalation in warfare. Guards hated the inmates with a passion. Inmates hated the guards with a passion. They hated anybody who associated with the guards with as much passion. The hate, it was like a tangible thing. It was what kept people motivated and going in that place. When the guards come to lock people up, they came with riot sticks and well trained. I don't know if you've ever heard a riot squad going through an institution. You can hear it from one end of the institution to the other. It shakes the institution. Well, they did that with pleasure. When they dragged the inmate out of his cell and started putting nightsticks to him, they did that with pleasure. So when the inmate came out of his cell to go to medical or to go for an interview, pulled his handcuffs off and stabbed a guard, the inmate did that with pleasure. It was escalation to insanity.

I guess the CSC learned by the time that place closed down, because when I came to this SHU I was amazed. I couldn't believe it. They managed to make good living conditions and the best security I'd ever seen in my life. The best security. Not just so inmates can't attack staff, but that inmates can't attack each other. There has not been one death in this SHU in the 10 years it's been open, compared to well over a dozen in the Millhaven SHU. There've been two minor stabbings. All it took was a few stitches to sew them up. That was it.

There's more than just the security. It's the old adage: "You can't just use a stick or you can't just use a carrot. You need both the carrot and the stick." It's also a thing of hope. I once read a quote from a warden of the most high-security Texas prison: "I never tell my lifers that they'll never get out, that they'll never see the street. You can't take away a man's hope and freedom and expect him to remain sane." And this man is one of the most well-respected wardens in U.S. prisons, amongst the wardens. It's not just somebody who decided to throw his opinion in.

There's nowhere you can move in this SHU without being underneath a gun slot. That's not to say that the guns are pointed at people all the time. There's an observation, kinda like an overhang on the wall, plexiglass, so the guard can see right down the wall throughout the whole room. He'll have a trap door where, if an inmate is stabbing another inmate, he can snap the trap door open and fire off a warning shot first, then tell the inmate he'll get it in the legs next, or something, if he continues to use the knife.

It's changed since I've been released from there, but when I first came to the Sask Pen SHU they had what they called "phases." Phase one being 23 and a half hour lock-up, phase two being roughly 16 hour lock-up with gym and yard and common room.

As far as security goes, there's massive amounts. Razor wire, barriers that were made in such a way that it would open two inches, three inches. You put your hands through so they could handcuff you and then open the barrier the rest of the way to let you through before frisking you. By doing it that way, you were observed. Your hands were observed from the moment they put the cuffs on till the moment you had your hands up being frisked. You couldn't take the cuffs off in that interim period as safety for the staff.

As far as safety for the inmates went, they went to a great deal more effort in keeping apart incompatibles, watching cliques, and being more attuned to what's happening with the inmate population.

I got into a couple of fights there. I got stabbed, but it was just a minor thing. It was funny the way it happened. We had a fist fight one night over absolutely nothing. Just a lot of tension, frustration, and we ended up scrapping it out. We shook hands and said it was over.

The next day I'm eating dinner and I feel someone punching me in the back. I jump off the table and I see a knife in his hand. It turned out, I found out later, that it wasn't actually a knife or even a decent piece of metal. It was a piece of pot metal that he had managed to take out of a radio. It bent after the first stab. It just kinda gave me a bunch of nicks and cuts. There's some truth that you've got to watch your back in a place like this.

Clifford Olson [who confessed that he had beaten, strangled or stabbed to death 11 children and is incarcerated in the SHU] wouldn't last one minute in the general population. The inmates, somebody would say: "I don't care if I get life or not." That person would kill him. There's strong segregation of sex offenders, especially heinous crimes like that.

There are sex offenders and whatnot in the SHU of some pretty bad crimes, but they're in a protective custody section where they all have something to be in protective custody for.

As far as prison rapes, that's one of the illogical things about inmates. Actually it's logical when you start to get deeper inside it. There's a definite paradox there. Inmates who have raped other inmates have been killed by other inmates. Usually it's by the inmate that's been raped. But it has happened that repercussions have been serious from other inmates. But there are also times the credibility of the inmate in the general population is such that he has said: "Well, the kid has been giving it to me this long and now he's crying wolf." If the inmate's status in the inmate population is such that it's in people's best interests to leave well enough alone, they'll leave well enough alone. It's always been frowned on and people have been checked in for it. People have used violence against other people because of it, but also I've seen personally the untruths, the illogics.

Things have become so much more civilized in the past decade. It's amazing how quickly a system can change when mandated to do so. When they make the decision to change and consider it a priority, they can change within a reasonable time frame. In the past decade, the system has definitely changed.

One of the biggest changes was with the CSC commissioner Ole Ingstrup. I'm not gonna say that he deserves more credit than previous commissioners, but he is the first one who put out an actual document called *Mission Statement*, mandating CSC to incorporate inmate input into various levels of decision-making. To me, personally, that was sort of a milestone. It was the first time I ever started writing letters to people in bureaucratic offices. It was the first time I ever started getting responses. It was the first time I said: "Hey, they're not doing the violence forever."

Back in '92, this institution was sort of a hot spot with integration. CSC was mandated to integrate sexual and non-sexual offenders. This institution took the mandate seriously. Just to show you what happened, so you can get a feel of the extent of what I'm talking about, Edmonton, Kent, Millhaven, every maximum across the country, has a divided prison population/protection population. Sex offenders, stool pigeons, all the people who are considered no good, are in one part. All the people who are considered the strongest, solid, won't rat out, supposedly don't have anything to hide, are in the population part. Every maximum across the country except for one. That's this institution.

This institution is medium now, but it didn't turn medium until after we had it integrated fully. A handful of inmates and three staff believed in the mandate given by Ottawa. Not just us, but it was given to all the prisons. The other prisons have been thus far incapable of managing to do that. We managed to do that, but not without a lot of problems. A hostage-taking being one of those problems. An inmate choosing to make his final position about sex offenders and rats known clearly, by taking hostages on a kamikaze type of thing.

It was during that period that Harvey came into this institution as a spiritual adviser. I went to him for help. At that time, I was not in contact with the Native population. I was voted in for the second time by the prisoners as inmate committee chairman, but I didn't have contact with a large segment of the population. That was the Native people, people who believed in Native spirituality, people who come from a Native spiritual background. Maybe they lost heavily, but they're still in touch with it.

Washico Chicala, Little White Man, is a nickname that people have given me. Washico is white man. Chicala is small guy. It's a nickname in the Native language. It's good to have a name in the Native language. There's no disrespect meant. Some people might think so, but I know better. It's a name of familiarity.

What happens out in the yard is the result of a lot of work. It's the result of pretty much a man with a vision coming into this prison, taking the latent energies of a lot of people and focusing them into this culture. I know of no inmate in here who knows Harvey, who doesn't love the man.

He doesn't wish to be called an elder, because he's not old enough. He has a history of coming from the streets. He's been in Native politics, quite deeply at certain points in his life, but he's gone past that. With all his deep insight into people, he can draw their spirituality out. What he tries to do is help, not teach us about ourselves, but draw out what we have.

I personally have stopped watching my back now for a lot of years. What happens, happens. I'm not going to worry about it. I'm not going to waste my energy worrying about it. I might as well not have a life if I'm going to walk around watching my back. The longer I live, refusing to raise my fist or pick up a knife, the more years that go by, the more I have nothing to worry about.

I have my hopes, my dreams, but I'm not in control. I'm in control of my life here. I'm in control of me, my thoughts, my feelings, how I want to feel about myself. I'm actually looking at my own mortality like an old man dying.

What do I want to be thinking as my last thoughts? That I'm in control of how I conduct myself, how I treat other people, how I ensure that I keep alive my feelings, the good feelings that I've found, how I ensure that I do the things I know work to keep them alive.

My future? I'm not in control of parole. I'm not in control of transfers or anything. I am in control of me and I'm happy like that. I'm tired of the politics. I'm tired of being involved in the mainstream, but I'm never, ever going to fall right out of the mainstream like I was when I was seven or eight. I'm never going to.

This Native culture is almost perfect for me, because everything is real. You live for the moment. Every day we remind ourselves, we remind each other, to live for the moment. If you think of something to do today to start building for the next week, for the future, if it takes a week to do it, a week to build a little log cabin like out there in the yard, or a month to build a medicine wheel, OK. We don't really think much further than that. Collectively we get together, we do what we can for the people who come. And what we get out of it is living together, and the good feelings we have living together.

There's one thing that I've often wished I could say to the public and that is: "Yes, a lot of us are animals. A lot of us act like animals. A lot of us, including myself, started out our lives that way and back with the way the prison system used to be, they didn't help too much for us to change that."

They wouldn't permit something like the medicine wheel out in the yard. They just wouldn't permit it back then. And anti-Christian stuff would never have been acceptable in the CSC. Today, as the system becomes more human, the people that the system is dealing with, the prisoners, are becoming more human. As they become more human they're starting to learn to teach each other how to become better.

I just wish the public could see, have a sense of CSC history, and see where we've come from and where we're going and help us. That's what I wish. That's all.

This picture of Kingston Penitentiary vividly illustrates a CSC prison, where offenders lose their freedom, where life consists of routine and more routine.

Strapping Table – The Correctional Service of Canada (CSC) museum, across the street from KP, has countless reminders of the days of hard time. If convicts laughed, talked or breached any one of the innumberable prison rules, they risked being strapped to this table, their bare buttocks lashed with the cat-o'-nine-tails or a paddle. One CSC official recalled: "The penalty for complaining about the food was six lashes. The prisoner might get three and would then be told, 'Any more problems and you'll get the other three.' In most cases, that was the end of it. No more trouble." The strapping bench, also called the flogging rack, was used from 1903 to 1968.

Contraband – This picture, also taken at the CSC museum, shows several types of weapons seized from prisoners throughout the years. Life in prison includes an atmosphere of coercion, intimidation and the constant fear of violence. Five percent of federal offenders are involved in gang activity inside the walls. A 1996 CSC survey of more than 4000 inmates revealed that one in five had been beaten or threatened, while seven percent had been assaulted with a weapon. In late June 1996, guards at KP found nine homemade knives hidden inside a refrigerator. They also discovered 90 litres of homemade booze. "We don't think they were planning any big Canada Day bash," said a prison official.

Author's Note

"The laws have got a lot stricter because people are fed up with crime, although there's too much media hype put on it."

– Claude Robinson, Edmonton Max

hile two-thirds of Canadians worry that crime is on the increase – a feeling attributed by some critical observers to profit-motivated, sensationalism-driven members of the media along with publicity-hungry, vote-starved politicians bent on public agitation – the statistics tell a different story.

The crime rate, compiled by the Canadian Centre for Justice Statistics (CCJS), dropped by 5 percent in 1994.

In 1995, police-reported crime (2.9 million cases) decreased for the fourth consecutive year, down 1 percent. The total drop in crime during those 48 months – 13.1 percent. Despite the falling numbers, however, crime in Canada remained 6.8 percent higher than it was a decade earlier.

Violent crime, reduced by 3.1 percent in 1994, fell another 4.1 percent in 1995, the largest annual decline since data collection began more than three decades previous. The decreases followed 15 consecutive years of increases in violent crime and left the 1995 rate 36 percent higher than in 1985. The CCJS, which noted a large increase in common assaults during the 10-year period, reported: "If this category is excluded from total violent crime, the increase from 1985 to 1995 drops from 36 per cent to 15.1 percent."

As for what proportion of the increase in violent crime over the past decade is due to actual increases in societal violence, the centre for justice statistics concluded: ". . . factors such as changes in reporting behavior by the public, police charging practices, and policy and legislative changes may all have contributed to the increase."

Homicides continued to account for less than 1 percent of violent crime. A 25-year low was recorded in 1994. In 1995, the rate moved downward again, to a level of 1.98 homicides per 100 000 population. As for the method of the madness, 31 percent of the victims were stabbed, 30 percent died by gunfire, others were beaten, strangled, torched or poisoned. Where an accused was identified, 47 percent of the victims were killed by an acquaintance, 36 percent by a spouse or other family member, and 16 percent by a stranger.

Youths made up 20 percent of all persons charged with crimes in 1994. During that period, the crime rate for youths decreased by 7 percent.

Overall, following three consecutive annual reductions, the youth crime rate remained stable in 1995, although the rate of juvenile delinquents charged with violent offences during the year increased by 2.4 percent.

A study of young offenders convicted during 1993-94 found that about 40 percent were repeat offenders. About 25 percent of them had three or more prior convictions.

Repeat young offenders receive increasingly harsher sentences from the courts. If they persist in their way of life, they too are destined to find themselves living a solitary existence inside the nation's toughest prisons. They too will be "prisonized".

In the beginning, if you stop and think about it, every male federal inmate was an innocent infant, minding his own business in a crib (if he was lucky), not a care in the world, his whole life ahead of him. Somewhere, somehow, something went terribly wrong – oftentimes irreversible emotional damage – usually inflicted during the formative years, in the home, long before he came into contact with the criminal justice system.

There is no question that we will always have crime – it is a social fact, a plague, doomed to be here until the end of time. There will always be once blameless babies who enter society and come into conflict with the Criminal Code due to rage, revenge, greed (the love of money), stupidity, a feeling of invincibility or recklessness. Others will find themselves on the wrong side of the law simply because the opportunity was there, they made a choice, or perhaps they were in the wrong place at the wrong time. As well, sociopaths, psychopaths and others with various psychological abnormalities are in no danger of becoming extinct.

Beyond those reasons – unrelenting poverty (in 1994, 19.5 percent of Canada's children under 18, 1.3 million, were living in such a vulnerable state, according to the Ottawa-based Vanier Institute of the

Family), unemployment, racism, divorce, inadequate parenting, unexplainable causes (bad seeds off good trees), peer pressure, illiteracy, learning and behavioral deficiencies could be added – lies the heart of the problem: parents, alcohol and drugs.

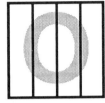ver the past several years, the profile of federally sentenced offenders has changed little: male, 32, convicted of robbery, limited education. Upon arrival at prisons throughout Canada, approximately 65 percent of offenders tested at lower than a Grade 8 completion level, 82 percent beneath Grade 10.

In 1995-96, there were 4402 new admissions to federal penitentiaries, a decrease of 8 percent over the previous year. Included in that total, robbery accounted for 24 percent of those entering prison gates, sexual assaults 14 percent, major assaults 12 percent and homicides 8 percent.

Native people, who represent about 3.9 percent of Canada's estimated 30 million inhabitants, comprised a highly disproportionate 12 percent of federal prison admissions in 1995-96, an increase from 11 percent in 1991-92.

"I think more parents should take more responsibility in their own families with their own kids and help them along and help themselves . . . you're a product of your environment."

– Claude Robinson

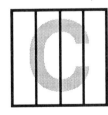hild maltreatment is an enormous problem. Dysfunctional families rife with alcohol and drugs, marital violence, parents who neglect, abandon, administer unabated abuse, fail to love, guide, discipline and protect, or instil values in their young during their crucial, clear-eyed, tender years are the root cause of what ails our society.

Damaged parents raising damaged kids. Tragedies in the making. An unconscionable absence of nurture in defiance of nature. They have effectively removed all hope for their children, dimissed their offspring's lives before they have had a decent chance to start, ensured that Canadian prisons are littered with the wreckage of their parental negligence. Humans, as somebody once said, are the only members of a race to fly without wings, talk to the stars and self-destruct their own children.

Parents have kids, batter them, desert them, treat them worse than animals, let them run wild, leaving the experts to ponder why crime won't take a holiday, why there are so many victims, why there are so many sons who end up behind bars.

lightly more than half of all federal inmates (50.2 percent) have been classified as having suffered child abuse. They were either physically, sexually or psychologically violated, neglected or witnessed family violence within their hate-filled homes.

In most physical or sexual abuse cases, the victimization began before the age of five and continued until the age of 16. Fathers were most often the abusers (75.7 percent), although perpetration by mothers (42.4 percent) and other family members (20.2 percent) was also reported. In addition, revealed an in-depth Correctional Service of Canada (CSC) national file analysis, 5.6 percent of the cases involved abuse by an authority figure outside of the family.

In an earlier intensive CSC interview-based study, "many offenders spoke of difficult and painful childhood experiences – detailing abuse and neglect they had witnessed and experienced."

"More specifically," the findings disclosed, "Seventy-nine percent of aboriginal offenders reported that they were hit by parents/caregivers (of which 41 percent said they were bruised), 58 percent stated that they were neglected by their parents/caregivers and 27 percent said they were sexually abused during childhood. Further, 57 percent of the aboriginal sample reported witnessing their father hit their mother (with 72 percent of these offenders reporting that their mother was bruised)."

Non-aboriginal offenders had similar horror stories. "Approximately 85 percent reported being hit by parents/caregivers (of which 56 percent said they were bruised), 38 percent said they were neglected and 24 percent indicated that they had been sexually abused."

As for witnessing abuse, "Forty-four percent of the non-aboriginal offenders said they had seen their father being 'really mean or cruel' to their mother (this phrase was used to identify psychological abuse) and 38 percent reported witnessing their father hit their mother (75 percent of these offenders indicated that the assault resulted in bruising)."

Child abuse, spawning an ill-fated, loathsome legacy of barbarism, a savage cycle, has taken an immense toll. In the nationwide CSC review, more than one-third (33.7 percent) of inmates who were abused, dehumanized as children, are listed as having since taken a voyage into the dark; spewing violence toward one or more members of their family, an appalling tradition that for many has put them behind bars.

Where child abuse ended, more tyranny began. The abused became the abusers, their future their past. When they were young they didn't know what love was. Sadly, as they got older, they didn't know what it wasn't.

"The constant partyin', drugs, alcohol, sort of starts to warp your way of thinking and the way you feel. You still know what the hell you're doin', but as for consequences of your actions, it just doesn't seem to matter that much."

– Rodney Munro, Sask Pen Special Handling Unit

ubstance abuse, a strong signal of simmering, deep-seated problems, is commonly one of the frightening outcomes of tortured childhoods. More than half of all federal inmates (53.7 percent) have been classified as having a severe substance abuse problem. More notably, 64 percent consumed alcohol or drugs on the day of their crime. In an extensive CSC inmate survey, more than 10 percent admitted using drugs every day in the six months prior to their crime, 17 percent had regular drinking binges.

he price of crime in Canada is staggering, the consequences horrendous. Too many shattered lives. Too many victims to count. An annual cost to society – conservatively estimated by the Vancouver-based Fraser Institute – of more than $16 billion. About $9.9 billion is spent annually for government-run justice systems, $1.9 billion (19%) of that to operate adult correctional services across the land.

The policing rate in Canada is 202 per 100 000 people, and private security guards measure 411 per 100 000 people at a cost of few more billion dollars.

There is not enough time or money to rehabilitate adult offenders or hard core youth who have already passed the point of no return.

An exhaustive 10-year CSC recidivism study of 43 000 releases from Canadian prisons determined that 64 percent of those re-entering society completed their sentence in the community and had not returned to prison. Another 3 percent remained under supervision, 33 percent returned to a federal institution for violating conditions of their release (12 percent), committing a new offence while under supervision (13 percent), or committing an offence after their sentence had ended (8 percent).

There is no easy answer, no simple remedy, no lone body can provide a comprehensive solution to crime, a worrisome collective dilemma. There are, however, duties and obligations to safeguard all children, our most precious resource.

The best and most effective cure is to focus on the future. Parental accountability – made mandatory by changes to federal legislation, studiously ignored for decades – should be at the top of the list, early intervention next.

The goal: to protect the weak, woundable and withering; salvage lives; prevent crime; avoid filling more prisons with more offenders and throwing away the key.

For centuries, disordered behavior has confounded experts involved with the study of crime. To borrow the words of English author G.K. Chesterton (1874-1936), which seem appropriate in this context, just maybe: "It isn't that they can't see the solution. It is that they can't see the problem."

Perhaps *In the Words of the Offender* will help.

– Peter Tadman